The 200

Inspiring Motorhome Destinations
Across Europe & North Africa

Julie and Jason Buckley

An OurTour Publication - OurTour.co.uk

Copyright ©2021 Julie and Jason Buckley

Published: February 2021

The authors have made every effort to ensure the accuracy of the information held within this book. However, much of the information given is personal opinion, and no liability can be accepted for errors contained within. Please do your own independent research before travelling to or staying in any of the places given in this book to be sure they are still accessible, safe and suitable for your specific needs.

All photographs copyright *ourtour.co.uk* (Julie and Jason Buckley). For large, full-colour versions of the location photos please see *tinyurl.com/the200*.

Maps © OpenStreetMap contributors. Used with thanks from *openstreetmap.org* under the Open Database Licence.

Contents

Introduction 1
Using this Book 2
Finding Great Places to Stay 6
   Finding Great Campsites 9
   Finding Great Aires 10
   Finding Great Wild Camping Stops 11
   Finding Great Business Stops 12
   Finding Great Tour de France Stops 13
Overview Map 14

ANDORRA 15
Stop #1: Ordino Arcalis 16

AUSTRIA 17
Stop #2: Hallstatt 18
Stop #3: Hochosterwitz Castle 19
Stop #4: Riegersberg Castle 20
Stop #5: Vienna 21

BELGIUM 22
Stop #6: Barrage de la Gileppe 23
Stop #7: Ghent 24
Stop #8: Thieu 25
Stop #9: Ypres 26

BOSNIA and HERZEGOVINA 27
Stop #10: Kravica 28
Stop #11: Mostar 29
Stop #12: Sarajevo 30

BULGARIA 31
Stop #13: The Rila Monastery 32
Stop #14: The Seven Rila Lakes 33
Stop #15: Veliko Tarnovo 34

CROATIA 35
Stop #16: Hvar Island 36
Stop #17: Krka 37
Stop #18: Pag Island 38
Stop #19: Plitvice Lakes 39
Stop #20: Povile 40
Stop #21: Split 41
Stop #22: Trogir (Okrug Gornji) 42

CZECH REPUBLIC 43
Stop #23: Český Krumlov 44
Stop #24: Mariánské Lázně 45
Stop #25: Prague 46

DENMARK 47
Stop #26: Aarhus 48
Stop #27: Copenhagen 49
Stop #28: Helsingør 50
Stop #29: Hornbæk 51
Stop #30: Jelling 52
Stop #31: Vandel 53

ESTONIA 54
Stop #32: Rõngu 55
Stop #33: Soomaa National Park 56
Stop #34: Tallinn 57
Stop #35: Viljandi 58

FINLAND 59
Stop #36: Kevo Nature Reserve 60
Stop #37: Kuopio 61
Stop #38: Kylmäluoma 62
Stop #39: Nagu/Nauvo 63
Stop #40: Rovaniemi 64
Stop #41: Sonkajärvi 65
Stop #42: Uusikaupunki 66

FRANCE 67
Stop #43: Beynac-et-Cazenac 68
Stop #44: Capbreton 69
Stop #45: Col du Lautaret 70
Stop #46: Comps-Sur-Artuby 71
Stop #47: Épernay 72
Stop #48: Le Reposoir 73
Stop #49: Monbazzilac 74
Stop #50: Paris 75
Stop #51: Port Grimaud 76
Stop #52: Rothéneuf 77
Stop #53: Saint-André-de-Rosans 78
Stop #54: Saintes-Maries-De-La-Mer 79
Stop #55: Saint-Jean-en-Royans 80
Stop #56: Soufflenheim 81
Stop #57: Taninges, Le Praz de Lys 82

GERMANY 83
Stop #58: Bastei 84
Stop #59: Berchtesgaden 85
Stop #60: Berlin 86
Stop #61: Dresden 87
Stop #62: Hamburg 88
Stop #63: Munich 89
Stop #64: Nuremberg 90
Stop #65: Oberwesel 91
Stop #66: Würzburg 92

GIBRALTAR 93
Stop #67: La Línea de la Concepción 94

GREECE 95
Stop #68: Acrocorinth 96
Stop #69: Athens 97
Stop #70: Diakofto 98
Stop #71: Diros 99
Stop #72: Galaxidi 100
Stop #73: Katakolo 101
Stop #74: Meteora 102
Stop #75: Methoni 103
Stop #76: Mezapos 104
Stop #77: Monemvasia 105
Stop #78: Porto Káyio 106
Stop #79: Vergina 107

HUNGARY 108
Stop #80: Balatonberény 109
Stop #81: Budapest 110

ITALY 111
Stop #82: Alberobello 112
Stop #83: Castiglione Falletto 113
Stop #84: Florence 114
Stop #85: Giardini-Naxos 115
Stop #86: La Spezia 116
Stop #87: Lake Orta 117
Stop #88: Marina di Ragusa 118
Stop #89: Montepulciano 119
Stop #90: Mount Etna 120
Stop #91: Palermo 121
Stop #92: Pisa 122
Stop #93: Rome 123
Stop #94: Syracuse 124
Stop #95: The Giau Pass 125
Stop #96: Turin 126
Stop #97: Venice 127
Stop #98: Vesuvius 128

LATVIA 129
Stop #99: Jūrmala 130
Stop #100: Klapkalnciems 131
Stop #101: Raiskums 132
Stop #102: Rīga 133

LIECHTENSTEIN 134
Stop #103: Vaduz 135

LITHUANIA 136
Stop #104: Druskininkai 137
Stop #105: Jurgaičiai 138
Stop #106: Vilnius 139

LUXEMBOURG 140
Stop #107: Luxembourg City 141

MOROCCO 142
Stop #108: Aït Mansour 143
Stop #109: Azrou 144
Stop #110: Chefchaouen 145
Stop #111: Erg Chebbi 146
Stop #112: Fez 147
Stop #113: Marrakech 148
Stop #114: Meski 149
Stop #115: Tafraoute 150
Stop #116: Tata 151

NETHERLANDS 152
Stop #117: Den Helder 153
Stop #118: Gouda 154
Stop #119: Kinderdijk 155

NORWAY 156
Stop #120: Aurlandsfjorden 157
Stop #121: Bergen 158
Stop #122: Dalsnibba Plateau 159
Stop #123: Eggum 160
Stop #124: Holmvassdammen 161
Stop #125: Nordkapp 162
Stop #126: Oldedalen 163
Stop #127: Oslo 164
Stop #128: Saltstraumen 165
Stop #129: Sand 166
Stop #130: Steinsvik 167
Stop #131: Trollstigen 168

POLAND 169
- Stop #132: Kazimierz Dolny 170
- Stop #133: Oświęcim 171
- Stop #134: The Wolf's Lair 172
- Stop #135: Warsaw 173
- Stop #136: Wieliczka 174

PORTUGAL 175
- Stop #137: Alvor 176
- Stop #138: Braga 177
- Stop #139: Cascais 178
- Stop #140: Coimbra 179
- Stop #141: Évora 180
- Stop #142: Faro 181
- Stop #143: Porto 182
- Stop #144: Silves 183
- Stop #145: Tomar 184

ROMANIA 185
- Stop #146: Bucharest 186
- Stop #147: Sibiu 187
- Stop #148: Sighișoara 188
- Stop #149: Transfăgărășan Pass 189
- Stop #150: Vatra Moldoviței 190

SAN MARINO 191
- Stop #151: City of San Marino 192

SLOVAKIA 193
- Stop #152: Tatranská Lomnica 194

SLOVENIA 195
- Stop #153: Bled & Vintgar Gorge 196
- Stop #154: Izola 197
- Stop #155: Kočevski Rog 198
- Stop #156: Ljubljana 199

SPAIN 200
- Stop #157: Ansó 201
- Stop #158: Barcelona 202
- Stop #159: Benarrabá 203
- Stop #160: Cangas de Onís 204
- Stop #161: Córdoba 205
- Stop #162: Donostia-San Sebastián 206
- Stop #163: Granada 207
- Stop #164: Guadix 208
- Stop #165: La Jarosa Reservoir 209
- Stop #166: Madrid 210
- Stop #167: Montserrat 211
- Stop #168: Nerja 212

- Stop #169: Port Lligat 213
- Stop #170: Santiago de Compostela 214
- Stop #171: Seville 215
- Stop #172: València 216

SWEDEN 217
- Stop #173: Älmhult 218
- Stop #174: Karlskoga 219
- Stop #175: Stockholm 220

SWITZERLAND 221
- Stop #176: Bern 222
- Stop #177: Chur 223
- Stop #178: Furkapass 224
- Stop #179: Gurnigel Pass 225
- Stop #180: Lauterbrunnen 226
- Stop #181: Sion 227
- Stop #182: Steingletscher 228
- Stop #183: Täsch 229

TUNISIA 230
- Stop #184: Aghir 231
- Stop #185: Bulla Regia 232
- Stop #186: Douz 233
- Stop #187: El Jem 234
- Stop #188: Ksar Ghilane 235
- Stop #189: Matmata 236
- Stop #190: Metameur 237
- Stop #191: Sidi Bou Said 238
- Stop #192: Tozeur 239

UNITED KINGDOM 240
- Stop #193: Canterbury 241
- Stop #194: Edale 242
- Stop #195: Edinburgh 243
- Stop #196: Fionnphort 244
- Stop #197: Sango Sands 245
- Stop #198: Whitby 246

UKRAINE 247
- Stop #199: Kolomyia 248
- Stop #200: Lviv 249

Destination Maps 250
- Maps A, C: Norway 250
- Maps B, D: Finland, Sweden 251
- Map E: Estonia, Latvia, Lithuania 252
- Maps F, J: UK, Netherlands, Belgium ... 253
- Map G: Denmark 254
- Map N: Hungary 254

Map H: Germany, Luxembourg, Czechia 255
Map I: Poland, Ukraine, Slovakia..........256
Map K: France.......................................257
Map L: Switzerland, Lichtenstein 258
Map M: Austria & Slovenia 259
Map O: Romania 260
Map S: Bulgaria....................................260
Maps P, T: Italy, San Marino 261
Map Q: Croatia, Bosnia & Herzegovina..262
Map R: Andorra, Gibraltar, Portugal, Spain... 263
Map U: Greece 264
Map V: Sicily... 265
Map: W Tunisia 266
Map X: Morocco................................... 267

And For More Inspiration... 268

About the Authors 269

Kamp Rožac, Near Trogir, Croatia

Introduction

Hi, we're Julie and Jason Buckley, authors of the *ourtour.co.uk* motorhome travel blog. We've been lucky enough to spend the night in our van in over 1,000 different places across Europe and North Africa in 15 years of campervan and motorhome travel, ranging from one-week holidays to multi-year full-time motorhome tours.

This book includes 200 of the most memorable places we've slept across 34 countries. With tens of thousands of potential places to stay, there are far too many for any of us to visit in a single lifetime. The 1,000 we've seen have barely scratched the surface, and with space for a mere 200 destinations we've aimed to give a flavour of the incredible options available to anyone travelling these varied continents on their own motorhome adventures.

What makes an 'inspirational destination' varies between each of us. We've stayed so many places which have felt extraordinary to us, it's been hard to narrow them down to the 200. We've tried to include as broad a selection as possible, representing different types of stopover, in both urban and rural settings, across varied landscapes from beaches to forests, deserts, mountains, rolling vineyards and mighty rivers. We've also included a handful of stopovers which inspired in another way, such as Oświęcim in Poland, trying to strike a balance between the lessons we can learn from Europe's darker past and the great sense of light, culture and beauty in the majority of places we've included.

In choosing the 200 locations, we've assumed you have a self-contained van, with its own toilet, washing, cooking, heating and sleeping facilities, which most modern motorhomes and many campervans have. With this level of autonomy, you're able to explore sleeping spots beyond the world of campsites, increasing your freedom, extending your experiences and lowering your costs by using aires, business parking and off-site 'wild camping' locations.

Using this Book

The countries included in the book are ordered alphabetically, as is each stopover within a country. Maps are provided from page 25014 onwards. Each stop has its own page with a summary at the top of the sleeping option we've used or recommend, along with the type of location (campsite, aire, business parking or wild/mixed car parking), GPS co-ordinates, what services are available and an indication of the cost. After a photo we've given a brief description of the location, building a picture of what you might find (to see full colour photos for all stops, head to *tinyurl.com/the200*).

Costs are per night for two adults, a motorhome and electricity staying out of season, and range from no cost (Free) to less than £10 (£), between £10 and £25 (££) and over £25 a night (£££). At the bottom of each location page there's a mini map, showing where the location is within Europe or Africa and the relevant country.

We've used the decimal degrees GPS co-ordinates format in this book, which looks like this: N42.63142, E1.48509. If you type these co-ordinates into your Sat Nav, web browser or mapping app like *maps.me*, you'll be presented with a map showing the precise location.

'All Services' means the location has a freshwater tap (usually drinkable but not always), somewhere to dispose of used (grey) water, empty a chemical toilet (black water) and hook up to mains electricity. A small number of remote locations have toilets which can't take chemicals, so a SOG Unit is useful (*www.soguk.co.uk*). Many places have no mains hook-up, so a solar panel or two is great for keeping your leisure batteries topped up.

Depending on the application you're using, you'll also see nearby public transport stations, tourist attractions and shops, cycling and walking routes. With Google Maps (*www.google.co.uk/maps*) and Bing Maps (*www.bing.com/maps*), for example, you can also create driving, walking and public transport maps around each location. Like the mapping websites above, all web addresses throughout the book are given in italics.

We've slept in all 200 locations in this book. For each location we've given the place we stayed plus, where possible, an alternative stopover in the area. We've checked whether all our locations and the alternatives remain available as of early 2021, and where our original locations are no longer available, we've made this clear in the text, occasionally including them anyway as examples of the kind of places which can be found.

As we've restricted the destinations to those we have direct experience of, some countries are completely absent from this book, or only have a small number of locations. This includes Ireland, Turkey, Iceland, Russia, Albania and several other countries in the Balkans. This is a reflection on us and not on the destinations themselves. Some countries, like Russia, are more difficult to visit requiring special insurance and visas, but others like Ireland have no such constraints and have fantastic reputations as motorhome destinations.

For each country we've given a one-page summary from a motorhome touring - perspective, including a **QUICK FACTS**

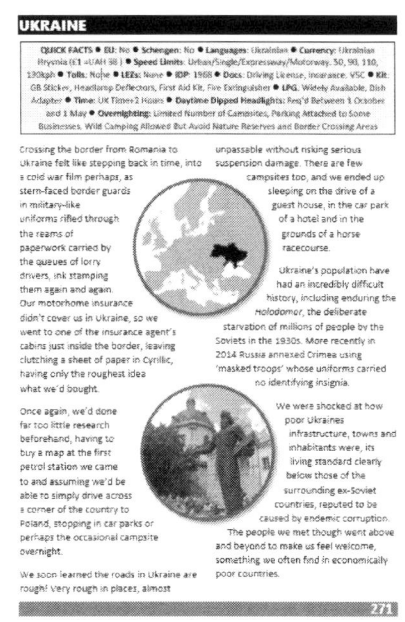

section at the top of the page which indicates the following:

EU: if the country is an EU member then UK-issued vehicle and breakdown insurance is likely to be easy to obtain. This extends to EEA countries too: Norway, Switzerland, Iceland and Liechtenstein, plus Serbia. You'll need to request a Green Card document from your insurer and carry a physical copy of it with your insurance certificate (if you tow a trailer you may need an additional Green Card for it). Outside the EU and EEA, you'll need to check if your insurer will extend your Green Card to the country you plan to visit. Some UK insurers will issue Green Cards for Turkey and Morocco, but few will cover other countries. You'll need to buy third-party insurance at the border for any country you don't have a Green Card for.

Schengen: this indicates whether the country is one of the European Schengen Area countries with no passport controls at their internal borders (in normal times). After 1 January 2021, UK citizens are restricted to 90 in a rolling 180 days access to the Schengen countries, without

3

applying for a visa. On tours longer than three months (or multiple shorter holidays out of the UK) you will need a visa, or to use 'waiting' countries like Croatia, Turkey, Morocco, Andorra, the UK and Ireland before you can legally re-enter Schengen. Also be aware that UK citizens will need an 'ETIAS' Schengen visa waiver from the end of 2022 onwards (*etias.com*).

Language: the predominant language(s) used in this country. Some countries have multiple, widely used official languages, Belgium, Spain and Switzerland for example. Learning a few words at least helps transactions and to draw out a few smiles all round: hello, please, thank you, how much and goodbye, perhaps. That said, good luck learning any Hungarian!

Currency: what currency is used in this country. Not all EU countries use the Euro. You can almost always obtain local currency from cash machines when you arrive. We use no-fee withdrawal cards like those from Starling Bank (www.starlingbank.com) to obtain cash abroad. Some countries prefer card payments, while some are still cash-dominant societies. Remember to spend or exchange any local currency before leaving a country unless you can use it later on in your travels.

Speed Limits: this is a general indication of the limits for motorhomes up to (and including) 3500Kg and those over 3500Kg Maximum Authorised Mass (MAM). Several factors can control the legal limit: the age of younger drivers, whether you're towing anything, the season, roadworks, the part of the country and weather conditions. Please treat the figures in this book as a rough guide only: locally signed limits should be followed.

Tolls: most countries have at least some toll roads, bridges and/or tunnels. Some are pay-per-use, some sell a window sticker called a *vignette* at fuel stations close to the border (or offer an electronic version) with allows unlimited use for a pre-determined number of days, weeks or months (or sometimes the current calendar year). Other countries require vehicles over 3500Kg to buy a special tracker box and pay for the distance travelled (different schemes operate in different countries; we've given the website to check for each of them).

LEZs: most countries have low-emission zones (LEZs) which prevent higher-emission classes of vehicle driving into them under certain (sometimes fiendishly complex) conditions. Italy has ZTLs too (restricted driving zones), which limit all non-local traffic from driving into the centres of towns and cities, for the purpose of preventing chaos rather than protecting air quality. We've given a brief indication of the system in each country. LEZs come with a variety of names across Europe: *Umweltzonen* (Germany) *Milieu Zones* (Netherlands) *Lavutslippssone* (Norway) *Miljozone* (Denmark) and *Miljözon* (Sweden). See *www.green-zones.eu* for a summary of Europe's LEZs.

IDP: UK citizens don't need to buy International Driving Permits (IDPs) for driving in EU countries after 1 January

2021. Countries outside the EU may require them, and we've indicated which version you'll need to buy from the Post Office. For more information see: *www.gov.uk/driving-abroad/international-driving-permit.*

Docs: the official documentation you need to carry to drive legally. Your MOT must be valid whenever you're outside the UK and can only be renewed in the UK. Take your original V5C too, we once had some 'fun' trying to cross from Ukraine to Poland with a colour photocopy of ours, with an official shouting "Xerox?, Xerox?!" at us. We suspect were only let off as we looked too embarrassed to be real villains.

Kit: the equipment you need to carry in/on your vehicle while in that country. If you plan to tour multiple countries across the seasons, it's worth packing everything they all require to save stress at borders: headlamp deflectors, a high vis jacket per occupant (accessible from inside the van), a first aid kit, fire extinguisher, M+S or 3PMSF winter tyres, snow chains, spare bulb kit, spare glasses if you need them for driving, a striped signal board for bike racks or rear boxes, two wheel chocks and a GB sticker. Sat Navs with speed camera alerts are illegal in some countries, as are dash cams, although anecdotally we've never heard of anyone being stopped for either.

LPG: butane and propane gas bottles (for cooking and heating as opposed to propulsion) vary across Europe and North Africa. To avoid sourcing and carrying several types of bottle and pigtail hose, many tourers fit self-refillable LPG bottles or a tank. Different countries use different styles of LPG refill 'guns' (of course, why standardise?), so you need to carry a set of screw-in brass adapters. Two downsides to refillable LPG bottles are: stations are rare in some countries (Finland and Morocco have none), and you have to drive to the refill point, you can't bring a new bottle to the van (unless you install a hybrid system), which could be handy for longer stays, at ski resorts for example. See *mylpg.eu* for a database of refill stations.

Time: the country's local time relative to the UK.

Daytime Dipped Headlights: some countries require you to drive with dipped headlights, or daytime running lights turned on during the day.

Overnighting: the types of location available for self-contained motorhomes to park for the night vary between countries (and within countries), as does the legality and local attitude to wild camping (freedom parking).

If you're looking for more practical information on sourcing and using a motorhome to travel the UK and Europe, our book *The Motorhome Touring Handbook* is available as a paperback and eBook on *amazon.co.uk*.

Finding Great Places to Stay

In France alone you could stay in a different campsite, aire or business every night for over a decade, and still you won't have exhausted all the places there are to stay. Add in the possibility of unofficial off-site parking (wild camping), and you've an even more enormous selection available. Extend this across the rest of Europe and North Africa, and you'd need several lifetimes to stay everywhere available.

Not all stopovers are created equal though, and the fun is in finding the best possible places to stay in the time available. Each of us will have different criteria for what constitutes a 'great place', and somewhere which feels wonderful one day might not feel quite so good another, when the rain's hammering down or the rest of the world has turned up for the weekend. These are questions we ask when deciding where to stay:

1. Do we know anyone who's stayed there who can recommend it?
2. Is it close to whatever we want to visit (city, beach, museum etc)?
3. Are public transport links available (*wikitravel.org* is a useful resource)?
4. Does it feel safe?
5. Are pets allowed?
6. What services does it have?
7. How much does it cost? We're happier to pay more for secure locations near cities.
8. Is it easy to get to? This applies around cities but also in remote areas or in the mountains.
9. Does it have shade (in high summer)?

Families travelling with children might want to check campsites allow them (most do) and whether facilities like playgrounds and pools are open out of season.

As an aside, we rarely book ahead when touring, only a handful of times in several years of full-time travel. This way we've experienced unbelievable flexibility, choosing to stay longer in locations we enjoy or to move more quickly when we don't like them, sometimes turning up and changing our minds straight away. This approach might not work so well if we always used campsites, if we were travelling in high season (which might be winter in ski resorts) or if we had a need to be certain we could stay in a specific place at a specific time.

In terms of what's nearby, there are a whole host of attractions or places of interest out there to discover, for example:

Beaches: parking directly on beaches isn't much recommended due to the risk of becoming stuck, or wet, but beach-side parking areas and campsites offer huge potential. The Atlantic coasts of France and Portugal offer fantastic sandy beaches, often with great conditions for surfing or kite surfing. For calmer and quieter beaches, it's hard to believe how unspoiled the Greek coves and bays on the Peloponnese and Pelion peninsulas are. Croatia's coast is a more rock-than-sand affair, but the Adriatic Sea more than makes up for it, with magnificently clear water (just keep an eye out for spiky sea urchins). We find some stretches of coastline easier to access than others in a motorhome. The French Riviera (south-east France), Italian Riviera (north-west Italy) and some stretches of the Costa del Sol (southern Spain) are developed more for package tourists and villa owners, with lots of traffic and fewer options (especially outside campsites) for overnight motorhome stays.

Mountains: the Alps are simply magnificent and readily accessible in a motorhome, whether you want to enjoy the views around the Mont Blanc massif, downhill mountain biking or zip lining at Pré-la-Joux or hiking (everywhere) in the summer, or snow sports in the winter. The Pyrenees and more minor ranges like the Sierra Nevada in Andalucia (Spain) and the Tatras Mountains (Slovakia) offer similar attractions, in a smaller but more laid-back way than the more frenetic Alps. As well as valley-based campsites, some ski resorts in the mountains provide high-altitude overnight parking (especially in summer when ski lifts have huge empty car parks) or paid aires (more useful in winter when electrical hook-up's needed to keep the heating fan spinning when it's -10°C outside).

Volcanoes: yep, believe it or not you can park your motorhome and sleep high on the side of active volcanoes in Europe, if you're mad enough. We've slept on Vesuvius (with fantastic views across the Bay of Naples) and on both the north and south slopes of Mount Etna on Sicily, surrounded by lava fields. Quite why we did this I struggle to explain, but we won't forget those nights in a hurry!

Canals and Rivers: in the UK, canals and rivers have largely been retired from working life, but not so much in Europe where enormous barges still ply the Danube, Rhine and a network of wide canals. Water-side campsites and aires offer calm places to sit and watch the waters, as working and leisure craft slide by. Marinas and harbours often allow motorhome parking too, sometimes free or maybe charging around £10 a night.

Lakes: some countries have huge networks of lakes and reservoirs. Portugal's *baragems* (dams) often provide quiet and free overnight parking. Poland and Finland both have large lake districts with 2,000 and 180,000 lakes restrictively, many of which have parking spots adjacent and offer wild swimming or kayaking in summer. Be aware of the potential for mosquitos though: Finland's are particularly big and thirsty!

Cities: Our tours have taken us to a wide range of cities, large and small: Berlin, Paris, Bucharest, Madrid, Vienna, Bern, Ljubljana, Oslo, Copenhagen, Rome, Tunis, Warsaw, Riga, Vilnius, Tallinn and more. Usually we avoid driving into cities and opt to use public transport from outer campsites or secure aires instead. Most cities have official facilities for motorhomes on the outskirts, within a short walk of a bus, train or tram stop. Some countries don't allow dogs onto public transport, or not on some services, so factor this into your plans if you're travelling with a beloved pet.

Archaeological Sites: the Etruscans, Romans and Greeks left behind fascinating reminders of their civilisations right across Europe and North Africa. We found that we couldn't normally stay at the site's parking area (except in Tunisia, where we found ourselves paying for an overnight guard to come and protect us), but we could use the daytime parking and find an overnight spot afterwards.

Vineyards: we've slept on campsites and aires set among vines in Switzerland, Italy, France and Bosnia & Herzegovina, taking advantage of the opportunity to sample their quality wines (and some rather rough home-brewed firewater too!).

Deserts and Dunes: for a feel of the real deal, a trip across the Straights of Gibraltar to Morocco or the Straight of Sicily to Tunisia is required. Both these countries have 'ergs', seas of sand dunes in the Pre-Saharan Steppe, which you can drive to without the need for a 4x4 or any specialist experience or equipment. At Erg Chebbi in Morocco, you can sleep right against the foot of the dunes, starting the day with a sunrise camel ride and ending it with a luxury meal in an adjacent Hotel Kasbah. Closer to home, the surprisingly high Dune du Pilat on the Atlantic Coast of France is fun to climb and sit atop, watching tiny boats in the sea below, and there are several campsites and aires nearby to spend a night or three.

Events and Festivals: I'll admit we're bad at forward planning, but on occasion we've happened across a local event which has transformed an otherwise pleasant location into a fascinating and memorable one. The Habits de Lumière festival at Épernay in France's Champagne Region wowed us with its huge animated dinosaur and captivating sound and light show. The Nomad Festival at M'Hamid in Morocco (*nomadsfestival.org*) had us running for cover as the racing camels came snorting our way!

We find our places to stay through a combination of word-of-mouth, books, tourist information, websites and smartphone/tablet apps. Over time we've gravitated towards technology, using apps on our phones more and more as mobile Internet access has become cheaper, faster and more widely accessible (no more trying to hook up to free WiFi at McDonalds!).

Apps have some big advantages over books: they can include a good range of photos, they're updated all the time by fellow travellers, so any last-minute closures or price changes are often easy to discover before arriving. Previous visitors also leave candid reviews, which are like gold dust when pre-assessing a place, although some folks are clearly very hard to please, leaving 1-star reviews because a previously-free aire has opted to start charging €5 a night, for example.

The following sections offer a few more hints and tips on finding your own great places to stay.

Finding Great Campsites

Camping Village Šimuni, Pag Island, Croatia (GPS: N44.46363, E14.96747)

There are a ton of books available for finding the best campsites in the UK and Europe, but the only books we make extensive use of are the current year's CampingCard ACSI (*campingcard.co.uk*) out-of-season discount camping books and card. This scheme lists hundreds of top-quality sites for reduced fees out of high season.

If we've been able to get a word-of-mouth recommendation from a fellow traveller for a campsite, we also find that's a proven way to source great sites.

When we don't have a direct recommendation, we also use websites like *searchforsites.co.uk*, *ukcampsite.co.uk*, *pitchup.com* and *park4night.com*. These usually have smartphone or tablet 'app' versions too. They all have user-submitted photos and reviews, which are perfect for finding the very best sites. They also allow us to view sites on a map, so we check whether they're close to a bus stop, beach, supermarket and so on. You can also apply filters to only show sites which accept motorhomes, allow children or dogs, are near a pub, allow fires and so on.

If you plan to tour the UK, the two big camping clubs offer top-quality locations, as well as smaller, more basic Certified Locations and Certified Sites (CLs and CSs):
Camping and Caravanning Club (*www.campingandcaravanningclub.co.uk*)
Caravan and Motorhome Club (*www.caravanclub.co.uk*)

Google Maps is also useful for finding campsites and reading user submitted reviews. Open *www.google.co.uk/maps*, centre the map on the area you want to stay and search for "camping" or "campsite". Tourist Information offices and websites are also a great source of information.

Finally, if you're heading to Morocco, *Campings du Maroc* by Pascal Samson, Emile Verhooste is the best guidebook available, but please be aware it's in French.

Finding Great Aires

Benarrabá, Spain (GPS: N36.549263, W5.279122)

Continental Europe has a huge range of motorhome-only parking locations called *Aires, Stellplatz, Camper Stops, Sostas* and *Área para Autocaravanas*, among other names. These are low-cost, no-frills and popular with locals and tourists alike, often placed close to the centre of towns and cities or near beaches or other attractions.

Many have service points, to allow emptying grey water and toilet cassettes and taking on fresh water. Some have electrical mains hook-ups. Few have a shower block (or a rule book) and they almost all have limits on how many days you can stay, and almost all of them operate on a first-come-first-served basis.

The main apps we use to find aires are *park4night* (associated website: *park4night.com*) and *CamperContact* (*campercontact.com*). Park4night, sometimes abbreviated as P4N, includes various types of stop including aires, businesses like pubs and farms, free/wild camping spots, campsites and even remote places which need a 4x4 to get to. CamperContact sticks to more formal aires. Both these apps have traveller-submitted reviews, and we tend to look for aires with 4 or more from 5 stars, and those with the most reviews.

Vicarious Books (*www.vicarious-shop.com*) sell a great range of paper-based aires guidebooks if that's your preferred format. We've used *All the Aires France*, *All the Aires Spain and Portugal* and more recently *Camperstop Europe*.

Finding Great Wild Camping Stops

Nærøyfjord, Norway (GPS: N60.90123, E6.86180)

With a self-contained vehicle there's often the option to go it alone, wild camping or freedom parking (whatever you want to call it) away from official areas. Unofficial off-site parking comes in a spectrum of locations, from vans stealth camping alongside the road in the centre of cities to motorhomes parked high in the mountains or alongside remote beaches, far from people. Some places are free of charge, others require a fee. We use the *park4night* app and word of mouth to find unofficial places to stay, sometimes asking the local police and tourist information. Others hunt out their own spots, using a moped or Google Maps for example. Some places formally allow legal, authorised overnight stays, many don't and it's down to locals whether they tolerate overnight stays. In some areas parking and sleeping overnight is legal but putting out levelling ramps or chairs is not and might attract the attention of the police (who mostly politely ask you to leave, but in some cases issue a fine).

caravanya.com is a useful resource for checking the legality and attitude to wild camping. Unofficial parking is possible out-of-season in many countries, and we've stayed in some out-of-this-world locations as a result, some of which are featured in this book.

11

Finding Great Business Stops

Berneux Dominique's Goat Farm at Pocé-sur-Cisse, France (GPS: N47.44473, E0.97048)

Keep an eye out for country-specific schemes where local businesses allow self-contained motorhomes to stay for free, with the unspoken assumption you'll procure some of their produce. The France Passion scheme is the most well-known (*www.france-passion.com*), where you buy a book each year and are issued a windscreen sticker. Some businesses in the scheme require you to call ahead, for others you just turn up and see if they have space for you. Usually you're expected to move on after 24 hours, and only a few locations have any motorhome services (for fresh and wastewater).

We've stayed at vineyards, a goat cheese producer, a mountain restaurant, a snail farm, lavender farm and an olive grower, all in the France Passion scheme. Some of the best-rated locations are listed in *park4night*, so we can read reviews from previous visitors. Other times we've just turned up and hoped for the best.

France Passion locations provide a unique way to get closer to local people and culture, with tastes, smells, sights and interactions which are otherwise hard to access.

The UK has a similar scheme called Britstops (*britstops.com*) which has a book listing business stops (mainly pubs), which allow an overnight stay typically in the car park in return for buying drinks or meals. We've used a few of these, finding mid-week stays at country pubs with large, flat car parks to be the best approach. The France Passion website lists more schemes in other European countries: *www.france-passion.com/en/france-passion/similar-networks*.

In a few of the lesser-visited countries we've occasionally winged it, spotting suitable parking outside a hotel, museum or restaurant and asking if we're able to stay overnight (sometimes for a fee).

Finding Great Tour de France Stops

Col du Grand Colombier, France (GPS: N45.90318, E5.76282)

When it comes to the iconic annual Tour de France cycle race, both the written and unwritten rules for places to stay are ripped up. While it's not a complete free-for-all, the opportunities to stay alongside the route multiply, and places where a cluster of motorhomes might not normally be welcome are transformed for a night or more into temporary communities, welcome to stay with an air of anticipation and celebration.

Once you've researched the stages being used (*www.letour.fr*), there are broadly two strategies for finding places to stay along the route:

1. **Stay-and-Wait:** this is necessary for the very best locations, parked up near the top of cols or in villages adjacent to finishes or mountain climbs. We've arrived four or five days early to find all the best (level) spots occupied. Some vans get in place over a week early, carrying a second toilet cassette and additional fresh water, drinks and food to keep them in comfort.

2. **Keep Moving:** here you simply drive the route the evening before and find a spot by the roadside, watch the caravan and racers the following day and then move to the next section once the road re-opens. This option makes servicing the van simpler but means you don't get to see the very best parts of the race with your own eyes.

Some towns and villages make additional parking available in fields for example, often for free, so you can get a space for a night or just during the day and carry your chairs and refreshments to the roadside to await the action.

We've also seen a couple of stages of Italy's Giro d'Italia, in the incredible Dolomites mountains, and found it to be easier to get in place just a night or two before, even on a mountain pass.

13

Overview Map

Map	Page	Map	Page
A, C	250	N	254
B, D	251	O	260
E	262	P, T	261
F, J	253	Q	262
G	254	R	263
H	255	S	260
I	256	U	264
K	257	V	265
L	258	W	266
M	259	X	267

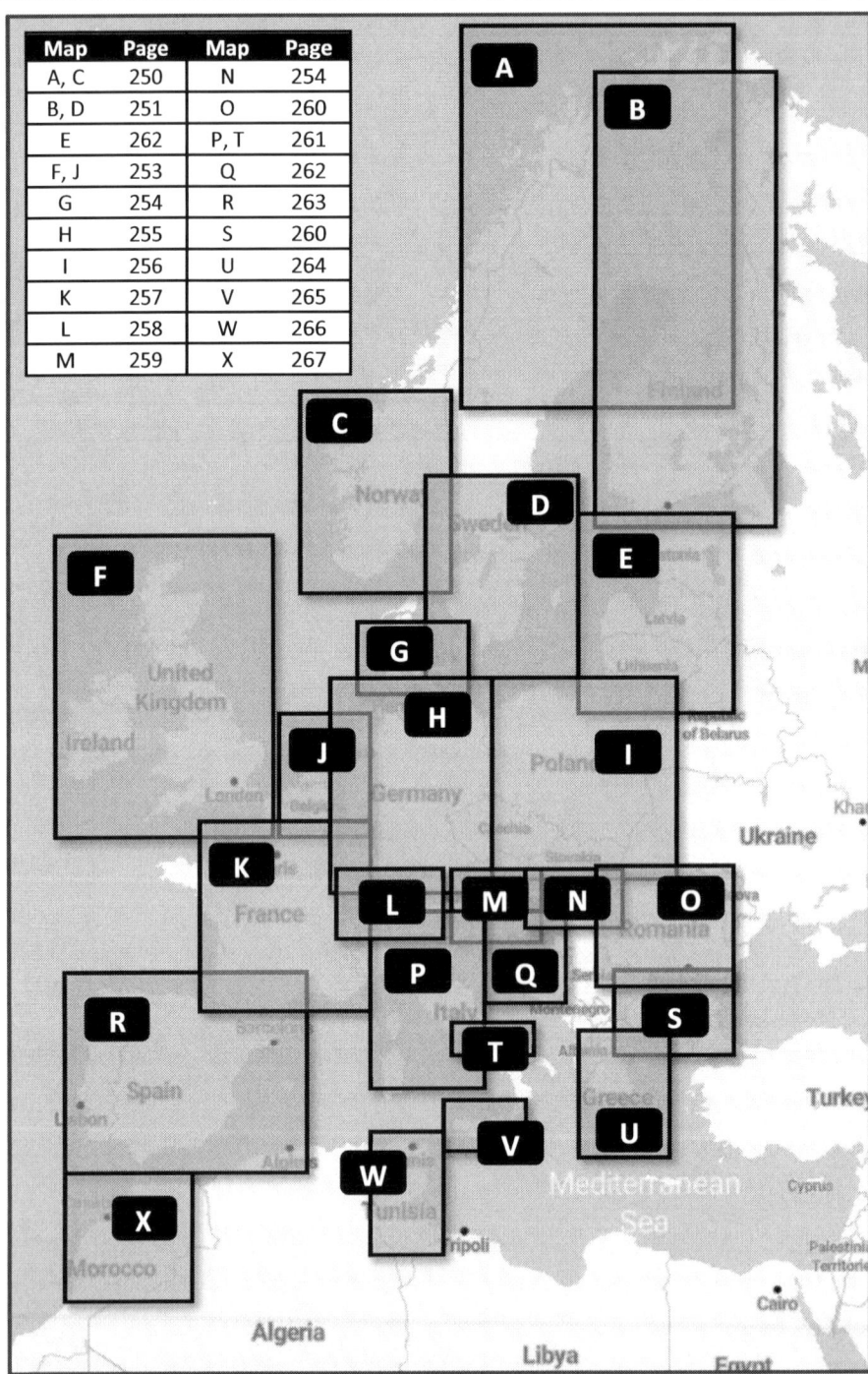

ANDORRA

QUICK FACTS ● **EU**: No ● **Schengen**: No ● **Language**: Catalan ● **Currency**: Euro (EUR, £1=€1.1) ● **Speed Limits ≤3.5t**: Urban/Single/Expressway/Motorway: 50, 60, 90, N/A kph ● **Speed Limits >3.5t**: Urban/Single/Expressway/Motorway: 50, 60, 90, N/A kph ● **Tolls**: No Toll Roads, but the Envalira Tunnel with France is Toll ● **LEZs**: None ● **IDP**: 1949 ● **Docs**: Driving Licence, Insurance, Passport, V5C ● **Kit**: GB Sticker, Headlamp Deflectors, Warning Triangle, Spare Bulbs, 3PMSF/M+S Tyres or Chains in Winter ● **LPG**: No Stations ● **Time**: UK+1 Hour ● **Daytime Dipped Headlights**: No ● **Overnighting**: Campsites, Some Official Aires and Tolerated Parking Areas

There are easier ways to cross between France and Spain than to head up into the mountains to the Principality of Andorra, but we'd recommend a trip up at least once to get a look at the lifestyle which gifts the inhabitants among the longest lifespans in the world (80.8 years for men and 85.4 years for women).

Andorra sits high in the Pyrenees, one of the few European microstates to avoid being absorbed by neighbouring countries over the centuries after (it's claimed) being originally formed as a buffer between France and the Muslim Moors occupying Spain from the 9th Century onwards.

The roads in Andorra are great quality, easy to navigate with only two main routes into and out of the principality: the CG1 to Spain and the CG2 to the French border via either the Envalira Tunnel or the hairpins of the Pas de la Casa. Access remains possible in winter but be prepared for snow and ice with winter tyres and chains or snow socks.

Andorra isn't in the EU so there are passport and customs controls at both borders, and limits on the amount of low-tax alcohol and tobacco you can take out of the country. There's no limit on diesel or petrol though, so make sure your brim your tank before crossing the border!

While Andorra isn't known for its architecture, which is generally modern, we found quaint stone villages just off the main routes and the country is peppered with small Romanesque churches with baroque altarpieces and paintings by the Catalan masters to explore.

Stop #1: Ordino Arcalis

Ski Station Car Park ● GPS: N42.63142, E1.48509 ● Overnight Allowed, Fantastic Views and Start of Hikes ● No Services ● Price Guide: Free ● **Alternative:** Official Aire at La Massana (*www.parquingbordadetorres.com*), GPS: N42.550952, E1.510418, Price Guide: ££, All Services

We entered Andorra from Spain, stopping for a night in the official motorhome parking at the River Shopping Centre in Sant Julia de Lorina, hoping to outrun the fireworks of the St Juan Fiesta which takes place in Spain on 23 June each year. Our spaniel Charlie was scared witless by fireworks, but we soon discovered Andorra celebrates the festival too and spent the evening jumping in unison with our wide-eyed pooch.

The following morning, we pulled up the *ourbumble.com* blog, put together by a couple of motorhome wild camping experts, and spotted a beautiful-looking location they'd used in a remote corner of the country, to the north-west along the CG-3 at the Ordino Arcalis ski resort (*www.ordinoarcalis.com*). It looked perfect, although once we read how they'd accidentally ripped off an external locker door on the mountain road to the ski area we made sure to triple-check ours were locked before setting off!

After negotiating a few hairpins (wide enough for a coach, so we had no trouble) we were so happy to find plenty of space on the grass with a magnificent valley framed by the habitation door. After a cuppa we headed out for a hike with Charlie, joining other hikers to walk under the chair lift to a stone shepherd's hut and small mountain lakes on the opposite side of the valley. On the return leg we couldn't resist the mountain restaurant, staring at the wonderful views around us.

Parking at the resort is likely to be at a premium in winter so although the road should be kept free of snow, overnight stays are likely only possible in summer.

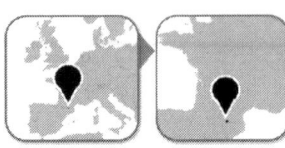

16

AUSTRIA

> **QUICK FACTS** ● **EU**: Yes ● **Schengen**: Yes ● **Language**: German ● **Currency**: Euro (EUR, £1=€1.1) ● **Speed Limits ≤3.5t**: Urban/Single/Expressway/Motorway: 50, 100, 130, 130kph ● **Speed Limits >3.5t**: Urban/Single/Expressway/Motorway: 50, 70, 80, 80kph ● **Tolls**: Yes, Vignette for ≤3.5t, Pay Per km for >3.5t With Electronic Box (*www.asfinag.at*) ● **LEZs**: Yes, But Not Currently Applicable to Motorhomes ● **IDP**: Not Needed ● **Docs**: Driving Licence, Insurance, Passport, V5C ● **Kit**: Headlamp Deflectors, Reflective Jackets, Warning Triangle, First Aid Kit (Dash Cams Prohibited) ● **LPG**: Good Availability, ACME or Dish Adapters ● **Time**: UK+1 Hour ● **Daytime Dipped Headlights**: Yes ● **Overnighting**: Campsites, Stellplatz, Some States Tolerate Wild Parking

The Alps sweep across Europe like a scythe, rising from the Mediterranean in France and Italy, building up to 4000m+ peaks as they swing north and then east across Switzerland and Austria before gradually dipping in the east. This makes Austria feel like a country in two halves to us: mountainous in the west and the (relatively) flat lush green pasture lands, forests and fields in the east.

Our journeys across Austria have so far missed the high-altitude delights of the Tyrol but we've still encountered beautiful rolling vistas, and descents long enough to see smoke billowing from our brakes, teaching us about the need to engine-brake in future.

Arriving from Hungary one year, a helpful local motorhoming couple advised us 'in-transit' wild camping is OK in Austria, allowing a single night's overnight stay in a motorhome. More research revealed the situation varies between federal states though, see *caravanya.com*.

We've used a combination of campsites, stellplatz and a few free parking spots in Austria. Over a couple of tours, we've visited the historic cities of Salzburg, Graz, Linz and Vienna, awash with imperial architecture reflecting Austria's previous power within the Austro-Hungarian empire, which was dissolved following defeat in World War 1.

If you use Austria's motorways, be aware that you'll need to either buy a vignette at the border if your motorhome's MAM is 3500Kg or less or obtain a GO Box if your van's heavier. Friends who weren't aware of this were stopped and fined over €400, ouch.

Stop #2: Hallstatt

Campingplatz Klausner-Höll (*camping.hallstatt.net*) ● GPS: N47.55322, E13.64704 ● All Services ● 1km Walk to Hallstatt ● Price Guide: £££ ● **Alternative:** Tolerated Parking in Obertraun, GPS: N47.558762, E13.679539, Boat to Hallstatt, No Services, Price Guide: ££

Hallstatt's a picture postcard Austrian village and World Heritage Site, a huddle of wooden houses and a spired church gathered on a narrow strip of land between the still waters of the Hallstätter See and the steep wooded mountains behind them.

Until the 1960s, access to the village was squeezed down a one-way road with traffic lights, but the opening of the 1km toll-free Hallstätter Tunnel has made access to the village easy in a motorhome.

We stayed in Campingplatz Klausner-Höll, about a ten-minute walk from the village. The site's not cheap (Hallstatt's a popular location) and has a reputation for a strict rule book! The main attraction for us was to simply to spend a night in this small paradise, but many others come to visit the Hallstatt Salt Mine. Dating back 7,000 years, it's the oldest in the world (*www.salzwelten.at*). Salt's still produced at Hallstatt although it's no longer the valuable 'white gold' it once was. Stood high above the village, the mine also has a 'Skywalk' with panoramic views across the mountains. A freebie hike's available too if you've the energy and want to escape the tourists down in Hallstatt. The Waldbachstrub Waterfall is a 3.5km uphill walk from the campsite in Hallstatt, about an hour one way.

4km further around the lake brings you to Obertraun (which has paid overnight mixed car and motorhome parking). From here the Dachstein Cable Car (*www.derdachstein.at*) delivers you to the Dachstein Ice Cave (Apr to Oct) and the Dachstein Mammut Cave (May to Nov).

Stop #3: Hochosterwizt Castle

Castle Car Park 4 ● GPS: N46.75519, E14.44654 ● No Services ● Price Guide: Free ● Castle Open April to November (*www.burg-hochosterwitz.com/en*) ● **Alternative:** Camping Weiser (*www.campingwieser.com*), GPS: N46.802083, E14.411956, Price Guide: £££, All Services

Austria's dotted with castles, *burgs* or *schlösser* in German, testament to more violent times when they were a necessity to escape marauding invaders. Burg Hochosterwitz drew us in when we read that we could offset the entrance fee with a free night's parking near the base, a win-win scenario for us and the Khevenhüller family who still own and maintain the medieval castle their forebears built.

Hochosterwitz stands on a 150m limestone rock, first mentioned in 860 AD, and was later used in the 15th Century as a refuge for the locals at a time the Ottoman Empire (which eventually shrunk down to modern-day Turkey) dominated the Balkans to the south.

The castle's fortifications twist back and forth around the rock forming a 620m walk upwards through 14 fortified gates, each with a plaque showing how the defences worked. It's claimed no attacks ever penetrated past the fourth gate, and that Hochosterwitz was the inspiration for Walt Disney's castle in Snow White. Even though several other European castles make this claim too, it's easy to see why this incredible fortress could have served to fire the imagination.

The castle has a centuries-old working blacksmith's forge, which carries out demonstrations in maintaining old armour and weapons as well as making new pieces. We really enjoyed walking the castle grounds with our dog, imagining life under siege. After a quiet night's sleep at the foot of the hill, the following morning we headed to Hallstätter See, visiting the Heinrich Harrer museum near Hüttenberg on the way (the Austrian climber and author of *Seven Years in Tibet* and *The White Spider*).

Stop #4: Riegersberg Castle

Castle Car Park ● GPS: N47.00797, E15.93299 ● No Services ● Shared Parking for Riegersburg Castle ● Price Guide: Free ● Castle open April to October (*www.dieriegersburg.at*), Entry Fee Applies ● **Alternative:** Gratz Stellplatz (*www.reisemobilstellplatz-graz.at*), GPS: N47.024492, E15.396444, Price Guide ££, All Services

Not all cities have convenient options for parking a motorhome, especially if you want a more secure overnight option than a car park or street-side parking. Since our visit to Graz, Austria's second-largest city, a useful stellplatz has been built. Only 200m from a bus stop, the stellplatz has direct access to the city centre, and if we visit Graz again, we'll certainly use it.

Without this facility we opted to stay the night an hour to the east at the medieval Riegersberg Castle, owned by the Princely Family of Liechtenstein, set among unlit countryside with night-time views of the Milky Way. The castle car park is free, but we paid the entrance fee to ride up the glass elevator to look around the fortress and peer out at the views.

Before we drove into Graz, we found that the city had (and still has) 'green' and 'blue' daytime parking zones, with the blue zones being cheaper and allowing longer stays (see *www.graztourismus.at*). Graz is the birthplace of Arnold Schwarzenegger and has a museum dedicated to him (*arnieslife.com*), but we'll remember the city for its futuristic and intriguing architecture, including the blue knobbly-roofed Kunsthaus, the Gratz Art Museum built in 2003. There's a great view of the Kunsthaus from the Schlossberg, where we enjoyed the skyline before descending the path to the city, crossing the wonderfully-quirky Murinsel, the Mur Island floating bridge, which partially sinks into the river Mur, built to celebrate Graz being the European Capital of Culture in 2003.

Stop #5: Vienna

Stellplatz (*www.reisemobilstellplatz-wien.at*) ● GPS: N48.13556, E16.31584 ● All Services ● 150m Walk to U Bahn (Train) into Vienna ● Price Guide: ££ ● **Alternatives:** Camping Wien West, Camping Wien Süd and Camping Neue Donau, All Similar Distances to the City

Vienna, the capital of Austria, is located to the east close to the border with Slovakia (and the old Iron Curtain) and regularly tops the charts as the world's best city for quality of life.

The city's stellplatz is located around 10km from the centre (the *Innere Stadt*). It's easy to access from the A2 and A21 autobahns, keeping driving stress levels down. From the stellplatz we walked 150m to the U Bahn train station into the centre. The journey took about 20 mins and costs roughly €2.50 per person each way (although we travelled for free thanks to a Dutch couple who gave us their still-valid *72 Stunden Wien* cards).

The custom-built stellplatz has 167 motorhome and campervan pitches and four service points. There are 10 showers and toilets available in a central block. Unusually for this type of location, you can book a pitch ahead of arrival. Dogs are allowed, and the site has daily bread and pastry deliveries at 8am in the reception building.

Vienna itself is a beautiful and relaxing city, which we found we could wander around on foot without needing to use public transport, following a walking tour we found in *Lonely Planet Austria*. Grand architectural statements draw your gaze as you walk: the Romanesque and Gothic St Stephen's Cathedral with its coloured-tile roof, the Hofburg imperial palace, the Rathaus town hall, the Schönbrunn Palace (summer residence of the Habsburgs) and many more. The baroque sculptures were a favourite for us: hulking great man-beasts straining under the weight of buildings or wrestling fierce animals.

BELGIUM

QUICK FACTS ● **EU**: Yes ● **Schengen**: Yes ● **Languages**: Dutch, French & German ● **Currency**: Euro (EUR, £1=€1.1) ● **Speed Limits ≤3.5t**: Urban/Single/Expressway/Motorway: 50, 70, 120, 120kph ● **Speed Limits >3.5t**: Urban/Single/Expressway/Motorway: 50, 70, 90, 90kph ● **Tolls**: Not on Motorways, Liefkenshoek Tunnel is Pay Per Use With Cash or Card ● **LEZs**: Central Antwerp, Brussels and Ghent ● **IDP**: Not Needed ● **Docs**: Driving Licence, Insurance, Passport, V5C ● **Kit**: Reflective Jackets, Headlamp Deflectors, Warning Triangle, (Fire Extinguisher & First Aid Kit Suggested) ● **LPG**: Good Availability, ACME Adapter ● **Time**: UK+1 Hour ● **Daytime Dipped Headlights**: No ● **Overnighting**: Campsites, Aires, Off-Site Parking Technically Not Allowed But Widely Overlooked Where No Prohibition Signs and Away from the Coast

Trappist beers first drew us into Belgium in our campervan, when we realised that Chimay, a favourite beer, was just over the border from France at Scourmont Abbey. Our enthusiasm got the better of us though and we arrived at the abbey with no tours available, while the Trappist monks were presumably busy brewing beer!

In the south of Belgium, the French we learned in school comes in handy, but in the north the locals speak Dutch (and often English too, thankfully!). To the east up against the border with Germany you'll also come across German language speakers.

We've travelled in Belgium several times over the years, visiting Ghent, Ypres, Tournai, Namur and the High Fens-Eifel Nature Park, coming across about WW1 battlegrounds and cemeteries, the industrial canal system with its giant boat lifts, towns packed with medieval architecture, the Redu satellite tracking station and let's not forget that Trappist beer! We've not yet visited Brussels by motorhome, but the Génération Europe Youth Hostel parking looks a popular budget option (GPS: N50.853131, E4.334484). Reservations are necessary at *www.lesaubergesdejeunesse.be*.

Belgium's also proved a very useful transit country for us. The motorways are toll-free for motorhomes, and although they've a reputation for having rough surfaces, we've found them to be mostly fine. If we're travelling to the French Alps, we tend to head from Calais down the toll-free A25 and A27 into Belgium, topping up with cheap diesel and LPG in Luxembourg before picking up the free A31 in France again.

Stop #6: Barrage de la Gileppe

Dedicated Motorhome Parking ● GPS: N50.587674, E5.969696 ● Free Electricity, No Other Services ● Price Guide: Free ● **Alternative:** Camping Wesertal (*www.camping-wesertal.com*), Price Guide: ££, Open April to October, GPS: N50.612191, E6.011491, All Services

A fellow motorhomer recommended this parking spot at the Gileppe Dam over towards the German border, east of Verviers (*www.gileppe.com*). The parking area for the dam has four dedicated motorhome parking spots with free electricity provided, and we really enjoyed our time here. We found the parking area busy with visitors during the day, but quiet and calm in the evening, giving us a great night's sleep.

Finished in 1875, making it one of the oldest in Europe, the dam was first built to supply the area's acidic water to support wool washing in Verviers. The dam was built with a huge 13.5m tall sandstone lion as a sentinel, now a famous landmark. It was quarried in Luxembourg and carved away from the site before being sawn into 183 blocks, each weighing up to seven tonnes, transported to the dam and re-assembled. These days the lake provides drinking water and produces a small amount of hydroelectricity.

There are views of the dam and the forests of the Ardennes to the south, which you can enhance from a panoramic tower near the parking area, plus an *Accropark* adventure course to enjoy. The other main attraction in the area is hiking and cycling. Various paths head out into woodland, including a 9.6-mile route circumnavigating the lake, and bikes are available for rent from the visitor's centre.

The *Parc Naturel des Hautes Fagnes* is also a few miles away, Belgium's oldest nature reserve. The park offers more hiking potential through moorlands, bogs and forests (*walloniabelgiumtourism.co.uk*).

Stop #7: Ghent

Shared Parking by Rowing Lake ● GPS: N51.050986, E3.680978 ● 24 Hours Allowed at the Time but Daytime Only Now ● No Services ● Price Guide: Free ● **Alternative:** Paid Aire on Braemkasteelstraat 5km from Centre at GPS: N51.037697, E3.7665675, Price Guide ££

We visited Ghent towards the end of our first long (two year) tour of Europe and by that point we'd cheerfully park up by the side of the road for a night, which is exactly what we did, alongside the man-made *watersportbaan* rowing lake about 4km from the centre. To be fair to us, tourist information advised it was fine at the time, although in the years that have passed it's been converted to daytime only motorhome parking now, but an aire is also available just a little further away (see details above).

Ghent (Gent in Dutch) was one of Europe's most important cities in the years spanning 1000 to 1550, larger even than London. During this period the Counts of Flanders were resident in the city's Gravensteen castle, built in 1180 and now a popular museum.

The centre of Ghent is one of the largest car-free areas in Europe, making the historic centre a pleasure to wander around on foot. Ghent University has around 44,000 students, giving the streets vibrancy during term time.

We picked up a walking tour from the modern tourist information office and, after pounding the streets sat with a drink, taking in the sunlit facades of the medieval Graslei, the quayside where ships have docked since the 11th Century on the right bank of the Leie river.

The 89-metre-tall Gothic Saint Bavo Cathedral was completed around the middle of the 16th Century and is also a major attraction, a five-minute walk from Graslei (*www.sintbaafskathedraal.be*).

Stop #8: Thieu

Motorhome Parking by Canal • GPS: N50.47133, E4.09005 • No Services • Price Guide: Free • **Alternative:** Small Canal-Side Parking Area a Short Distance Away, GPS: N50.472357, E4.105901, Price Guide: Free, No Services

We remember the village of Thieu, in Wallonia, as the land of the boat lifts! The free parking area is very popular with motorhomes, located on an old dock directly adjacent to two incarnations of a section of the Canal du Centre: the new canal to the front and the older, 19th Century one to the rear.

The older section of the canal was dug between 1884 and 1917 and has four UNESCO-listed hydraulic lifts, one of which is a mere 4-minute walk away from the parking area. These lifts were needed to link up the Meuse and Escaut rivers, allowing coal to be moved by barge. The natural height difference between the rivers, coupled with a lack of water, made locks impractical, so these industrial hydraulic giants, which still work, were constructed instead, each lifting boats up by around 15m.

In 2002 a modernisation programme was completed, bypassing the four old lifts with the world's tallest (at the time) Strépy-Thieu funicular lift. This remarkable new lift is around a 25-minute walk from the parking area and is well worth waiting for a boat to be slowly hauled up into the air while another is lowered alongside. The tallest boat lift crown's been taken by the Three Gorges Dam ship lift in China, completed in 2016, but that one's quite hard to drive to!

The whole area has a relaxing ambience, aided by the lime, maple, chestnut, walnut and ash trees planted alongside the old canal when it was built. It's only a couple of hours' driving from Dunkirk and makes a great stopover for a night or two. A cycle path runs all the way to Mons, roughly 45 minutes each way.

Stop #9: Ypres

Cobbled Car Park ● GPS: N50.84811, E2.88049 ● No Services ● Price Guide: Free ●
Alternative: Paid Aire Camperplaats Zillebeke Vijver 2.4 km from Centre at GPS: N50.83557, E2.90511, Price Guide £, All Services

Ypres looks old. Walking into the market square (the Grote Markt), the impressive Cloth House stands like a transept-less cathedral. Pale stone and yellow brick medieval and renaissance buildings stand around the edges of the square. The whole place looks four hundred years old but was sadly reduced to rubble during World War 1 and completely (and very well) rebuilt after the fighting.

Prior to that an idea was floated to retain the destroyed town as a monument to soldiers killed in the Ypres salient. The Cloth House was left in ruins for a while, leaving a stark reminder of what had taken place just a few years beforehand.

Just off one end of the market square stands the Menin Gate memorial. Built in 1927, it carries the names of 54,332 men killed in the salient with no known grave.

The moving Last Post ceremony takes place here every evening at 8pm (*www.visitflanders.com*).

As we drove towards Ypres, we passed sign after sign, each pointing towards a cemetery, museum or memorial of the Great War. We failed to find the motorhome aire, so opted to wing it in a cobbled car park. Arriving late, Ju legged it into tourist information and asked about the large commonwealth war cemetery nearby. "Which one?" the lady answered, "there are 157 of them?". The following morning, we visited Tyne Cot Cemetery, learning that 245,000 soldiers from the British side and 215,000 from the German side were killed, wounded or went missing in just 100 days to gain only five miles of land (*www.cwgc.org*).

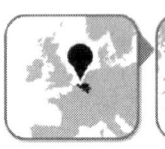  

BOSNIA and HERZEGOVINA

QUICK FACTS ● **EU**: No ● **Schengen**: No ● **Languages**: Bosnian, Croatian & Serbian ● **Currency**: Convertible Marka (BAM, £1=2.14KM) ● **Speed Limits**: Urban/Single/Expressway/Motorway: 50, 90, 130, 130kph ● **Tolls**: Yes on A1 Motorway (*www.jpautoceste.ba/en/toll*), Pay Per Use With Cash (BAM, EUR) or Card ● **LEZs**: None ● **IDP**: 1968 ● **Docs**: Driving Licence, Green Card Insurance, Passport, V5C ● **Kit**: Headlamp Deflectors, Warning Triangle, Fire Extinguisher, First Aid Kit, GB Sticker, Winter Tyres (15 Nov to 15 Apr) ● **LPG**: Good Availability, Dish Adapter ● **Time**: UK+1 Hour ● **Daytime Dipped Headlights**: Yes ● **Overnighting**: Campsites, Parking at Restaurants, Vineyards & Farms, Some Paid Aire-Type Stopovers, Wild Camping & Car Parks

Bosnia & Herzegovina (abbreviated to Bosnia below) is perhaps not the first place most of us would think of to travel to in our motorhomes. It's not in the EU, and no insurers that we know of will issue a Green Card for it. This means we need to buy 3rd-party insurance at the border, and ours cost us €55 for 5 days back in 2012 (the equivalent of around £3,200 a year!).

Our only exposure to Bosnia before we arrived was memories of news reports of the 1992 to 1995 war which erupted when Slovenia and Croatia declared independence from Yugoslavia following the fall of communism. Infighting started between ethnic groups, fuelled by historical religious and political tensions, over whether to remain with Yugoslavia or seek independence.

Today the mixture of Eastern Orthodox Christians, Roman Catholics, and Muslims co-exist peacefully again.

We had no trouble with the roads in Bosnia or finding places to stay overnight. Checking the *Park4Night* app, there are even more places to stay now, plenty to allow for a ten-day journey across the country.

Our memories of Bosnia are of friendly, welcoming people and an air of vibrancy, especially in Sarajevo where the cafés sell delicious *Cevapi* (lamb and beef kebab in a pita with raw diced onion) and intense Bosnian coffee. We left with life-long memories and were very glad we shelled out that €55.

Herzegovina, which contains Mostar, forms roughly 25% of the country. This area is located to the south and was merged with Bosnia in 1853. There's never been a strictly defined border between the two.

27

Stop #10: Kravica

Car Park for Kravica Waterfalls ● GPS: N43.15849, E17.60839 ● Near Studenci ● Price Guide: £ ● Car Park Warden Collects Money, Charges for Daytime and Overnight Stays ● Separate Entrance Fee to Visit Waterfalls

We entered Bosnia from Croatia, crossing at Brgat, south-east of Debrovnik. The sun was hammering down and we felt like the anvil, sweating and nervous as we reached the Bosnian side of the border crossing up in the hills. When we're travelling in the Schengen Area we rarely see a 'real border' but this one was very real! It came complete with guards supping cold beers (it was 10am) and a plain-clothes insurance man asking for payment in Euros or Croatian Kuna, helpfully for us as we had no Bosnian Convertible Marks.

Clutching our insurance, we rolled into Bosnia, excited and wondering what we'd find. A Czech lady we're met earlier (who had a Bosnian father) asked us why we were going to Bosnia "there's nothing there?" she queried.

At first, she seemed correct, as we drove through miles of countryside, too edgy to pull into Trebinje as we passed. At Stolac we found some courage and pulled in and were helpfully guided to a bank by a policeman. A walk up the hill to the old town was abandoned when Ju spotted an overgrown, rusting minefield sign. Instead we grabbed chairs at an outside café, the walls above pock-marked by bullets.

In the next town we pulled in to give Charlie a walk when some locals caught our attention and invited us inside, showing us a photo of the Kravica Waterfalls when we mentioned the sweltering heat. With their instructions we found a small paradise, a large bowl of greenery into which beautifully cool waterfalls fell. Bars around the edge were full of locals watching young lads demonstrate their courage diving from the rocks into the water below.

Stop #11: Mostar

Campsite Autocamp Paradise ● GPS: N43.26911, E17.86447 ● Located in Blagaj, 10km South of Mostar (Drive or Bus into Centre) ● Price Guide: ££ ● All Services ● **Alternative:** Camping Neretva, Price Guide: ££, GPS: N43.362257, E17.815146 at Sjeverni Logor, 3km from Centre of Mostar (*neretva-camping.business.site*), All Services

Mostar's star attraction is the Stari Most (the 'old bridge'), built in the 16th Century during Ottoman rule, hence the Islamic curve of the architecture. The bridge was destroyed in 1993 and rebuilt in 2004. Locals and Red Bull-fuelled travellers alike demonstrate their nerve diving from the bridge into the Neretva river below. We came to Mostar via the town of Međugorje, a town placed on the map by an apparition of the Virgin Mary in 1981 and now a major pilgrimage destination for Catholics.

We opted to use day parking in Mostar and walk into the centre, past a lively array of hawkers, coffee-sellers and tourist shops selling mortar shells and confusing Yugoslav war maps. Where the buildings hadn't been re-rendered, bullet and shrapnel marks peppered the walls. Off the tourist drag we came across a graveyard full of white marble columns pointing skyways like square pencils, each carved with a name and the year 1993 or 1994. Black and white photos of young men smiled out from each of them, an incredibly sad sight. Mostar seemed to us like a face burned by fire, beautiful but scarred.

Asking at tourist information we were given the address of Autocamp Paradise about six miles to the south. When we arrived the owner, Sacha, was stood in the road, beckoning us into a spot besides his vines. He parked us in the shade of a cherry tree, even pruning branches to help us open the door! Our stay there proved memorable to say the least as Sascha reminisced about life under communism and Tito, providing fascinating insight as he plied us and fellow campers with cold beer and home-made *grappa*.

Stop #12: Sarajevo

Campsite Autocamp Oaza (*hoteliilidza.ba/oaza-villas-camping*) ● GPS: N43.82950, E18.29685 ● 7km to City, Tram Stop 15-Min Walk then 45-Min to Centre ● Price Guide: ££ ● All Services ● **Alternative:** Camping Sarajevo, Price Guide: ££, GPS: N43.838889, E18.264444, 10-Min Walk, Bus then Tram to Centre (*camping-sarajevo.com*), All Services

We knew Sarajevo before we arrived for three reasons: as the place where WW1 started when Archduke Franz Ferdinand was assassinated after his car took a wrong turn into a dead-end street, the location of the 1984 Winter Olympics and holder of the title of 'longest siege of a capital city in modern times', enduring almost four years of being practically cut off from the world from May 1992 to Feb 1996. 14,000 soldiers and civilians were killed, including 1,500 children.

This latter period dominated our thoughts during our visit. Sarajevo is now largely a Muslim city, and the melodic call to prayer (the *adhān*) rang in our ears as we walked to the tram stop. The ancient tram rattled its way through 'sniper alley', the main boulevard into the city and infamous during the siege for gunmen shooting civilians as they crossed it, part of the daily horror.

From a hillside looking out over the city we visited the forest of graves in the Martyrs' Memorial Cemetery Kovači, and within the city streets we came across the 'red roses', coloured resin used to fill in mortar impacts in the street. At one point we stopped to read the names on a plaque, realising this was the site of the Trznica Markale massacres, where civilians shopping at the market were twice deliberately targeted with mortars.

Despite all this tragedy, Sarajevo felt like a city being quickly reborn. We ate delicious *cevapi* surrounded by full street cafés, bustling with young life.

BULGARIA

QUICK FACTS ● **EU**: Yes ● **Schengen**: No, But In Process of Joining ● **Language**: Bulgarian ● **Currency**: Lev (BGN, £1=2.15Лв) ● **Speed Limits ≤3.5t**: Urban/Single/Expressway/Motorway: 50, 90, 120, 140kph ● **Speed Limits >3.5t**: Urban/Single/Expressway/Motorway: 50, 80, 90, 100kph ● **Tolls**: Yes, Vignette or eVignette (*www.bgtoll.bg/en*), Plus Some Bridges and Ferries to Romania Charged Separately ● **LEZs**: None, But Vehicles >4t Cannot Enter Sofia 7am to 9pm ● **IDP**: Not Needed ● **Docs**: Driving Licence, Green Card Insurance, Passport, V5C ● **Kit**: Headlamp Deflectors, Warning Triangle, Reflective Jackets, Fire Extinguisher, First Aid Kit ● **LPG**: Good Availability, Dish Adapter ● **Time**: UK+2 Hours ● **Daytime Dipped Headlights**: Yes ● **Overnighting**: Campsites, Paid and Free Car Parks, Wild Camping

From the border post onwards the 1,000-year-old Cyrillic language gave Bulgaria an edgy, fascinating feel to us: Република България, the Republic of Bulgaria.

For nearly 500 years Bulgaria was submerged into the Ottoman Empire, although the Turkish Islamic influence has, to our eyes at least, been largely razed from the country.

There's plenty of evidence of more recent times, however, when Bulgaria was a communist state allied to the USSR between 1946 and 1990. Huge stone monuments celebrate Russian army success and promote the power of the working people. Aging Russian trucks, cars and the occasional horse-drawn cart still occupy the streets, alongside more modern VWs and Opels.

Being in the EU, UK insurers generally provide cover so Bulgaria's on the main motorhome tour overland route between central Europe and Greece or Turkey. The roads are generally in good condition and wild camping is widely allowed. There's also a network of campsites, although these are limited in number and you'll need to plan your route carefully if you don't want to wild camp some nights.

Your budget isn't likely to be badly dented by Bulgaria, especially if you do stay off-site some nights. Fuel prices are the lowest in the EU, and the cost of living is among the very lowest too. We'll never forget an ex-pat couple we met telling us how they'd bought a house there for £1,400 (telling us that was in the early 90s, and prices have gone up since!).

Stop #13: The Rila Monastery

Car Park for Monastery ● GPS: N42.132690, E23.339588 ● On Route 107, 21km East of Rila ● Price Guide: £ ● No Services ● Need to Leave before 9:30am ● **Alternative:** Camping Bor, 1km East of Monastery, GPS: N42.1401, E23.3532, Price Guide: ££, All Services

The Rila Monastery is one of the most famous sights in Bulgaria, one we didn't want to miss and very were happy to find we could stay the night right outside. We'd spent the night before free camping in the mountains of the Pirin National Park, six miles from the Bankso ski resort (GPS: N41.76619, E23.42575) surrounded by nature, so were already used to the cooler temperatures up at 1,147m in the Rila Mountains, where the monastery is located.

Around 60 Eastern Orthodox monks live and work at the monastery. At one point we sat and watched with interest as one of them blessed a car parked beside us, lifting the bonnet to sprinkle holy water onto the engine.

During 500 years of Ottoman rule the monastery acted as a kind of historical store, helping Bulgaria retain its language and cultural identity, and has been a UNESCO World Heritage site since 1983.

Set among forested hills, the monastery is heavily visited but given our parking spot a few metres from the gates we could choose our moments to wander around in peace, taking in the architecture and frescos painted across the outer walls, some depicting terrified sinners condemned to hell.

Just outside the monastery lies British writer James Bourchier's grave, a long-time supporter of the Bulgarian people. There is also a grave in the main church to Boris III, the king during World War II who refused to allow Hitler to deport Bulgarian Jews in WW2.

Stop #14: The Seven Rila Lakes

Car Park for Chair Lift ● GPS: N42.24274, E23.32441 ● Price Guide: £ ● No Services ● Some Single-Lane Stretches on Access Road ● **Alternative:** Camping Verila at Sapareva Banya (*camping-verila.com*), GPS: N42.291811, E23.251076, Price Guide: ££, All Services

The Seven Rila Lakes are a series of small glacial lakes resting between 2,100m and 2,500m above sea level. In other words, they're up high in the mountains, with snow lying in patches even in late June. If you can get high enough on the paths, all seven lakes are visible. We can't vouch for this though as we failed to start out early enough in the day and ran out of time.

The route to the lakes is along a mountain road. Usually these types of road tend to degrade the higher they get but this one strangely shifts nature from single-track-with-passing-places to a great quality dual-width road as it reaches higher up. At the top a car park attendant took a few Lev from us and directed us to a side area away from the main chair lift car park, where we could sleep on flat ground, surrounded by trees. Brown Bears inhabit these mountains (along with vipers), so night-time dog walks were brief, deliberately noisy and very jumpy!

The following morning the chair lift attendant advised us to be back by 4pm, and we headed off along the well-trodden mountain path. We found ourselves accompanied by a well-dressed lady in heels clutching a bottle of vodka and glasses, but you will need walking gear to make it to the top! The lakes appear one above the other along the hike, The Lower Lake, Fish Lake, Trefoil, Twin, Kidney, Eye and The Tear, although we only got to see the lower four before having to turn back.

The high-altitude landscape and cool air make for a wonderful summer walk, but the lakes are normally frozen from October to June, the ice sometimes 2m thick, so we'd recommend timing your visit for the warmer months. The Bulgarian tourist board has great photos of the lakes: *bulgariatravel.org/en/the-seven-rila-lakes*.

Stop #15: Veliko Tarnovo

Campsite (*www.campingvelikotarnovo.com*) at Dragijeo, 20-Min Drive from Veliko Tarnovo ● GPS: N43.0697222, E25.7530556 ● Price Guide: ££ ● All Services ● Open May to Sep ● **Alternative:** Camping Kapinovo Monastery (*www.kapinovski.bg*), 20km South of Veliko Tarnovo, GPS: N42.975930, E25.746959, Price Guide: ££, All Services

Along with Sakar Hills Campsite (*www.sakar-hills.com*), Camping Veliko Tarnovo is often mentioned by fellow motorhome travellers passing through (or staying a while) in Bulgaria. The site was created from scratch by British couple Nick and Nicky Kinson after they toured through Bulgaria on honeymoon in their Swift motorhome, taking their first guests in 2009. The site is located on a hillside near the village of Dragishevo, where you can wander the old streets or visit a coffee bar, taste the village cherries and get a feel for typical Bulgarian rural life.

The village is about a 20-min drive from the centre of Veliko Tarnovo (Great Tarnovo). The owners will arrange a taxi if you don't want the hassle of finding a parking place. The town has two universities and has a good range of bars and restaurants to cater for students and tourists, so it's a bustling place at times.

This area of Bulgaria gets very warm in summer, with average highs of between 26 and 30°C from Jun to Sep. The bars were spraying a fine mist of water on their outdoor guests during our visit to help cool them off. We took in the views of the Yantra River from the Tsaravets Castle and enjoyed simply wandering the streets taking in the architecture, monuments, cityscapes and the hillside views.

Since 2013 the city has a multimedia visitor's centre and tourist train, or if you're feeling more active the campsite hosts can arrange bird watching, rock climbing and 4x4 trips.

CROATIA

QUICK FACTS ● **EU**: Yes ● **Schengen**: No, But In Process of Joining ● **Language**: Croatian ● **Currency**: Kuna (HRK, £1=8.27KN) ● **Speed Limits ≤3.5t**: Urban/Single/Expressway/Motorway: 50, 90, 130, 130kph ● **Speed Limits >3.5t**: Urban/Single/Expressway/Motorway: 50, 80, 90, 90kph ● **Tolls**: Yes, Pay Per Use Motorways With Cash or Card (*hac.hr/en/toll*), Tolls Higher for >3500kg MAM, But No Electronic Box Required ● **LEZs**: None ● **IDP**: No Needed ● **Docs**: Driving Licence, Insurance, Passport, V5C ● **Kit**: Headlamp Deflectors, Reflective Jackets, Warning Triangle, First Aid Kit, Spare Bulbs, Snow Chains in Winter ● **LPG**: Good Availability, Dish Adapter ● **Time**: UK+1 Hour ● **Daytime Dipped Headlights**: Yes from Last Sunday in Mar to last Sunday in Oct ● **Overnighting**: Wild Camping Illegal, Enforced on the Coast. Many Quality Campsites (*www.camping.hr*). Some Businesses Allow Overnighting

A combination of warm Mediterranean climate, the pure blue waters of the Adriatic Sea, beautiful Venetian-built ports, stunning inland waterfalls and relatively low cost of living make Croatia (or *Republika Hrvatska* to the locals) a beautiful, calm and interesting country to relax for a while.

The country is easily accessible overland from Slovenia or Hungary, or via a ferry from Italy, perhaps to Dubrovnik or Split, and then driving the coastline northwards. As Croatia isn't yet in the Schengen Area, expect border controls and queues at busy times of the year.

Once you're in the country, you've the option to stay on the mainland or to take in some of the country's islands. Croatia's coastline is fragmented into 1,000 islands, 48 of which are inhabited. Some are accessible by bridges from the mainland, while others are reached by ferries which run like bus services: you arrive at the quayside and wait in line, pay for your ticket and get on the next available boat which has room.

Careful to control the integrity of the coastline, the police actively enforce wild camping laws, effectively restricting motorhomes to campsites. Out of season, the CampingCard ACSI discount card is very useful, with low-cost access to over 80 sites in Croatia.

Keep an eye out for 'mini camps' too, smaller sites for up to 200 people (*www.camping.hr/ok-mini-camps*). If you see that a site is 'FKK', it means it's a naturist destination (*Freikörper-Kultur*), which are popular in Croatia.

Stop #16: Hvar Island

Camp Vira (*campvira.com*) ● Set on Rocks by the Sea ● GPS: N43.19087, E16.43060 ● Price Guide: ££ ● All Services ● **Alternative:** Camping Jurjevac at Stari Grad, Simple Municipal-Style Site, GPS: N43.18269, E16.59282, Price Guide: ££, All Services

Ferries run from Split to the western ports on Hvar Island in about two hours, but we opted to use the shorter 35-minute crossing at the eastern end of the island, from Drvenik to Sućuraj. This ferry has the advantage of being shorter and cheaper but meant we had to drive 77km of relatively narrow, winding mountain roads to reach Hvar Town. The route's picturesque, through pines, orchards, vineyards and lavender fields, but requires concentration to save your wing mirrors. After using day parking to visit the popular old Venetian port, we retreated to Camp Vira, 3km to the north. Upon arrival we enjoyed our first (and only) golf-buggy tour of the shady site, settling in before enjoying snorkelling the crystal-clear Adriatic waters.

From Camp Vira we headed half an hour away to the more intimate Stari Grad, staying at a simple site a short walk from the yachts floating by the quayside. Ambling into town one evening we ate in the narrow streets at the unpretentious Jurin Podrum restaurant, where King Edward VIII dined in 1936 with Wallis Simpson, having recently abdicated. On the same trip the couple swam naked in a bay on the island of Rab, said to have kick-started Croatia's naturist tradition. Back at the campsite we were lucky to spend an evening chatting with a Czech family, who relayed how they'd fled their home country during communist rule, over the Slovenian mountains with just a suitcase each. They'd managed to emigrate to the USA and find work, although they were unable to return home until after the Velvet Revolution many years later.

Stop #17: Krka

Kamp Krka (*camp-krka.hr*) ● 3km to Krka Waterfalls Entrance ● GPS: N43.80029, E15.94143 ● Price Guide: ££ ● All Services ● **Alternative:** Autokamp Slapovi Krke, GPS: N43.791924, E15.970463, Price Guide: ££, All Services, 10-Min Walk to Krka Lozovac Entrance

Croatia has two waterfall-based national parks, Krka and Plitvice Lakes. They're both well worth a visit, with Plitvice being the most impressive (in our opinion, see page 39) but Krka having the advantage of allowing swimming in some parts, a definite plus when the sun's burning down from high in the sky.

Krka's located about 10km from Sibenik in the Dalmatia area of Croatia (yep, the same part of the world that the spotted dogs originate from). We stayed a couple of miles away from the Lozovac entrance to the park, where you can park for free during the day (day parking: GPS: N43.795596, E15.968595). We opted for nearby Kamp Krka as it took the CampingCard ACSI during our stay. We'd topped up with groceries from a Lidl en-route as the site is remote, surrounded by pines, vineyards, olive and fig groves, Mediterranean scrub and a few villas.

For information and entrance prices, go to *www.np-krka.hr/en*. There are three levels of access to the park, and we opted for the middle one, giving us access to the famous, mesmerising *Roški Slap* pictured above (*slap* is Croatian for waterfall), but not the boat excursions other than the ride from Skradin to Skradinski buk.

We spent a few hours ambling along the sun-dappled boardwalks which provide access throughout the park, peering at fish in the turquoise waters, eating a picnic we'd brought with us and enjoying the cool air before heading back to our van and returning to the coast.

37

Stop #18: Pag Island

Camping Village Šimuni (*www.camping-simuni.hr/en*) ● Large Site Directly by the Sea ● GPS: N44.46363, E14.96747 ● Price Guide: ££ with CampingCard ACSI ● All Services ● **Alternative:** Tonchi Ranch Farm Stop at Košljun, GPS: N44.405454, E15.066595, Price Guide: ££, No Services, Two Pitches

The landscape of Pag Island is like nothing we've seen before or since, a harsh, wind-blasted world of white stone, herbs and scrub being picked over by sheep whose milk goes into one of the island's famous exports: *paški sir*, a hard cheese.

We used the road bridge to the southern end of the island, leaving after our stay via the ferry back to the mainland at the northern end. When we arrived at the town of Pag we came across a *ražanj*, a wood-fired spit. We'd seen these at roadside eateries across Croatia and took the opportunity to pick up some roasted pork, happy to wait 40 minutes while it was cooked to perfection.

At the campsite further north we met up with a couple travelling south in a Winnebago nicknamed *The Beast*, complete with slide-outs, a sofa, washing machine and karaoke machine, and had a blast over a couple of days, drinking far too much and singing all night (we were the only two rigs on the huge site, so no other ears were assaulted). In the morning the campsite breakfast came with free alcoholic shots, just what we needed!

After leaving the site we visited Sirana Gligora cheese factory (*gligora.com*), where we enjoyed a tour and tasting session, learning that they only make *paški sir* at certain times of the year as that's when the sheep produce milk. Only sheep can survive the harsh conditions on the island and they create some wonderful cheeses which are flavoured by being wrapped while maturing in lavender, rosemary, olive, cherry and grape pulp (the latter being known in the factory as *drunk cheese*).

Stop #19: Plitvice Lakes

Borje Camp ● 16km from South Entrance to Plitvice Lakes National Park ● GPS: N44.76533, E15.68946 ● Price Guide: ££ ● **Alternative:** Camping Korana, 13km from Lakes (Bus Runs from Site to Lakes), GPS: N44.881264, E15.621373, Price Guide: £££

Plitvice Lakes is Croatia's oldest national park and has been on the UNESCO World Heritage list since 1979 (*np-plitvicka-jezera.hr*). It's the country's most popular tourist attraction, offering a chain of 16 azure, green, grey and blue lakes, each joined by waterfalls which flow over natural dams of *travertine*, formed by moss, algae and bacteria. *Veliki slap* is the highest waterfall at 78m, and tourists (us included!) line up to get a photo stood in front of it. The lakes are crossed by wooden walkways, hiking trails and at one point an electric boat ride, all located in a mountainous area between the Mala Kapela and the Lička Plješivica mountain ranges.

The wider area around the park supports brown bears and grey wolves and there are no campsites at the lakes. We opted to drive to the national park and park outside, visit and then drive to Borje Camp 16km to the south. Other sites run buses to the lakes if that suits your plans better. Allow a few hours for your visit, it's quite a large area.

This beautiful national park has a darker past too, as the location where Croatia's 'Homeland War' started. The first victims of the war died here in March 1991 when Yugoslavia started to break apart. Serbs living in Croatia declared independence from the rest of the country and occupied buildings at the park. In response, not having an army at the time, Croatia sent in the police and both sides suffered a casualty. A bloody four-year war followed which eventually saw Croatia win, retaining its pre-war borders, thanks in part to the controversial figure of Ante Gotovina, who is revered as a national hero in Croatia.

Stop #20: Povile

Camping Punta Povile ● Coastal Site 3km from Novi Vinodolski ● GPS: N45.11476, E14.81478 ● Price Guide: ££ ● All Services ● **Alternative:** Privately-Owned Overnight Motorhome Parking by Beach, GPS: N45.116854, E14.833958, Price Guide: £, No Services

Povile sticks in our memories not for any impressive tourist attractions nearby (it's a small fishing village), but simply as an idyllic location to park up and stay a while soaking up the sun, supping a cold *pivo* (beer) and enjoying being alive.

Camping Punta Povile is located a couple of miles from the centre of Novi Vinodolski with its bars and restaurants, and more importantly for us, a Lidl complete with low-cost lager and fridge-filling food to enable us to stay put on this lovely little site for a few days.

Our pitch was on a rocky promontory with no shade, but a wonderful view out along the coast. The ocean below our pitch offered a curious snorkelling experience, with the top few inches of sea being a layer of cold, fresh water, giving a strange semi-translucent affect when mixed with the warmer salt water below. The average sea temperature in Croatia in June is around 22°C, but with the cold upper layer of water a wetsuit was appreciated!

Standing cooking fresh vegetables and meat over our BBQ in the evening sunshine was such an uplifting experience. Charcoal BBQs aren't often allowed on campsites in summer, so ours got a rare outing. This was one of our top campsite pitches in years of touring.

The forested Krk Island is visible from the campsite and is accessible via a toll bridge (you only pay to get on, leaving is free) to the northern end. The island is well worth a visit too, including the tiny historic Krk City, surrounded by walls and a castle built by the Frankopan Family over several centuries and generations. On a later tour we stayed at Camping Krk, a 20-minute walk from Krk City (GPS: N45.02140, E14.59250).

Stop #21: Split

Camping Stobreč Split (*www.campingsplit.com*), 10km (15-Minute Taxi) from Centre of Split • GPS: N43.50473, E16.52940 • Price Guide: ££ • All Services • Easy to Access Without Driving into the City • **Alternative:** None

We drove to Split overland from the north the first time we visited, travelling via Italy and Slovenia. On the second occasion we arrived on a ferry across the Adriatic from Ancona in Italy, sleeping in a pet-friendly cabin on the 11-hour crossing.

About half of the old town in central Split is formed by Diocletian's Palace, a Roman-era sea-facing fortress and retirement residence built on the site of a previous Greek settlement. Modern Split has absorbed and expanded around the palace, so it's no longer a stand-alone entity, but is instead wonderfully enmeshed into the modern world. Restaurants, shops and homes cluster inside the walls, enlivened with tourists enjoying the sunshine and ambience. The palace was listed as a UNESCO World Heritage Site in 1979 and has featured in several *Game of Thrones* episodes.

There are a few car parks listed on park4night within walking distance of Split, but none officially allow overnight parking (comments from some of those chancing it report being fined), and some are height limited (OK for a small camper van). In search of a safe and quiet harbour we opted for the town's only campsite at Stobreč, about six miles from the old town, set against the sea with a small beach and a swimming pool.

Advised by the site that our small dog wouldn't be allowed on the bus, we arranged for a taxi into the city and took our time looking around the palace and having a drink beneath its walls. If you've bikes the route into the city is largely along the promenade but has a short steep hill to tackle on the return journey.

Stop #22: Trogir (Okrug Gornji)

Kamp Rožac (*camp-rozac.hr*) ● Stone Beach by the Sea, 2km Walk to Trogir ● GPS: N43.50524, E16.25766 ● Price Guide: ££ with CampingCard ACSI ● All Services ● **Alternative:** Various Car Parks Around Trogir But No Official Overnight Options

Our first visit to Trogir was back in 2012 during a summer heatwave. We bought a bag of ice from a vending machine and draped it over our panting pooch, to little effect. The extra-ordinary architecture of the town, packed onto a small island accessible by bridges, was lost in a battle against a blazing sun. On our second visit in 2016 we made a more sensible decision to arrive in April, and to park up at Kamp Rožac a 2km walk away from Trogir on the adjacent island of Čiovo.

In our first two years of touring we moved overnight spot on average every 1.5 days, and although we've slowed down over the years, even we were surprised to find we stayed for almost three weeks at Rožac.

What was it about Rožac we enjoyed so much? A combination of things: the site was quiet and low cost out of season (we were waiting for our new ACSI card to be posted to the site), we were parked overlooking the Adriatic, with dolphins appearing several mornings, the calm sea offered fun for our inflatable kayak and snorkelling gear (look out for urchins though) and a series of interesting and friendly British and Irish couples and families happened to arrive, so we had lots of people to chat with.

Trogir's the big tourist attraction nearby, but once we'd toured the small town, we found ourselves eating great quality, inexpensive meals in the far quieter sea-facing restaurants at Okrug Gornji. Okrug hosts a Fisherman's Festival in August and Okrug Summer Nights in mid-June to early September includes live music

CZECH REPUBLIC

QUICK FACTS ● **EU**: Yes ● **Schengen**: Yes ● **Language**: Czech ● **Currency**: Czech Koruna (CZK, £1=30Kč) ● **Speed Limits ≤3.5t**: Urban/Single/Expressway/Motorway: 50, 90, 110, 130kph ● **Speed Limits >3.5t**: Urban/Single/Expressway/Motorway: 50, 80, 80, 80kph ● **Tolls**: Yes, Vignette for <3.5t, Pay per km for >3.5t With Electronic Box (*mytocz.com*) ● **LEZs**: None ● **IDP**: Not Needed ● **Docs**: Driving Licence, Insurance, Passport, V5C ● **Kit**: Headlamp Deflectors, Reflective Jackets, Spare Wheel or Tyre Repair Kit, Warning Triangle, First Aid Kit, Winter Tyres ● **LPG**: Good Availability, Dish Adapter ● **Time**: UK+1 Hour ● **Daytime Dipped Headlights**: Yes ● **Overnighting**: Campsites (*camp.cz*), Some Aires, Wild Camping Illegal But Possible

We toured the Czech Republic (or Czechia for short) back in 2012, when databases of places to stay were in their infancy. On a tight budget, and not knowing many of the free and low-cost places to stay, we only stayed in a few locations before heading to Germany.

Looking at *park4night.com* now, there's a great number of free and paid parking places, mostly car parks or campsites, and only a few aires with service points. The CampingCard ACSI scheme lists 14 Czech campsites with low out-of-season fees and *eurocampings.com* lists 107 campsites in the country.

The main draw of Czechia for us were the historic towns: Český Krumlov, Tabor, Prague and Mariánské Lázně. Although the country was a communist state between 1948 and 1989, we didn't spot any of the huge monuments still evident in other ex-socialist countries. We were treated to architecture from the 14th to 17th centuries, in a range of styles from gothic through to brutal tower blocks.

To get a closer look at socialist history, the Museum of Communism in central Prague (*muzeumkomunismu.cz*) attempts to reconstruct life for the 15 million Czechoslovakian citizens who lived under communism.

We found eating and drinking out to be inexpensive in Czechia, with pints of craft lager costing little more than £1, and branded beer in supermarkets even cheaper (the original Budweiser beer is brewed in České Budějovice, known as Budweis in German). We were surprised to find Tesco supermarkets in Czechia too, even more taken aback to find alcohol stills for sale inside.

Stop #23: Český Krumlov

Official Overnight Parking ● Pop-Up Summer Parking on Grass ● GPS: N48.81548, E14.30875 ● Price Guide: ££ ● No Services ● **Alternative:** Parking Behind Bus Station, No Services, GPS: N48.816059, E14.309117, Price Guide: ££, 10-Minute Walk to Old Town

When we arrived at our overnight parking place a 10-minute walk from the centre of Český Krumlov we were curiously greeted by the attendant in German. Before the first part of the 20th Century most inhabitants were German, but most were forcibly expelled after World War 2.

During the communist era after WW2 the town fell into disrepair. The Vltava river which curls around the old town was polluted and dead by the late 1950s. The inhabitants heated their homes with coal, leading to fume-laden air as little breeze flowed through the valley in the colder months.

Traffic was a nightmare, with logging trucks and horse drawn carriages sharing the narrow streets with cars and pedestrians. Locals accessed everything they needed inside the town, only venturing out to the hospital or train station.

Fast forward to now and things have changed out of all recognition. The town has been thoroughly renovated, and the river runs clean, ridden by shouting canoeists in colourful life jackets. The cobbled streets are full of life although mainly for the benefit of tourists, and we enjoyed a meal and a few dark craft beers sat outside one of the many restaurants.

The town's main campsite is Kemp Krumlov a 2km walk to Vnitřní Město, the inner city (*www.kemp-krumlov.cz*). The site is relatively inexpensive, but reviews indicate that the motorhome pitches are basic. The site is open May to September.

Stop #24: Mariánské Lázně

Secure Paid Car Park ● GPS: N49.95902, E12.70183 ● Price Guide: ££ ● No Services ● Some Noise Until Midnight ● **Alternative:** Camping Stanowitz (*www.stanowitz.com/en*), GPS: N49.944033, E12.728114, Price Guide: ££, 3.5km (45-Min Walk) to the Springs, All Services

Mariánské Lázně (Marienbad in German), to the far west of Czechia, is famous for one thing: mineral water. Mention of the city's curative waters goes back nearly 700 years, and they're still pumping them out, claiming they fix everything from kidney disorders and sterility to cancer (we kid you not, see for yourself at *www.marianskelazne.cz*).

The city has over 100 naturally carbonated springs, with 16 of them available to taste for free, and all tasting quite awful (in our humble opinion!). The springs are named too, so you can wrinkle your nose as you try to force down some Rudolph, Pirate, Edward VII or Ambrose. The advice is to sip just a little: and get your doctor's advice first. Flavoured *Spa Wafers* are made and sold in the town, which helpfully mask the water's taste.

The town's beautiful and grand buildings are separated with leafy gardens and parks, a great place to relax and explore.

We stayed in a basic lorry, bus and motorhome parking area a short walk from the centre. When we went to pay the guardians, they'd one eye on a TV watching the 2012 London Olympics, telling us "it's very safe here", and that they released a fierce dog overnight! We nodded back, smiling, remembering not to step outside after dark.

Stop #25: Prague

Camping and Caravan Yacht Club Campsite ● Located on Císařská Louka, a Mile-Long Artificial Island in Central Prague ● GPS: N50.06167, E14.41423 ● Price Guide: £££ ● **Alternative:** Camping Prague (*www.campingpraha.cz*), on Outskirts. 35-Min Bus+Train or Bus+Metro to Centre, GPS: N50.098705, E14.684665, Price Guide: ££ with ACSI

Prague made it easy for us to visit by motorhome, with the Camping and Caravan Yacht Club Campsite located close to the centre, on an island in the Vltava River just a short water taxi ride from the city's tram network.

We arrived in Prague at the end of July, in high season, the streets and monuments thronged with fellow tourists, tour groups being led around by harassed-looking leaders with a raised umbrella or flag.

We spent a couple of days exploring the city. The first day we did no research and just took in the vibrant feel of the place, joining the crush on the Charles Bridge and Staroměstské Náměstí (the old square) with its astronomical clock, the location of Christmas and Easter markets. A cool local lager eased us back to the ferry and our motorhome, where we utterly failed in our attempts to watch the opening ceremony to the London 2012 Olympics (these days 4G internet makes watching TV abroad much simpler).

On our second day, re-invigorated despite the booming music of late-night party boats on the adjacent river, we made a more concerted effort to explore, again with our dog Charlie in tow. Climbing the cobbled steps, we watched the guards changing outside Prague Castle before taking it in turns to peer into the soaring interior of the gothic St Vitus Cathedral. After a half hour rattling along on the city's #41 Historic Tram, we ate lunch and headed back to the van before the rain came, treated to the quieter evening charms of jazz from a passing boat.

DENMARK

QUICK FACTS ● **EU**: Yes ● **Schengen**: Yes ● **Language**: Danish ● **Currency**: Danish Krone (DKK, £1=8.16KR) ● **Speed Limits ≤3.5t**: Urban/Single/Expressway/Motorway: 50, 80, 130, 130kph ● **Speed Limits >3.5t**: Urban/Single/Expressway/Motorway: 50, 80, 80, 80kph ● **Tolls**: Yes, But Only on Øresund and Storebælt Bridges (*www.oresundsbron.com* and *storebaelt.dk*) ● **LEZs**: Yes in Copenhagen, Frederiksberg, Aarhus, Aalborg and Odense (*miljoezoner.dk/en*) ● **IDP**: Not Needed ● **Docs**: Driving Licence, Insurance, Passport, V5C ● **Kit**: Headlamp Deflectors, Warning Triangle ● **LPG**: Very Limited Availability, Bayonet or Dish Adapters ● **Time**: UK+1 Hour ● **Daytime Dipped Headlights**: Yes ● **Overnighting**: Campsites and Paid Aires, Wild Camping Illegal But Allowed in Some Forests (*eng.naturstyrelsen.dk/experience-nature*) and Often Tolerated Elsewhere for One Night Unless Explicitly Signed

Although no car ferries run direct from the UK to Denmark, it remains the easiest of the Scandinavian countries to get to by motorhome. After a ferry from England to the Netherlands, toll-free motorway takes you all the way to the Danish border on the Jutland Peninsular in eight or nine hours. On a longer tour, numerous ferries cross from Denmark to Norway or Sweden, or you can take the incredible Øresund Bridge to Sweden.

Our memories of Denmark are of a beautifully clean and safe country, where we enjoyed learning about the history of Carlsberg in Copenhagen, discovering modern sculpture in the ARoS Aarhus Art Museum, watching new ships being hand-built to match the 900-year-old real thing at Roskilde Viking Ship Museum, coming face-to-face with the 2,200 year old Tollund Mann at Museum Silkeborg Hovedgården and learning about Bluetooth at Jelling.

We found Denmark easy to travel by motorhome. The roads are in great condition and toll-free, except for the Storebælt Bridge linking the country's two largest islands, Zealand and Funen. We kept our costs down sleeping in a combination of free parking spots and paid marina parking, but there's a great range of paid aires and campsites, with over 70 sites listed in the CampingCard ACSI scheme alone.

The PinTrip scheme also offers 24-hour free stays at over 600 businesses including distilleries, a Christmas tree plantation and an ice cream maker, allowing you to get close to the real Denmark (*pintrip.eu*).

Stop #26: Aarhus

Paid Marina Aire ● GPS: N56.13956, E10.21995 ● Price Guide: ££ ● All Services Plus Showers ● 3km, 15-Min Cycle Ride to ARoS Art Museum ● **Alternative:** DCU-Camping Blommehaven (*www.dcu.dk/en/campingplads/dcu-camping-blommehaven*), GPS: N56.110536, E10.231736, Price Guide: £££, 5km South of Central Aarhus

Aarhus is Denmark's second-largest city, located on the east coast of the Jutland Peninsular. It has a dedicated motorhome aire with six places at the marina a few km south of the centre. We rented two basic bikes from the city, a simple process of depositing a 20 DKK coin, no need for credit cards or any registration, and you even get the money back when you return the bike. Access to the aire was a bit more of a convoluted process, requiring us to buy a *Tallycard*, something we'd never come across before (or after).

We were drawn to Aarhus by the ARoS modern art museum and were blown away by the clever nature of the sculptures it hosted. A giant squatting boy towered over us, his expression changing as we walked beneath. A sign told us we could no longer scratch the paint work on a brand-new sports car parked in one area, as it was already scratched almost paint-less by previous visitors. A giant chandelier almost filled one room, made entirely of (unused) tampons. Rectangular holes in the walls of a mirror room revealed yet more mirrors, making the room appear to float. A huge set of coloured steam irons arranged into the petals of flowers smoothly opened and closed automatically, as though responding to the sun.

The ARoS offered a great view of the Aarhus skyline too, in a rainbow of colours as we walked a circular rooftop walkway in stained glass, experiencing our emotions change with the different hues.

Stop #27: Copenhagen

Free Car Park ● GPS: N55.66475, E12.52962 ● Price Guide: Free ● No Services ● Opposite Entrance to Carlsberg Exbeerience ● Overnighting Not Allowed ● **Alternative:** DCU-Copenhagen Camp Absalon (*www.dcu.dk/en/campingplads/dcu-copenhagen-camp-absalon*), Open All Year, GPS: N55.670984, E12.433969, Price Guide: £££, 7km West of Central Copenhagen (600m Walk to Brøndbyøster Station, then 20-Min Train Ride), All Services

We arrived in Copenhagen from Malmö via the five-mile-long Øresund Bridge (and tunnel, as it dives below the sea for a further two and a half miles). The city's official aires were closed for the winter, and we opted to wing it for a night, parking on the road opposite the entrance to the Carlsberg Exbeerience (great name but now re- branded to Visit Carlsberg, *www.visitcarlsberg.com*).

We wouldn't recommend doing the same (the city has an all-year campsite, quieter and safer), but we enjoyed learning about the history of Carlsberg, including the fact they'd needed to remove the swastika from their brand after it was adopted by the Nazis (it's still carved onto the sides of the huge iconic elephants nearby). The fact a few drinks were thrown into the mix didn't do any harm!

The following morning, we walked into the centre of the city, gobsmacked by the number of bicycles on the road or parked up everywhere. The city has around 560,000 bicycles, more than the number of residents. Half of all city journeys are by bike along dedicated lanes safely separated from the road (430km in total).

The famous Tivoli Gardens were closed at the time, and we didn't have the legs to walk out to The Little Mermaid statue, but we did enjoy the colourful and iconic 17th and 18th Century houses and moored historic wooden boats alongside the Nyhavn Canal.

Stop #28: Helsingør

Paid Car Park at Kronborg Castle ● GPS: N56.04040, E12.61610 ● Price Guide: ££ ● No Services ● **Alternative:** Helsingør Camping (*www.helsingorcamping.dk*), GPS: N56.043226, E12.604713, Price Guide: £££, Open All Year, All Services

With a motorhome you get to sleep in some unusual places! At Helsingør we stayed overnight besides 'Hamlet's Castle', the UNESCO-listed Renaissance Kronborg Castle. Shakespeare used the English version of the name in his play, Elsinore Castle, although the Bard never visited Denmark.

Helsingør is strategically placed at the entrance to the Øresund, a two-mile-wide strait between Denmark and modern-day Sweden (when Kronborg was built the area on the other side was also Danish). Taxes would be collected on shipping passing through the straight, providing up to two-thirds of Denmark's state income. These days you can take a ferry to Helsingborg, an alternative route to the Øresund Bridge and the busiest car ferry route in the world.

The short distance across the straight is all that separated Danish Jews from safety in neutral Sweden during WW2, and over 7,200 of them (plus 700 non-Jewish relatives) were spared the concentration camps in a three-night secret escape in 1943, hidden on fishing boats, private pleasure craft and ferries.

The castle parking area, set among grass and trees, proved a calm and quiet place to visit the imposing castle and the nearby port town. As well as providing several (relatively) low-cost beer and wine shops for visiting Swedes, the town's dry dock has been transformed into the Danish Maritime Museum. Also, one of the town's churches still has an English cannonball embedded in an inside wall where it landed during an 1801 conflict.

Stop #29: Hornbæk

Beach-Side Parking ● GPS: N56.092693, E12.46783 ● Price Guide: Free ● No Services ●
Alternative: Gilleleje Camping (*www.gillelejecamping.dk*), GPS: N56.104649, E12.342115, Price Guide: £££, 9km from Hornbæk, All Services

By the time we reached the beach-side parking area a short walk from the small resort town of Hornbæk, we'd been on the road for ten months and had slept in 170 different places. The simple pleasure of staying at an out-of-season, sandy and deserted beach was just what we needed.

After the usual post-arrival chill out and cuppa, we set off along the beach towards the town, passing thousands of washed up plate-sized pink jellyfish. Above a thatched cottage by the path a battered Danish flag flew to remind us where we were.

In town we tracked down a seafood diner/cafe/restaurant/takeaway (you ordered your food at an outside window and decided for yourself where on the premises you ate it) recommended in our Lonely Planet guidebook.

Heated by the sun through a huge glass window, we tucked into an enormous pile of deep-fried plaice, battered fishcakes and chips, having ignored all the fantastic-looking fresh seafood on offer. On one wall a black and white photo showed a group of men using a rope and an iron contraption to haul a pool table-sized chunk of ice from the sea.

Having arrived through Norway and Sweden, where strong alcohol is only sold through government shops, we enjoyed the novelty of ordering a 10cl bottle of 45% proof *Akvavit*, a colourless eye-wincer of a drink. We asked the chap serving us whether we should drink it before or after the meal. He just smiled enigmatically and shrugged, suggesting either would do. After a quick taste of it, we think the real answer he was trying to discretely tell us was this: neither!

Stop #30: Jelling

Car Park at Hybylund, 36km SE of Jelling ● GPS: N55.58042, E9.78613 ● Price Guide: Free ● Small Sloping Site By the Sea ● No Services ● **Alternative:** Harbour Aire at Vejle, 13km SE of Jelling, GPS: N55.706973, E9.552261, Price Guide: ££, All Services

Our guidebooks told us that every Dane goes to Jelling at some point in their life, as it's revered as the birthplace of Christianity in Denmark, the monarchy and all that is Danish. On a personal level we wanted to find out why everyone now has a Danish Viking King on their phone.

We followed the signs to the UNESCO-listed site and parked up in the free car park (daytime parking: GPS: N55.75613, E9.41680). In fact, everything here is free, you can wander around the church and new visitor's centre explaining the history of the place, all for nothing (*en.natmus.dk*). The lack of entry fee doesn't detract from the quality of the place though, it seems that the government keep it free because it is such an important place to the Danish people.

Jelling was a Viking settlement over 1,000 years ago. Not just any Viking lived there though, it was the royal seat of King Gorm the Old, the first in a millennium-long chain of monarchs that still sit on the throne today. How do we know they were here? Well, they left their mark, literally. Gorm and his son Harald Bluetooth both had runes carved into huge boulders, which still sit outside the church today, now protected behind glass in atmosphere-controlled boxes.

So, why do we all have a Viking King on our mobiles? The engineer Jim Kardach, who helped create the Bluetooth system, spotted the name of King Harald in a Viking book, and chose to name the system after him. The Bluetooth symbol combines the Viking runes for H and B.

Stop #31: Vandel

Car Park ● GPS: N55.71309, E9.21811 ● Price Guide: Free ● 6km from Legoland at Billund ● No Services ● **Alternative:** LEGOLAND Camping (*www.legolandholidays.dk*), GPS: N55.731171, E9.136048, Price Guide: £££, 460m Walk to LEGOLAND Park Entrance, All Services

Lego's a Danish invention, created at Billund in 1932 with the name derived from the words *leg godt*, meaning "play well" (*www.lego.com*). The first plastic bricks were produced in 1948 (before that they were wooden) and these days the company makes a profit of roughly a billion pounds a year, but it's still based in little Billund in central Jutland.

With a population of less than 7,000 people, the town almost feels like it's built from Lego. It's everywhere! There are Lego factories, Lego murals, Lego offices, a Lego theme park, a Lego hotel, a Lego campsite, a Lego house and even huge pieces of Lego besides the street.

Our research turned up the fact all the car parks around Billund were a no-go area for overnight stays, so we scouted out an overnight parking area four miles away at Vandel, and then used a free car park about 1km from Billund for the day.

We'd heard that entrance to the theme park was free for a couple of hours before closing time and when we arrived we found a queue of locals waiting to get in (*www.legoland.dk/en*)! We had to leg it around in the short time available to get onto a ride, then look around the fantastic miniature cityscapes, models of Concorde and Mount Rushmore and life-sized animals all crafted from Lego. The darkness was falling too, creating some difficulty actually seeing anything!

If we had kids, we'd have happily paid the entrance fee, but with our pooch waiting in the van our quick evening visit satiated our Lego curiosity, for now!

ESTONIA

QUICK FACTS ● **EU**: Yes ● **Schengen**: Yes ● **Language**: Estonian ● **Currency**: Euro (EUR, £1=€1.1) ● **Speed Limits ≤3.5t**: Urban/Single/Expressway/Motorway: 50, 90, 90, 90kph ● **Speed Limits >3.5t**: Urban/Single/Expressway/Motorway: 50, 90, 90, 90kph ● **Tolls**: Not for Motorhomes ● **LEZs**: None ● **IDP**: Not Needed ● **Docs**: Driving Licence, Insurance, Passport, V5C ● **Kit**: Headlamp Deflectors, Warning Triangle, Fire Extinguisher, Two Wheel Chocks, Winter Tyres ● **LPG**: Good Availability, Dish Adapter ● **Time**: UK+2 Hours ● **Daytime Dipped Headlights**: Yes ● **Overnighting**: Campsites, Some Aires and Businesses, Free Camping Legal With Restrictions (Notably for 24 Hours Outside Hearing and Sight Range of Houses)

We arrived in Estonia via Poland and the other Baltic countries, squeezing between Kaliningrad and Belarus to avoid additional insurance and visa concerns. Coming from the north, ferries cross to Estonia from Finland and Sweden.

We found Estonia much like the other Baltics in terms of the ease of free parking, able to sleep against the sea, by lakes and in forests with no issues at all. Estonia legally allows overnight stays in nature (with limitations) under their Everyman's Right (*www.eesti.ee/en/housing-and-environment/nature-protection/everymans-right-and-public-access-to-natural-areas*).

Our overall memory of Estonia was of a safe, welcoming place for motorhome travellers. The roads were generally good quality, with dirt roads in more remote places. We loved the mix of legal free camping and access to formal facilities when we wanted them.

The towns and cities had character, well restored after being repeatedly fought over by the Germans and Russians in WW2. The capital, Tallinn, lies on the Baltic cruise liner routes, attracting large numbers of tourists and has been heavily polished as a result.

Estonia was a natural route for us to travel up to and across the Gulf of Finland to Finland and onwards up to the North Cape in Norway, an incredible tour route. If you're travelling this way with a pet dog, be aware Finland requires a worming treatment before entry, like the UK, which we found easy and inexpensive in Estonia. It also makes a lot of sense to stock up on long-life groceries, as they're far cheaper in Estonia than in Scandinavia!

Stop #32: Rõngu

Hospital Car Park ● GPS: N58.13981, E26.24586 ● Price Guide: Free ● No Services ● 500m Walk to Town ● **Alternative:** Soontaga Forest Camp (details on *loodusegakoos.ee*), GPS: N58.021879, E26.067821, Access via 4km of Gravel Road, Price Guide: Free, Dry Toilet

In retrospect, it seems very odd that we just opted to pull into a hospital car park and sleep for the night near the hamlet of Rõngu. The parking area was very quiet though, set besides an orchard, and it seemed quite natural at the time to spend an evening there, a demonstration of how easy-going the Baltics felt for freedom parking. Our journey had taken us through Valga-Valka, where we'd chosen not to sleep as a festival was taking place, and we spotted the hospital car park as we drove along the road on our way north.

Valga-Valka is a fascinating place, a town split in two by the Estonian-Latvian border. 100 years ago, there was no border, no Estonia (or Latvia), just the town of Walk. A national spirit started to form in the late 19th Century, and when the Russian revolution took place Estonia and Latvia took the opportunity to declare independence. After the fighting was over a new border was drawn up, with majority populations deciding which side each town was placed, except for Walk, which had a fairly-even split. The answer was formed by a British diplomat: divide the town in two, following the route of a small stream.

At this point people of Walk suddenly needed a passport to walk to the other end of town, and a different currency to buy from the shops. Customs posts were squeezed in between houses. When the Soviets later occupied the region, this problem was removed, only to be re-introduced when the USSR fell, and removed again when the towns joined the EU. Today, zebra-striped poles still mark the location of this quirky border.

Stop #33: Soomaa National Park

Kõrtsi-Tõramaa Campfire Site ● GPS: N58.43074, E25.03012 ● Price Guide: Free ● Electricity, Cooking Fire, Firewood, Dry Toilet, Water ● Located Near the Soomaa National Park Visitor's Centre ● Access via 16km of Good Quality Dirt Road ● **Alternative:** None

Estonia doesn't just allow free camping it positively encourages it. Perhaps harking back to the country's communist years, simple, free camping locations are maintained out in nature for all to use (the *loodusegakoos.ee* site catalogues them).

Like many of these sites, the Kõrtsi-Tõramaa Campfire Site in the Soomaa National Park is accessed via an unpaved road. 10 miles of it. After visiting an Autoekspert shop to fix a minor radiator leak (*www.autoekspert.ee*, like Halfords) we tackled the road, finding it to be in good condition but dusty and limiting us to around 20mph. The park has a reputation for heavy flooding in the spring though (we saw photos of people kayaking down the road), so check the conditions first.

The site itself was a grass field with a wooden hut containing firewood, and a large cooking fire pit with a grill. Before leaving the UK, we'd fitted a 'SOG Unit' to our van (*www.soguk.co.uk*), which means we don't use any chemicals and can empty into the natural (long-drop) toilets provided at remote sites like this one.

A 'Beaver Trail' walking route leads from the site across paths and raised boardwalks into the forest. Signs suggested we might spot black woodpeckers or beavers, but the closest we got to wildlife was seeing where they'd gnawed away at tree trunks. There are bears, wolves and elk in the forest, but they stayed away too. That said, there was no lack of mosquitoes. The Soomaa is called the 'Land of Bogs' in English, and it's a perfect breeding ground for mozzies; come armed with Jungle Formula and practice a quick hand swatting motion!

Stop #34: Tallinn

Tallinn City Camping (*www.tallinn-city-camping.ee*) ● GPS: N59.44800, E24.80888 ● Price Guide: £££ ● All Services ● **Alternative:** Pirita Harbour Camping (*www.piritatop.ee*), GPS: N59.466640, E24.823670, Price Guide: ££, All Services

Tallinn is Estonia's capital, a port city set on the Baltic Sea with direct ferry access to Helsinki, 50 miles to the north in Finland (or to Stockholm in Sweden). The city has a population of only 440,000, around the same as Bristol. Centrally, Tallinn has retained a medieval feel with cobbled streets, the flowing, flower-like decoration of the orthodox cathedral, Disney cylindrical towers on the town walls and a thousand vibrant cafes and restaurants, all spilling out into the squares and streets.

We had fun eating a huge ox rib and supping mead sat outside the medieval-themed III Draakon in the town hall square (*Raekoja Plats*) before walking up Toompea Hill for a view over the town and cruise ships docked in the distance. The town has several museums and galleries, including the Vabamu Museum of Occupations and Freedom which documents German and Soviet rule in the 20th Century, and the Kadriorg Art Museum, a beautiful baroque palace built for Catherine I of Russia by Peter the Great.

From Tallinn we took a ferry to Finland, having first stocked up at a Rimi hypermarket (*www.rimi.ee*), and brimming our LPG tanks as we wouldn't see another refill station for over 1,000 miles until we reached Alta in the Norwegian Arctic.

The 'campsites' listed above are basic aire-style locations (asphalt, no marked pitches), but are only 4 or 5km away from the centre. If you can't walk, and have a dog, they are allowed on public transport, but technically they need to be in a carrier or wearing a muzzle.

57

Stop #35: Viljandi

Lake Parking ● GPS: N58.35911, E25.60298 ● Price Guide: Free ● No Services ● 1.6km Walk from Centre ● **Alternative:** Sammuli Camping (*www.sammuli.ee*), GPS: N58.338303, E25.589298, 7km Walk or Cycle from Centre, Price Guide: ££, All Services

Sometimes we get lucky and meet up with travellers who furnish us with some of their favourites places to stay. This happened on our way to Viljandi, spending an evening chatting with a couple who'd spent decades travelling. During the evening they recommended some places to stay, including this quiet place by the lake.

Arriving in the sunshine of mid-June, the boat owners on the lake were out in force bailing them out, fixing motors and paying no attention whatsoever to our arrival in their midst.

The lake has a 13km 'Green Way' path around it, and a set of stacked stones nearby are carved with the names of winners of an international running race which takes place around it each year, (the Grand Race, *viljandijarvejooks.ee*).

We walked the route, finding it's nothing like as flat as it looked from our parking place! Afterwards we refuelled with an inexpensive and delicious restaurant meal.

The town's huge ruined Teutonic castle also drew us upwards, with beautiful views of green countryside beyond the lake. The town itself was a neat and clean affair, with clues of a tougher past here and there: leafy squares cleared of house rubble after WW2 bombings, and the statue of a mayor and his dog, deported to Russia for 'anti-Soviet activities' (huge numbers of Estonians were deported during and after WW2). More recently the boarded-up windows of beautifully detailed buildings, many built by wealthy Baltic Germans, make it clear the town is awaiting new investment and new life.

FINLAND

QUICK FACTS ● **EU**: Yes ● **Schengen**: Yes ● **Languages**: Finnish, Swedish, Sámi ● **Currency**: Euro (EUR, £1=€1.1) ● **Speed Limits ≤3.5t**: Urban/Single/Expressway/Motorway: 50, 80, 100, 100kph ● **Speed Limits >3.5t**: Urban/Single/Expressway/Motorway: 50, 80, 80, 80kph ● **Tolls**: None ● **LEZs**: None for Motorhomes ● **IDP**: Not Needed ● **Docs**: Driving Licence, Insurance, Passport, V5C ● **Kit**: Reflective Jackets, Headlamp Deflectors, Winter Tyres ● **LPG**: No Refill Stations ● **Time**: UK+2 Hours ● **Daytime Dipped Headlights**: Yes ● **Overnighting**: Campsites, Aires and Businesses, Free Camping Legal With Restrictions Under Right of Public Access Law (*Jokamiehen Oikeudet*)

Finland is one of Europe's most sparsely populated countries with just over 16 people per km² (compared with the UK at 280 people/km²). With 72% of the land covered in forest, longer drives on arrow-straight roads feel like an endless corridor of trees. The country has over 180,000 lakes and over 46,000km of coastline. Finland's 'Everyman's Right' law enables free camping (with restrictions) across much of the country, providing a huge number of places to stay overnight. Databases like *park4night.com* list out only a small percentage of the available spots to stay.

These facts play out on the ground with a wonderland for motorhome-based nature-lovers. Keep an eye out though, reindeer like to amble around on the routes in the north and have zero road sense. Elk, bear, wolves and lynxes all roam the forests (we saw plenty of reindeer, but only glimpsed a single elk). To avoid any encounters at speed we didn't drive in the dark, but in the far north it was light 24 hours a day, and one couple we met saw lots of wildlife by driving at night.

Nature aside, we were challenged by the Finnish norm of being naked in saunas, made to laugh out loud at the World Wife Carrying Championship, loved the sensation of crossing the Arctic Circle and enjoyed learning about the indigenous Sámi people who live at those high latitudes.

We travelled through Finland in June and July. From Helsinki, we headed west to the Turku Archipelago before turning north east and crossing the Finnish Lakeland. From there we headed north to the Kylmäluoma National Park, crossing into the Arctic at Santa's hometown of Rovaniemi, and finally into Norway near the Kevo Nature Reserve, 250 miles inside the Arctic Circle.

Stop #36: Kevo Nature Reserve

Nature Reserve Car Park (*www.nationalparks.fi/en/kevo*) ● GPS: N69.39365, E26.11219 ●
Price Guide: Free ● No Services ● **Alternative**: Trail Car Park, GPS: N68.895424, E26.967095,
Price Guide: Free, 3km from Siida Sámi Museum in Inari, No Services

Our overriding impression of Finland was of vast areas of raw nature, with functional towns designed to service the needs of the people. We drove for hours through forests, slept alongside and wild-swam in lakes, and didn't do anything like as much hiking as we should have (we're blaming our elderly dog).

Nature seemed to define the indigenous Sámi people who traditionally lived in an area which spans modern Norway, Sweden, Finland and Russia. They live through coastal fishing, fur trapping, sheep herding and reindeer husbandry, all of which we learned about at the Siida Museum in Inari. We can't claim it was all work mind you, we had fun trying to lasso reindeer horns in the area outside along with friends we'd met in their motorhome in Estonia and who were following a similar route, gravitating towards the North Cape in Norway.

The car parks around Inari don't allow motorhomes to stay overnight. After spending a couple of hours in the museum (including refuelling with coffee and a blueberry-topped *pulla*, a cardamom-flavoured bread), we headed to a K Market to get the deposit back on empty drinks cans before leaving the country.

Our plan was to cross the border at Karigasniemi in Lapland, and the car park for the Kevo nature reserve proved a convenient place to spend a quiet night beforehand (with 24-hour light and eye masks) before heading west. The reserve has a 2km nature trail, as well as more serious 63km and 86.5km hiking routes.

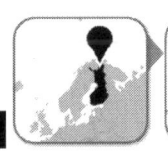

Stop #37: Kuopio

Spa Hotel Rauhalahti Car Park (*www.rauhalahti.fi*) ● GPS: N62.86711, E27.64403 ● Price Guide: Free ● Electricity Available for a Fee ● 750m Walk to Lumberjack Lodge and Sauna ● **Alternative:** Rauhalahti Holiday Centre (*www.visitrauhalahti.fi*), GPS: N62.8640342, E27.6392019, 1.2km Walk to Lumberjack Lodge, Price Guide: £££, All Services

We admit it, we failed miserably at our first attempt at nakedness in a sauna in Finland. The test came when we arrived at the Spa Hotel Rauhalahti, which allows motorhomes and caravans to overnight in their car park for free, even providing hook-up for a fee. The hotel is attached to a lumberjack lodge and the world's biggest smoke sauna, all located besides a lake an easy 750m walk through the forest.

The Jätkänkämppä Lumberjack Lodge (*jätkä* = lumberjack, *kämppä* = lodge) is a beautiful building fashioned with hand-cut logs which used to accommodate 70 Finnish workers, cutting trees for paper. It was transferred to its current location in 1987. The lodge's original smoke sauna was too small and old to be moved, so a new one was built next to it, which burned down in 1997 and has since been rebuilt again, big enough for 70 people.

Quite what the Finnish Sauna etiquette is eluded us during our visit, as we fumbled with swimwear and towels in the separate changing rooms by the sauna, eyeballing the cold lager on tap by the benches. Stepping into the sauna, the smoke was remarkably absent, whereas the darkness and heat were very much present, as were all the body parts of our Finnish hosts. Thankfully a few folks retained clothes, and we also discovered swimwear was required to jump into the lake outside (ice swimming is possible if you arrive in winter and are hardy enough!). Traditional evenings take place every Tuesday with access to the sauna, a buffet and music. If you're lucky you might catch a lumberjack demonstration too.

61

Stop #38: Kylmäluoma

Kylmäluoma Campsite (*www.hossa-kylmaluoma.fi*) ● GPS: N65.58525, E28.89866 ● Price Guide: £££ ● In Hossa National Park ● Price Includes Free Use of Saunas and Wood Fires in Cooking Huts ● All Services ● **Alternative:** Campsite Karhunkainalon Leitintäalue, GPS: N65.468290, E29.517146, Price Guide: £££, All Services

The Hossa National Park lies to the east of Finland, about 30 miles from the Russian border and roughly 60 miles south of the Arctic Circle (*www.nationalparks.fi/hossa*). Once the sole realm of the indigenous Sámi people, the park was established in 2017 to celebrate Finland's 100th anniversary of independence from Russia.

With 90km of marked trails, the park has plenty of walking opportunities, although we were content with strolling around the lake adjacent to our campsite pitch, keeping an eye out for the reindeer which wandered past at some point each day, and fending off the hungry (but thankfully slow-moving) mosquitoes.

The Kylmäluoma Campsite was a perfect stopover for us on the way north, and the place where we finally overcame our reluctance to take a naked sauna. The site has male and female saunas which were heated each afternoon and available to all guests, on the unspoken assumption you'd strip before entering. After making a mess of emptying the toilet cassette, daftly flinging effluence everywhere, one of us (mentioning no names) needed a fully clothed shower, followed by a clothes-less sauna to get over the ill-smelling experience.

The site also has a set of cabins with fire pits, free wood (very sharp axes are provided) and cooking facilities where you can use your extendable cooking fork (we kid you not) to sizzle away at Finland's favourite vegetable: the sausage.

Stop #39: Nagu/Nauvo

Free Car Park ● GPS: N60.18810, E21.90201 ● Price Guide: Free ● No Services, Service Point (*ajokaivot* in Finnish) in Turku (GPS: N60.44415, E22.22378) ● **Alternative:** Solliden Camping (*www.solliden.fi*), GPS: N60.3163505, E22.3014923, Price Guide: £££, All Services

Depending on how you count them, there are somewhere between several hundred and tens of thousands of islands, skerries and islets in the Turku Archipelago, one of the largest in the world. The islands are a natural paradise, covered in birch, pine and spruce trees, with strawberries and lingonberries growing wild beneath them.

We opted to follow the Turku Tourist Board's suggested 155-mile route through the archipelago, open in June, July and August (*www.visitturku.fi*), crossing between islands via 12 bridges and 9 ferries, all but one of which were free.

We were a little concerned we'd not fit on the ferries until we sat waiting in a queue for one, and a huge lorry cruised into the priority lane alongside us. The boarding process is simple: with no tickets or payment, we just waited for a ferry to arrive, waited our turn and then drove on as directed. The ferry to Nagu even had second side-decks above the main one to allow more cars to fit on, we were most impressed.

The spot we picked to sleep on our first day in the islands at Nagu (or Nauvo in Swedish, the predominant language here) was one of the few free camping places we could find. The islands each look like a leaf on Google Maps, with a single main road across them and small side roads generally leading to a single sea-front home or boathouse, not suitable for parking next to.

Locals were heading to their summer cabins around us, taking small boats across the sea packed with cool boxes, baskets and bags. The sea sometimes freezes around these islands in winter, hard to believe as we lay soaking up the sun on rocks dipping down into the ocean.

63

Stop #40: Rovaniemi

Santa Claus Village Car Park (*santaclausvillage.info*) ● GPS: N66.54329, E25.84074 ● Price Guide: Free ● No Services ● **Alternative**: Napapiirin Saarituvat Camping (*saarituvat.fi*), GPS: N66.517120, E25.845967, Price Guide: £££, 6km from Centre of Rovaniemi, All Services

The Arctic Circle in winter's a tough place to be, with lakes frozen hard enough to drive over. Even after being cleared of snow, the roads ideally need metal studded tyres to ensure grip and cars have engine heaters plugged into electrical outlets. In the summer it's a much tamer creature and needs no special equipment or knowledge.

The circle is a line of latitude at 66°33'48.4" around the north of the planet, above which the sun can be seen at midnight in summer, and doesn't rise fully in winter, known as the Polar Night. In Finland, this line passes through the area around Rovaniemi.

Although the line isn't fixed, and is currently drifting northwards at around 15m a year, the Finns know what us tourists want and have drawn a big thick white line through the Santa Claus Village, a few miles north-east of Rovaniemi for us to get selfies with. They've also built a large flat car park where we, along with representatives of half the nations of the motorhome-owning world, free-camped for the night on the way north.

Did we mention Santa? Ah yes, he lives here in the capital of Lapland! You can come meet him, Mrs Claus and his reindeer, or visit the post office which handles his annual 500,000 items of international mail. If you're hardy enough to venture here in the colder months (winter tyres are mandatory from 1 Nov to the end of Feb), you can have a crack at dog sledding, visit the Arctic SnowHotel (*arcticsnowhotel.fi*), take a Northern Lights Safari, go snowmobiling or take a dip in a frozen lake.

Stop #41: Sonkajärvi

Lakeside Car Park • GPS: N63.67156, E27.53456 • Price Guide: Free • No Services • By Frisbee Golf Course • **Alternative:** Official Caravan and Motorhome Parking in Car Parks Close to the Centre During Wife Carrying, Check *www.sonkajarvi.fi* For Details

Legend has it that back in the 17th Century a thief named Rosvo-Ronkainen ran a gang in the area around Sonkajärvi in central Finland. He tested would-be members by getting them to either steal a woman from one of the local towns or carry a heavy sack over a course of stones, stumps, fences and springs. Whether anyone chooses to believe either option or not, the Finns are hell-bent on having a laugh at the Wife Carrying World Championship event held annually in July.

The rules of wife carrying (*eukonkanto*) are many, but briefly each male competitor must carry his 'wife' (who can be any lady over 17 years old and weighing at least 49kg) over a 253.5m course including a metre-deep pool and two fences. Dropping of your 'wife' is permitted, as long as you pick her up again before continuing. The winning couple receives the wife's weight in beer.

As well was being great fun, the agility, determination and strength of some of the couples had to be admired. Most competitors opted for the 'Estonian' method of carrying, with the female upside down and her legs wrapped around the man's neck, leaving his hands free to sprint. The poor women get a serious face-full of water in this position when they leap into the pool near the start! We got the chance to say hello to the winning couple at our event, a huge muscular Russian and his petite 'wife' and were very impressed with his bone-crunching handshake!

During breaks in the athletics, spectators can try their hand at sauna water throwing, perusing a traditional market or enjoying the beer terrace.

65

Stop #42: Uusikaupunki

Santtioranta Camping (*www.santtioranta-camping.fi*) ● GPS: N60.80996, E21.39777 ● Price Guide: £££ ● All Services ● Communal Male and Female Showers ● **Alternative:** Free Car Park, GPS: N60.798310, E21.415252, Price Guide: £££, Leisure Boat Dock, No Services

Juhannuspäivä is Midsummer's Day in Finland (the Summer Solstice), a day of celebration, taking place on a Saturday each year between the 20th and 26th June. Traditionally a fire is lit on the Friday evening and we'd heard talk of raucous partying accompanying the big day so were keen to be on a campsite, to see what took place.

The day just happened to coincide with the result of the UK's vote to leave the EU, which added another dimension to the evening as we chatted with fellow Brits on the site and Finnish locals about their views on the result.

Although the level of partying turned out to be low key, we were treated to a campsite fire (a *kokko*) managed by a local fireman named Pasi. At 11pm it was lit, still bright daylight at this latitude. Pasi explained the fire would ward off evil spirits and asked for a good harvest, although he was more interested in breaking his record for how long the lit fire stayed upright. A collection of people gathered on the campsite beach, which only allows alcohol on this one day of the year.

Also part of tradition is not to sleep on Midsummer's Eve, and we were helped in this by a friendly local lady named Suvituuli, who took us under her wing and gave us a twilight tour of the town until 3am, when it started to get fully light again. As we walked everyone we passed said hello (*hei*) and our host explained the old wooden houses had been rebuilt further apart after several fires and pointed out a hotel which had a drinking den beneath it during Finland's prohibition era (from 1919 to 1932).

FRANCE

QUICK FACTS ● **EU**: Yes ● **Schengen**: Yes ● **Language**: French ● **Currency**: Euro (EUR, £1=€1.1) ● **Speed Limits ≤3.5t**: Urban/Single/Expressway/Motorway: 50, 80, 110, 130kph ● **Speed Limits >3.5t**: Urban/Single/Expressway/Motorway: 50, 80, 80, 90kph ● **Tolls**: Yes on Motorways, Pay Per Use With Cash or Card ● **LEZs**: Several in Crit'Air Scheme (*www.certificat-air.gouv.fr/en*) ● **IDP**: Not Needed ● **Docs**: Driving Licence, Insurance, Passport, V5C ● **Kit**: GB Sticker, Headlamp Deflectors, Warning Triangle, Fire Extinguisher ● **LPG**: Good Availability, Dish Adapter ● **Time**: UK+1 Hour ● **Daytime Dipped Headlights**: No ● **Overnighting**: Campsites, Business Parking, Aires, Unofficial Parking Possible Where Not Regulated/Out of Season/Away from Heavily Visited Areas

France is more than twice the size of the UK, with around the same population, so has plenty of space and a wonderfully welcoming approach to motorhomes, or *camping-cars* in French.

As well as several thousand campsites, we also have the option to stay on a huge network of no-frills official motorhome parking locations called 'aires'. *Campercontact.com* lists almost 8,000 of these, over 3,500 of which are free. More than 2,000 vineyards, farms, restaurants and other businesses allow free overnight stays to self-contained motorhomes who are in the France Passion scheme (*www.france-passion.com/en*).

France offers a stunning variety of landscapes including the mountains of the Alps and Pyrenees, Atlantic surf beaches and calmer coves on the Med, rolling lavender fields of Provence, wetlands of the Camargue, the enormous Dune du Pilat and of course sweeping vineyards across the country.

The towns and cities are accessible, vibrant and full of culture, packed with parks, museums, music venues and, of course, myriad cafes and restaurants. Unless you're heading into the mountains to ski, snowboard or hike, France is at its best from late spring to early autumn, when the towns are still vibrant, and the weather is kinder. For the low-down on all things French, including the weather, tips on avoiding toll roads and understanding the French way of life, the *about-france.com* website is very useful.

Also look out for our book *Motorhome France* on *amazon.co.uk*, for specific advice on touring this magnificent country.

Stop #43: Beynac-et-Cazenac

Official Aire ● GPS: N44.844748, E1.145575 ● Price Guide: Free ● 10-Min Walk to Beynac Château ● No Services ● **Alternative**: Camping La Plage Vézac (*www.camping-laplage.fr*), GPS: N44.824824, E1.171337, Price Guide: ££, By the Dordogne River

Motorhome travellers are spoiled for choice on a tour along the Dordogne River, with aires, campsites, businesses and parking areas all accomodating overnight stays. It really is a paradise, especially in the shoulder seasons when there aren't many tourists, but the trees still have their leaves and the evening sun reflects golden chateaux and medieval houses from the still waters of the river.

We've visited a few of the towns and villages in the Périgord region where some have been beautifully restored if at the expense of attracting hordes of tourists. Others appear immaculate and yet more genuine, such as Beynac-et-Cazenac. The town's château stands high on a limestone cliff above the river, which oddly once formed the border between England and France.

The free parking area set back from the river is the location of our first 'wild camping' experience at the start of our first two-year tour. It's been more formalised since as a motorhome stop-over, but at the time we spent a half-sleepless night alone, imagining crazed axemen wandering the woods around us in the night! No-one bothered us, of course, and we gradually grew more relaxed with off-site parking after that.

There are lots of attractions in this area, including famous caves (Les Combarelles, Cave of Font-de-Gaume, Lascaux II and so on), and the area is well-known for *fois gras* and truffles, and for the walnuts which sometimes fall wild onto paths for easy foraging.

Stop #44: Capbreton

Municipal Aire ● GPS: N43.63672, W1.44721 ● Price Guide: £ ● Open All-Year, Price Varies with Season ● All Services ● **Alternative**: Camping Domaine de Fierbois (Capbreton), GPS: N43.633246, W1.446178, Price Guide: ££, Open Jun to Oct, All Services

The municipal motorhome aire at Capbreton is a large tarmaced parking area, with a couple of basic service points. On the face of it, there's not much to get excited about, and yet Capbreton's become a favourite of ours and we've stayed here several times over the years.

The surfer vibe's a big part of the draw. The aire's separated from the Atlantic by an expanse of protected dunes, and the sound of the waves crashing on the beach echoes across the aire day and night, like a surfer's lullalybe. One end of the parking area is reserved for cars, and surf boards are often strapped to them when they arrive. Some turn up attached to the sides of bicycles, with a wetsuit-wearing rider loping off towards the sea. On occasion, someone takes to the air with a paramotor, hung below a wing with a big fan strapped to their backs, roaring along the beach.

The sands are wide and endless, with a view of Spain and the foothills to the Pyrenees rising to the south. Walking north brings you to a set of concrete blockhouses, a legacy of the Nazi's formidable Atlantic Wall, now standing tilted and decorated with colourful graffiti. There are hundreds of these crumbling structures along the French coastlines, reminders of a less peaceful past.

Further on (or you can take the cycle paths from the aire) and you're brought to the town of Capbreton, with its large pleasure craft marina and fishing port, seafood market, restaurants, casino and ice cream parlours. A *pelota* (handball) court on the ride into town reminds us we're close to the Basque Country here, with Biarritz just 40km south.

Stop #45: Col du Lautaret

Large Flat Parking Area ● GPS: N45.03250, E6.40758 ● Price Guide: Free ● No Services ●
Alternative: Camping Municipal d'Arsine (*www.neuillysurmarne.fr*), GPS: N45.031619, E6.363399, Price Guide: ££, Summer Only, All Services

This is an out-of-this world location, at 2,058m above sea level with panoramic views of the Parc National des Écrins. For cyclists the start of the route to the D902 Col du Galibier is a short distance away, frequently the highest point of the Tour de France. Alternatively, just an 850m walk from the parking area brings you to the Lautaret Alpine Botanical Garden, with around 2,300 species from mountains around the world.

We arrived at the Col du Lautaret from the west, finding the road easy with just a few hairpins and a couple of stretches of tunnel, one of which was quite narrow but easily passable in a motorhome. The parking area is set back a couple of hundred metres from the main road (the D1091) so there's traffic noise during the day but it's beautifully silent at night. It's unpaved and has no services or bins, so plan to bag up and take all your rubbish with you. The nearest fill/empty point is Camping Municipal d'Arsine, a 10-minute drive west.

Marmots entertained us each day, whistling as they scampered around on the hillside adjacent. A short walk (a few seconds) from where we were parked, we could gaze up at the icy mass of the Glacier de la Meije.

There's a popular café at the col itself, but we were still recovering from a *racelette* the night before, a traditional meal of melted cheese and potatoes we ate at Auris en Oisans – La Station (paid aire at N45.05170, E6.07832). Other than that, hiking, stargazing, sun-bathing, cooking and watching the football World Cup on our satellite TV kept us entertained.

70

Stop #46: Comps-Sur-Artuby

Municipal Aire ● GPS: N43.70599, E6.50707 ● Price Guide: Free ● All Services Except Electricity ● 30-Min Drive from the Gorges du Verdon ● **Alternative**: Municipal Camping du Pontet de Comps sur Artuby, GPS: N43.714209, E6.498814, Price Guide: ££, All Services

The Provence area in south-east France has a well-deserved reputation for sun-warmed lavender fields, sweet-smelling pine forests, olive groves and butter-coloured stone hilltop villages. But among all this bucolic tranquillity lies a Provençal wild side, from rugged deep-cut gorges to the wind-blasted heights of Mont Ventoux, all of which are accessible in a motorhome (with a bit of courage).

We'd read about the Gorges du Verdon in our guidebook, including the circular 'corniche' D23 route to the south of La Palud-sur-Verdon. That route sounded just a little too much, so we opted to drive the easier route on the southern side of the gorge. Not without trepidation we'd driven up the D952 from the Lac de Saint-Croix, wondering just how good an idea driving our 20-year-old, non-turbo, 3.1 tonne motorhome around these roads might be. Before we knew it, we'd managed to find our way onto the D23 on the north side. Argghhh! Unfairly, and loudly blaming the satnav, we continued onwards anyway, pulling over whenever we could to let faster cars past, taking in increasingly stunning views of the deepening gorge. The road didn't feel dangerous, although it was a little narrow at times, and we were enjoying it just up until the point we found ourselves facing no-entry signs. Double-whoops, it turns out the D23 must be done clockwise, resulting in us backtracking 30km and finding the turn-off for the southern route along the D71.

After an exhilarating day's driving, we were very happy to find plenty of space in the free and quiet aire, set back from the road at Comps-Sur-Artuby, the nearest town to the eastern end of the gorge.

Stop #47: Épernay

Aire ● GPS: N49.036070, E3.951655 ● Price Guide: Free ● 1.2km to Avenue de Champagne ● Service Point in Épernay (GPS: N49.055424, E3.954520) ● **Alternative**: Municipal Camping (*www.epernay.fr*), GPS: N49.057437, E3.949969, Price Guide: ££, All Services, Closed in Winter

France's Champagne region lies only three hours south of Calais, to the east of Paris. Unsurprisingly, the area is full of vines flowing over low hills, well-kept historic villages and small Champagne houses, some of the 260 which make the iconic wine. For the big names though, you need to head to Reims or Épernay, or both.

We opted for Épernay, for its reputation as the Capital of Champagne, and were surprised at the sheer number of motorhomes parked in an overflow area near the town's aire. As we walked the 2km to the tourist office on Rue Guillaume-de-Machault, we spotted signs for the town's Habits de Lumière festival, which takes place over three days in mid Dec each year, and we'd just happened to be there at the same time, woo hoo!

The festival takes places along the UNESCO-listed Avenue de Champagne, which is lined with famous producers including Moët et Chandon, Mercier, Paul-Etienne Saint Germain and Pol Roger (many of which offer tours). Beneath the street lie more than 200 million bottles of champagne in 110km of cellars, bonkers!

The festival changes each year, but we were treated to a magnificent sound and light show, with a dragon story projected onto the front of the Hôtel de Ville (the town hall). The Champagne flowed as a smoke-snorting mechanical dragon stalked the street giving children a ride in its huge mouth. It was magical stuff, something we'll remember for ever.

Stop #48: Le Reposoir

Municipal Aire ● GPS: N46.00986, E6.53626 ● Price Guide: Free ● All Services Except Electricity ● **Alternative**: Car Park at Le Reposoir Monastery, GPS: N46.007457, E6.538276, Price Guide: Free, Flat, No Services

We've been lucky to witness the Tour de France at a few places over the years, but we've chosen Le Reposoir as a favourite because of how welcoming the village was, the location near to a mountain climb and the festival taking place in the build-up. Oh, and the fact France happened to win the football World Cup the day of the race, sending the locals into raptures of celebration!

Le Reposoir is a commune of 500 people, normally a quiet corner of Auvergne-Rhône-Alpes south of Cluses. We arrived four days before the tour was due, finding ourselves in a melee of motorhomes. Thankfully we were squeezed into the aire by a local, who proceeded to magic up space for around 150 arriving motorhomes in every conceivable parcel of land around the village over the following days.

The village's multi-day fête included a chainsaw sculptor, tightrope walker, ham-roaster, speed lumberjacks, a choir and fireworks, all well-watered with wine and beer by an outdoor bar. A jovial atmosphere bubbled away in the aire too as our fellow *camping-caristes* enjoyed lunch sat at tables between the vans.

On the day of the race spectators walked from the heaving temporary car parks to line the mountain road. The Tour's famous caravan arrived first, a series of vehicles sporting all kinds of huge sculptures, pounding out music, blowing their horns and flinging small gifts at a baying crowd! The riders themselves were announced by a buzz of helicopters, tiny in the distance, weaving around to follow the athletes below. Eventually, under a roar of blades and screams of support the lycra-clad heroes flew past at outlandish climbing speeds. Once again all was calm, at least until that famous football match took place later!

Stop #49: Monbazzilac

Les Avinturiers, Domaine de La Lande Vineyard (*www.les-avinturiers.fr*) ● GPS: N44.788286, E0.495878 ● Price Guide: Free ● All Services Except Electricity ● 24 Hours Max ● **Alternative**: Domaine de Cavaroque, GPS: N44.784018, E0.475094, Price Guide: Free, 24 Hours Max, All Services Except Electricity

The Domaine de La Lande vineyard is one of our favourite France Passion stopovers, south of the Dordogne and the town of Bergerac in South West France. The owner was very welcoming, helping us site our van and get level with wooden ramps he provided, then inviting us to an evening's *dégustation* (wine tasting) before leaving us to get settled in, right next to the lines of vines. As we popped the kettle on we were still excited by the sight of a family of wild boar crossing the road as we'd arrived, pootling along in size order.

Later as we nervously attempted to use our rusty school-days French in the tasting room, we gathered the owner enjoys his own motorhome travels, heading down to Spain in the winters. After setting up the aire in 2001, complete with a custom-built service point fashioned from a barrel, it had proven so popular he sells almost all his wine to passing motorhomes, a win-win situation for him and us.

The wine itself was a sweet white, made from grapes which are affected by the "noble rot", a kind of helpful grey fungus which infects the grapes as they ripen and leads to a fine, concentrated sweetness. Neither of us are wine buffs, but we liked the taste and bought a couple of bottles to say thank you for our stay. The host encouraged us to take our dog for his evening walk among the vines, which had started to yellow in the late autumn.

The vineyard only asks that you arrive before 6:30pm. As well as the service point, they advertise picnic tables and a BBQ too, what more could we ask?

Stop #50: Paris

Camping de Paris (*www.campingparis.fr*) ● GPS: N48.86949, E2.23577 ● Price Guide: £ With Huttopia Camping Card ● All Services ● **Alternative**: Municipal Site: Camping de la Haute-Île (*www.neuillysurmarne.fr*), GPS: N48.8538988, E2.541338, Price Guide: ££, All Services

We found Paris a very easy capital city to visit by motorhome. We opted to stay at Camping de Paris, which is set under trees alongside the Seine, on the edge of the Bois de Boulogne city park and to the west of the centre. The site felt secure, with gates which were closed overnight, allowing pedestrian entry via a code.

Access was via motorway and dual carriageway almost to the site entrance, and traffic was light on a Sunday. The site is covered by the Greater Paris LEZ, so a suitable Crit'Air sticker is needed depending on the time of day you arrive (*www.certificat-air.gouv.fr* and *www.green-zones.eu*). The site is part of the Huttopia Group, which offers a discount card for their 43 campsites across Europe (*europe.huttopia.com*). You could consider using the municipal site in Neuilly-Sur-Marne (details above, about 13km from the centre) as another low-cost option.

Camping de Paris runs a frequent shuttle bus (a *navette*) to the Porte Maillot metro station, from where you can access the entire city. We found this website helpful for navigating the metro system: *parisbytrain.com/paris-metro*.

Paris is packed with places to visit, from the iconic Eiffel Tower and Louvre to less well-known attractions. We enjoyed a free view of the city from the rooftop of the *Galeries Lafayette* on Boulevard Haussmann. For a look at the ultra-modern face of Paris, we wandered around the La Défense business district. The huge Père Lachaise Cemetery offered a more historic, thoughtful experience. If a visit to Versailles interests you, you can take a train from Paris to the palace, which we did and enjoyed.

75

Stop #51: Port Grimaud

Camping de la Plage (*www.camping-de-la-plage.fr*) ● GPS: N43.28167, E6.58625 ● Price Guide: £££ ● All Services ● On the Saint-Tropez Gulf ● **Alternative**: Camping des Mûres (*www.camping-des-mures.com*), GPS: N43.283717, E6.591706, Price Guide: £££, All Services

Until the end of the 18th Century, the Côte d'Azur (the French Riviera), area was remote and impoverished, surviving from olive and flower growing and fishing. Fast forwards 200 years to today, and although the wonderful climate and scenery remain, everything else has changed. Having long been the haunt of royalty, artists, film stars and the mega-wealthy, we'd normally avoid this stretch of coastline as being traffic-packed, and beyond our budget.

Fortunately for us our friends felt otherwise and convinced us to join them at a beach-side campsite looking across the sea to Saint-Tropez, a magnificent spot. From the campsite, a 30-min walk south brought us to Port Grimaud, a 1960s creation, a fascinating complex of sea channels fronted by fisherman-style houses with pleasure boats moored alongside every door.

From Grimaud a foot ferry carried us across the gulf to Saint-Tropez, where we wandered around staring at the supercars and mega-yachts, before being drawn into one of the many restaurants for a meal and a cold beer in the sunshine. The town's fortress holds an interesting naval museum, and the Plage de l'Escalet is a popular spot to enjoy the crystal-clear turquoise waters.

Later, back at the vans, we enjoyed a beach-side BBQ watching yachts race out on the gulf and cooling our feet in the nearby lapping waves. Not a bad life!

Stop #52: Rothéneuf

Aire Camping-Cars Des Ilots • GPS: N48.68054, W1.96357 • Price Guide: £ • 5-Min Walk to Beach • All Services • **Alternative**: Aire in St-Malo, GPS: N48.643502, W1.994000, Price Guide: £, Includes Free Bus to Centre of St-Malo or 3.5km Walk/Cycle, Service Points Available

We'd been on the road pretty-much non-stop for two years when we arrived in Rothéneuf in Brittany. Our funds were running out and we needed to head back to the UK to look for work. Having spent all that time travelling amazing places in incredible freedom, we were feeling a little low as things came to an end and reality called. Thankfully we'd met up with an Australian couple (with Maltese ancestry) who were nearing the end of a three-year tour of Europe and were feeling much the same. We'd been in touch through our respective blogs, and it was a great feeling to catch up at long last.

Our friends knew how to travel, and as well as having a good-sized motorhome (complete with a huge flat screen TV), one of them drove a car so they had flexible transport. This meant we could stay in the leafy ex-campsite aire at Rotheneuf and drive into Saint-Malo, rather than stay in the port's more central car-park style motorhome aire.

It also meant we could visit the best sites for donning wetsuits and heading into *La Manche* (literally 'the sleeve', the French name for the English Channel), with me collecting mussels and my more adept Australian mate picking off a massive fish with his spear gun and prising oysters free with his knife.

We spent a couple of evenings in the aire, enjoying the oysters and fish cooked on a BBQ, watching a film on that huge telly, supping a few beers and taking it easy after filling our days exploring Saint-Malo, walking the coastal path and inspecting the work of Abbé Fouré. He was a deaf and mute priest who, over 25 years, carved sculptures from granite rocks by the shore using only a hammer and chisel, creating "The Hermit Village" which contains about 300 carved figures.

Stop #53: Saint-André-de-Rosans

La Ferme de La Condamine ● GPS: N44.32717, E5.33210 ● Price Guide: Free ● Farm Selling Fruit, Olive Oil, Jams etc ● All Services ● **Alternative**: Domaine des Lauribert (*www.lauribert.com*), GPS: N44.348658, E4.971347, Price Guide: Free, Vineyard, All Services

The kind owner of La Ferme de La Condamine, in the France Passion scheme, couldn't have been more patient and helpful with us as we worked out what all the jars of home-made produce were at this beautiful France Passion farm. Clutching a bag of fresh apricots and some olive oil, we wandered back to our motorhome afterwards parked in the sunshine besides fragrant lavender fields. In return for buying some top-quality food, we were granted a free night's parking in a fabulous location in Provence.

We'd spent the day before investigating Glanum (*www.site-glanum.fr/en*), the remains of an ancient city outside Saint-Rémy-de-Provence. While we'd visited the 'big' Roman sites in France, like the amphitheatre at Nîmes and the Pont du Gard to the north-east of the same city, we'd never heard of Glanum and were intrigued. The site isn't huge and is easy to walk around. Its first inhabitants arrived in the seventh Century BC, drawn to the source of an underground spring.

Around the fourth Century BC a tribe of Celto-Ligurian people, the *Salyens*, built a town there and named it Glanum in honour of their Celtic god, Glanis, who was associated with the healing spring. In the second Century BC the Greeks brought wealth and their own Hellenistic style of building and finally the Romans colonised it in the very early years of Augustus' reign, just about the time Jesus was walking the planet. The town was finally abandoned in 260 AD and lay buried in the earth for 17 centuries, before being discovered and excavated in 1921.

Stop #54: Saintes-Maries-De-La-Mer

Municipal Aire ● GPS: N43.45399, W4.43827 ● Price Guide: ££ ● Direct Access to Camargue Reserve ● All Services Except Electricity ● **Alternative**: Les Poissons D'Argent Camping, GPS: N43.561962, W4.164753, Price Guide: ££, 3km Walk or Cycle to Aigues Mortes, All Services

Saintes-Maries-De-La-Mer is the capital of the Camargue region, on the Mediterranean coast between Montpellier and Marseille. The Camargue is Europe's largest river delta, a huge plain filled with *étangs*, salt-water lagoons, separated from the sea by sandbars. The area is home to over 400 bird species, including one of the few European habitats for the Greater Flamingo.

The Camargue is also famous for its white *Camarguais* horse breed, and for the black bulls reared either for the bloodless *course camarguaise*, in which participants attempt to snatch rossettes from between the bull's horns, or for export for the *corrida*, bull fighting in Spain.

Saintes-Maries-De-La-Mer attracts up to 500,000 visitors in high season, and each May and October holds feast days which attract large numbers of Gypsies. Motorhome parking is regulated and the town provides a campsite and two large aires, one of which has direct access to the *Digue à la Mer* dyke path, the other being based closer to the town centre.

We opted for the aire nearer the dyke, by chance avoiding the mosquitos which sometimes invade the area. Walking a few miles across the dyke we were treated to flamingoes, egrets, black-headed gulls, gull-billed terns and a whole host more we failed to identify. The *Camarguais* horses made an entrance too, but there was no sign of the bulls from the dyke.

Stop #55: Saint-Jean-en-Royans

Aire on Mixed Parking ● GPS: N45.0202, E5.2905 ● Price Guide: Free ● All Services Except Electricity ● 6 Miles from Combe Laval ● **Alternative**: Vercornoix France Passion Location, Saint-Jean-en-Royans (*www.vercornoix.com*), GPS: N45.030805, E5.301539, Price Guide: Free, Sells Local Produce, Fresh Water and Electricity Available

The Vercors Massif extends out of the south-west of Grenoble, forming a natural barrier to road traffic which, despite huge effort, still hasn't been tamed to this day. Looking at a map of the Vercors it's not immediately obvious just how incredible some of the roads are, many of which are impassable in a motorhome!

We were drawn to the area by the descriptions and photos of these 'balcony roads', precipitous routes cut into ledges and tunneled through sheer cliffs. Our plan was to plot a route through the massif, staying to the easier roads and running or cycling the more precipitous sections. It didn't entirely work out!

We started out with Cognin-Les-Gorges, where we could easily park and run up 3.5km of the D22 to the spectatular Gorges du Nan, a jaw-dropping sight.

We then headed to Romans-sur-Isere to get our wheel bearings replaced (it's always 'fun' getting repairs done abroad), then back to the aire at Saint-Jean-en-Royans from where we could cycle the 10km up to the incredible Combe Laval. So far, so good, but it came apart a little when we drove north along the D103 the following day, which deposited us onto the eastern section of the D531, the Gorges de la Borne. That route is amazing, but not something we're planning on repeating in a motorhome, with lots of traffic and narrow cliff-road, with overhangs we felt might peel back the roof at any time!

Stop #56: Soufflenheim

Municipal Aire ● GPS: N48.832429, E7.960286 ● Price Guide: ££ ● All Services ● **Alternative**: Chapel Car Park near Climbach, GPS: N49.014228, E7.857840, Price Guide: Free, No Services

The Maginot Line was built by the French along their border with Germany during the 1930s to deter an attack by their neighbours. It's a series of formidable defences, including huge underground networks of rooms, tunnels and retractable gun turrets. It looked impregnable to us, but proved useless when Germanany invaded France via Belgium instead. The French had envisioned this, and expected to repel an invasion via that route. However, the Germans proved them wrong by attacking through the Ardennes region, which the allies had wrongly believed impenetrable for large scale operations.

Some of the bunkers are maintained and open to the public (*www.visit.alsace*). We were introduced to one of them by our German friends, the Four-à-Chaux fortress near Lembach, named after an earlier lime quarry and kiln on the site. We'd been travelling in convoy with their motorhome along the *Deutsche Weinstraße* (the German Wine Route) and easily reached the fortress from there, being only 9km from the German border.

There's not much evidence of the Four-à-Chaux from the outside, just a concrete entrance buried in the ground. Behind the steel doors lie 3km of galleries, 30m below the surface, with all the facililties for over 600 men to live for months, including dormitories, toilets, kitchens, power station, an ammunition workshop, a well and a hospital. The air's cool inside, down to 13°C, and it gets damp so good shoes and a coat are recommended.

The fortress was bombed in the 1940s and later surrended. It was renovated and reoccupied in the 1950s for use against the Cold War threat from the USSR.

Stop #57: Taninges, Le Praz de Lys

Ski Aire ● GPS: N46.140956, E6.603687 ● Price Guide: Free in Summer, ££ in Winter ● All-Year Service Point, Including Electricity ● **Alternative**: All-Year Aire at Mieussy, GPS: N46.159675, E6.549366, Price Guide: Free (Paid Services), No Grey Drain, Bucket into Black Water Drain Only, No Electricity

The motorhome ski aire at Le Praz de Lys-Sommand was a baptism of ice for us! Our tour would take us through the winter and we fancied spending a few days high in the Alps to see the mountains under snow. Our van is 'winterised' with water tanks located in a heated space between its two floors, and is fitted with Mud & Snow tyres, M+S-marked on the sidewall (not as good as 'full winter' 3PMSF tyres). We'd also bought and practised fitting snow chains and had external silver screens to cover our cab windows.

The roads up to the aire at 1,400m above sea level were clear of snow, as was the aire when we arrived. With the sun shining on our solar panel, we happily parked up and didn't think to hook-up to the electricity. We'd arrived the day before the school holidays though and all the sockets were soon taken! We'd also come with only 12 litres (6kg) of gas. The night temperature fell to -10°C and snow came down heavily. Ill-prepared, we had fun with frozen locker doors, flat leisure batteries and a build-up of ice on the roof. Thankfully our neighbours helped us out. A snow plough arrived each morning and cleared the aire, allowing us to drive off on our chains and escape to lower altitude to lick our wounds.

A few days at altitude taught us a lot, and we enjoyed messing around with a plastic sledge, eating out in the nearby ski resort and feeling amazed at how warm we were inside the van (when we'd got the heating working!) with a blizzard raging outside.

GERMANY

QUICK FACTS ● **EU**: Yes ● **Schengen**: Yes ● **Language**: German ● **Currency**: Euro (EUR, £1=€1.1) ● **Speed Limits ≤3.5t**: Urban/Single/Expressway/Motorway: 50, 80, 130, 130kph (Recommended, Some Autobahn Sections Have No Speed Limit) ● **Speed Limits >3.5t**: Urban/Single/Expressway/Motorway: 50, 80, 80, 100kph ● **Tolls**: Only for Motorhomes Over 7.5t ● **LEZs**: Large Number of Locations in Umweltzone Scheme ● **IDP**: Not Needed ● **Docs**: Driving Licence, Insurance, Passport, V5C ● **Kit**: Reflective Jackets, GB Sticker, Headlamp Deflectors, Warning Triangle, First Aid Kit ● **LPG**: Good Availability, ACME Adapter ● **Time**: UK+1 Hour ● **Daytime Dipped Headlights**: No ● **Overnighting**: Campsites, Business Parking, Stellplatz, Unofficial Parking Tolerated Away from Nature Reserves & Tourist Hotspots

With around half a million motorhomes, Germany outstrips even France for the number of *wohnmobiles* on the road. The country has almost 4,800 *stellplatz* (the equivalent of French aires) listed on *campercontact.com*, along with over 1,100 campsites listed on *www.eurocampings.co.uk*. If you prefer printed books, have a look at *bordatlas.de*.

When you consider that the motorway network is in great condition and is free to use, LPG refill stations are widely available, and the fact German towns are invariably safe and pristine, the country has an awful lot going for the motorhome traveller.

The only potential fly in the ointment is the ever-widening LEZ scheme. To enter many towns and cities you'll need an environmental sticker, an *umweltplakette*, colour-coded to reflect the emissions of your vehicle. Depending on the level of sticker you have will restrict which areas you can drive in. Also be aware you'll need full Alpine-marked winter tyres (a snowflake symbol inside a mountain), to drive in Germany in snow and/or ice conditions, M+S-marked tyres are being phased out.

Germany has a number of routes created for tourists to follow: the Romantic Road (*Romantische Straße*), the Wine Route (*Weinstraße*), the Fairy Tale Route (*Märchenstraße*), the Alpine Route (*Alpenstraße*), the Black Forest High Road (*Schwarzwaldhochstraße*) and so on. Alongside visiting some of Germany's historic cities, these routes have provided much inspiration for us during our tours of Germany.

Stop #58: Bastei

Park and Ride Car Park #2 (*saechsische-schweiz.de*) ● GPS: N50.98669, E14.05581 ● Price Guide: ££ ● No Services ● **Alternative**: Official Bastei Stellplatz (*www.reisemobilpark-bastei.de*), GPS: N50.984872, E14.056854, Price Guide: ££, All Services

Half an hour's drive south from Dresden brought us to Saxon Switzerland, the *Sächsische Schweiz* national park, a popular hiking area with over 1,000 peaks for climbers, the highest one at 562m. Swiss artists named the area after its tall, fluted sandstone rocks reminded them of home. The name was banned during the Nazi era but was re-introduced afterwards.

The park and ride car park we slept in is much nicer than it sounds, flat and set among fields on the edge of a forest. It's about a mile away from the walking area and officially allows overnight motorhome parking. A stellplatz with services has also been created since then, near to the same spot, so you've a choice of where to stay. A bus takes you to the start of the walks, dropping you in the forest close to the edge of a cliff with views of the eroded grey limestone cliffs rising from the woods.

We followed the throng of people over the famous Bastei Bridge which links a series of the peaks together, and found ourselves at another viewpoint, more impressive than the last with sheer cliffs on three sides. It looked out over the River Elbe 194m below, and an expanse of woodland either side of its banks. Our guidebook wasn't wrong when it said that this is one of the most breath-taking spots in Germany.

The Königstein Fortress is another famous landmark in Saxon Switzerland, used for centuries as a prison and now drawing 700,000 visitors a year. The spa town of Bad Schandau is also a local attraction, with a popular farm stopover nearby at Gohrisch (*www.ferienhof-mandry.de*).

Stop #59: Berchtesgaden

Reisemobilstellplatz Rasp (*www.reisemobilstellplaetze-berchtesgaden.de*) ● GPS: N47.65104, E13.07115 ● Price Guide: ££ ● All Services ● **Alternative**: Camping Resort Allweglehen (*www.allweglehen.de*), GPS: N47.648357, E13.039838, Price Guide: ££, All Services

Berchtesgaden lies to the far south of Germany in the Bavarian Alps, a 20-min drive of hairpin bends to the Austrian border, or two hours on foot. This beautiful part of the world is protected as the Berchtesgaden National Park, with sublime views of rolling green pastures and pine forests, towered over by endless flanks of grey-white mountain cliffs and peaks.

Most visitors to the area (us included) will probably be intrigued by the famous *Kehlsteinhaus* (Eagle's Nest), one-time haunt of Adolf Hitler (although he had a fear of heights and spent most of his time at the *Berghof*, his summer home at nearby Obersalzberg). The Berghof is no more, having been bombed, looted and burned before being demolished by the Bavarian government in 1952, along with around 50 other Nazi-era buildings.

The Kehlsteinhaus survived though and can be visited via a small convoy of buses which run up and down a single-track road which itself cost over €150m in today's money. From the top a marble-lined tunnel leads you to an elevator (wartime dignitaries would have been driven through it in their cars). The ornate lift climbs the remaining 124m to leave you up in the thin air at 1,834m above sea level, peering down on the tiny buildings below. We enjoyed the magnificent views, and were fascinated by the red marble fireplace given to Hitler by Mussolini and badly damaged by soldiers, who chipped off pieces as souvenirs. For more information, plan a visit to the Dokumentation Obersalzberg museum (*www.obersalzberg.de*).

85

Stop #60: Berlin

Stellplatz Berlin (*www.stellplatz-berlin.de*) ● GPS: N52.59540, E13.28920 ● Price Guide: ££ ● 15-Min Walk to S and U-Bahn into Berlin ● All Services ● **Alternative**: Stellplatz am Plötzensee (*stellplatz.ploetzensee.de*), GPS: N52.543260, E13.329183, Price Guide: ££, All Services

Both the *stellplatz* listed above are outside of the Berlin *umweltzone* (low emission zone), located to the north-west of the city centre with easy access from the *autobahn*. We pre-booked our place at Stellplatz Berlin, one of the few places we've booked across Europe, as we were arriving in peak season. As expected, the parking area proved popular with all 90 spaces taken by the evening.

The city is a 20-minute ride on the *S-Bahn*, the commuter train, with the nearest station at Tegel, a 15-minute walk. Tickets are sold at the station, and you must 'validate' each ticket in a stamping machine before boarding. On a second visit we used the U-Bahn boarding at the Alt-Tegel station, again a 15-minute walk away.

Berlin's a large city, so we opted to take an open-top bus, especially as it was 35°C and walking for miles wouldn't have been fun. The bus ran on a 2.5-hour loop, taking in all the big sights. The following day we returned for a look around on foot, visiting Checkpoint Charlie on the Berlin Wall, the Brandenburg Gate, the Reichstag, the DDR (East Germany) Museum and the Holocaust Memorial.

Berlin has far more to offer than our brief visit could take in, including five world-class museums on the UNESCO-listed Museum Island, the Gedenkstätte Berliner Mauer memorial to the Berlin Wall and the 1936 Olympic stadium where Jesse Owens won four gold medals.

Stop #61: Dresden

Official Stellplatz ● GPS: N51.063022, E13.728650 ● Price Guide: £ ● No Services ● 30-Min Walk to Centre of Old Town ● **Alternative**: Official Parking at Alberthafen Restaurant, GPS: N51.064140, E13.715595, Price Guide: £, 40-Min Walk to Old Town, No Services

As the rain fell on a cloud-heavy July morning, history drew us to Dresden. Heading south from Berlin, the *autobahn* split and offered us either Leipzig or Dresden, only the memory of a war time bombing at the latter city steered us that way. We know, we know, we really should do more guidebook reading, but we were visiting hundreds of places one after the other, and sometimes (usually) we run out of research-steam.

The parking area we chose was alongside the Elbe, already occupied by a few other motorhomes. Reading up a little on the events of February 1945, our expectations for the city weren't high. Over the course of three days, in what would later become a highly controversial series of attacks, British and American bombers dropped thousands of tons of explosive and incendiary devices, deliberately creating a firestorm within the city and killing over 22,000 people. The *altstadt* (old town) was utterly destroyed, the city's Renaissance, Baroque and 19th Century heart ripped out. More moving were the horrific accounts of survivors of the man-made horror.

Walking into the city, we found it beautiful, orderly, and clean, but knowing what it had once been we felt a little sad. Coming across the impressive Frauenkirche church, we marvelled at how it's been beautifully rebuilt, having been left in ruins for 50 years by the communist DDR government as a war memorial. The Zwinger was also destroyed but rebuilt by 1963, beautiful gardens surrounded by Baroque palaces.

87

Stop #62: Hamburg

Hamburg Stellplatz (*www.wohnmobilhafen-hamburg*) ● GPS: N53.543303, E10.025689 ● Price Guide: ££ ● On-Site City Bus Tours or 2-Min Walk to S-Bahn ● All Services ● **Alternative**: Campingplatz Buchholz Hamburg, GPS: N53.590016, E9.931405, Price Guide: £££, All Services

Industrial port cities tend to have a rough edge to them, and Hamburg, on the river Elbe where it meets the North Sea, is no different, with its strip clubs and (legal) brothels on the infamous Reeperbahn, otherwise known as *die sündigste meile* (the most sinful mile).

There is, of course, much more to the city though, and whenever we talk of Hamburg, we laugh at how much we enjoyed Miniatur Wunderland (*www.miniatur-wunderland.com*), Hamburg's innocent and fun museum of the world's largest model railway, and much more. Miniatur Wunderland must be seen to be believed. Constructed over 17 years (so far) with a spend exceeding €20m, the model landscape takes in a fully functioning airport and cruise ships sailing along water-filled fjords where the tide ebbs and flows. Lights simulate day and night, shining out from the tiny cars, cities and towns. Fun's everywhere, with the Space Shuttle landing at the airport and tiny figures engaged in fights, or more 'friendly behaviour' in the fields or running from dinosaurs! We were in there for hours on end.

On another day we bought a day ticket from the nearby S-Bahn station, which also included a ferry across the Norderelbe, with views of the giant docks. Walking the city, we took in the Außenalster man-made lake and the *rathaus* (town hall), recovering from our exploits with a cold beer on the BLOCKBRÄU brewery roof terrace (*www.block-braeu.de*).

Stop #63: Munich

Allianz Arena Stellplatz ● GPS: N48.22112, E11.62497 ● Price Guide: ££ ● 15-Min Walk to Fröttmaning Station ● All Services ● Not Available Match Days ● **Alternative**: Munich Olympics Stadium Stellplatz, GPS: N48.17035, E11.53923, Price Guide: ££, 15-Min Walk to Toni-Merkens-Weg Train Station, No Services

Munich, or *München*, is the capital of the State of Bavaria (*Bayern*) in the south of Germany, from which the country's highest mountain (the Zugspitze at 2,962m) is visible in the distance. In a motorhome the city is easily accessible, using public transport from a range of stellplatz and campsites a few kilometres outside the centre, avoiding the umweltzone.

Munich ranks as having among the best quality of living in the world and like all of Bavaria, the city feels immaculate, safe and welcoming. Despite being heavily bombed in WW2, the city's traditional buildings were rebuilt and make for a great walking tour on a sunny day.

The Deutsches Museum proved a highlight for us, the world's largest museum of science and technology, with the basement full of industrial mining machinery, the kind one of our father's used as a coal face worker for 20 years (*www.deutsches-museum.de*). We spent four hours in the museum and could easily have been there for days.

Outside the museum we enjoyed taking in the city centre before heading to the *Englischer Garten*, a large and beautiful park where we indulged in Bavarian hospitality, including a couple of *maß* of *weißbier* (each glass was a full litre, 1.75 pints of white beer) and a *schweinshaxe* (roasted port knuckle, which our dog loved too!). Neither of these were likely to enhance our lifespans but were delicious at the time!

89

Stop #64: Nuremberg

Official Stellplatz ● GPS: N49.42298, E11.10705 ● Price Guide: Free ● No Services ● 10-Min Walk to U-Bahn Station to Centre ● **Alternative**: Official Stellplatz, GPS: N49.474757, E11.093831, Price Guide: Free, 15-Min Walk to U-Bahn Station to Centre, No Services

A brief search for safe, free places to stay in Nuremburg turned up this official stellplatz by the edge of a large park. Once settled in we were surprised to find the park encompasses the old Nazi Rally Grounds, and we were a stone's throw from the *Zeppelinfeld*, the grandstand from which Adolf Hitler gave speeches to crowds of over 100,000 in the 1930s.

With our dog in tow, we opted first to visit the city, buying a family ticket for the U-Bahn. Nuremburg was once the unofficial capital of the Holy Roman Empire and the Imperial Diet met at Nuremburg Castle, one of Europe's most formidable medieval fortifications which still stands on a ridge above the city. This reputation was seized upon by the spin-masters in the national socialist party, building the population into a frenzy before finally initiating WW2.

Sadly, the city's old town was almost completely reduced to rubble by 521 British bombers, who dropped over a million incendiary devices in a single raid as the war drew to a close in 1945. Photos inside a rebuilt church showed it as a skeleton. 1,800 people were killed, and the lake alongside the stellplatz was half-filled with the rubble from the town. The following day we felt our hairs stand on end walking the cracked, discoloured steps of the *Zeppelinfeld* before spending hours in the Documentation Center Nazi Party Rally Grounds museum, learning about how the party came to power, and later abused it (*museen.nuernberg.de*).

Stop #65: Oberwesel

Campingplatz Schönburgblick (*camping-oberwesel.de*) ● GPS: N50.10267, E7.73581 ● Price Guide: £ ● On the Bank of the Rhine ● All Services ● **Alternative**: Camping Loreleyblick at Sankt Goar (*hotel-winzerhaus.de*), GPS: N50.142382, E7.721656, Price Guide: ££, Direct View of the Rhine, All Services

After a weekend watching friends driving at bonkers speeds around the open-to-all Nürburgring racetrack (we were tempted to have a go in our van but were too afraid!), we needed somewhere calmer to recover. Heading 90 minutes south-east, we hit the mighty Rhine, parking directly on the grassy riverbank at Oberwesel.

When we arrived at the site, we used our CampingCard ACSI to get a discount, before realising the site allowed self-contained motorhomes to stay for half the 'camping' price, if we agreed not to use the shower and toilet block. We'd paid by this point, but learned that some German campsites also function like *stellplatz*.

With a windscreen full of Rhine, we were able to sit and gaze at the enormous barges powering their way along the river, wondering about the lives of the crew, and how they got their car, perched on the barge roof, onto the shore. We read up and learned that the Rhine's one of the world's most frequented inland waterways, carrying 10 million tonnes of material a year (*www.ccr-zkr.org*), but we still don't know how they move their car!

Oberwesel was once on the frontier between the Roman Empire and the untamed Germanic tribes to the east, protected by the fortifications of the *Limes Germanicus*. After the retreat of the Romans, the town had a tumultuous past, including being annexed by France in 1802. These days the town is dominated by the red church, the Schönburg, and the city's 16 defensive towers, with a backdrop of hills flowing with vines, and holds an annual fireworks festival in September.

91

Stop #66: Würzburg

Mixed Parking ● GPS: N49.79896, E9.91916 ● Price Guide: Free ● No Services ● 25-Min Walk to Centre of Old Town ● Noisy ● **Alternative**: Official Stellplatz, GPS: N49.797886, E9.923191, Price Guide: ££, All Services, On the Bank of the Main River

Würzburg sits at the northern end of the Romantic Road, which runs all the way south to Füssen in the Alps. It occupies a bend of the Main River, with the hills to the north combed green with vineyards.

We arrived in Würzburg via tiny Mödlareuth, a town once split in two by the Iron Curtain (hence being dubbed 'Little Berlin') and now presenting a section of the wall and fascinating history to visitors (*moedlareuth.de*).

The area we initially parked in Würzburg was busy with cars and we only just found a space, meaning to move to the official stellplatz nearby on the river, but that plan was aborted after we were drawn into a couple of cool glasses of local white wine on the Alte Mainbrücke, the city's 500-year-old bridge, busy with locals in the late afternoon sunshine.

From the bridge we could relax and take in the enormous barges slowly making their way along the river beneath us, the pastel-coloured buildings along the river and the Fortress Marienbad, a castle heavily fortified with bastions after having been stormed by the Swedes in 1631. We enjoyed wandering the compact old town on foot, not needing to use public transport, but didn't find the energy to visit the main attraction, the Würzburg Residence (*www.residenz-wuerzburg.de*). Like the rest of the city, it was heavily damaged in an RAF bombing raid in 1945, the town being largely being rebuilt by women.

GIBRALTAR

QUICK FACTS ● **EU**: No ● **Schengen**: No (Expected to Join in 2021) ● **Language**: English ● **Currency**: Gibraltar Pound (GIP, £1=£1) ● **Speed Limit**: 50kph ● **LEZs**: None ● **IDP**: Not Needed ● **Docs**: Driving Licence, Insurance, Passport, V5C ● **Kit**: Headlamp Deflectors ● **LPG**: None in Gibraltar, Nearest Station in Campamento in Spain ● **Time**: UK+1 Hour ● **Daytime Dipped Headlights**: No ● **Overnighting**: Only Car Parks in Gibraltar, Otherwise Use Parking, Aires or Campsite at La Línea de la Concepción in Spain

You're right, Gibraltar isn't a country, it's a British Overseas Territory, but it's unique enough we've opted to treat it as one in this book! The name 'Gibraltar' is derived from the Arabic جبل طارق, Jabal Ṭāriq meaning the 'Mount of Tariq' (named after an 8th Century Moorish military leader).

Seized by an Anglo-Dutch force back in 1713, Gibraltar's been a British territory for over 300 years, and it's a pretty weird part of Britain at that. We can attest to how odd it feels to be in North Africa in the morning, then finding ourselves picking up English bacon in a Morrisons supermarket a few hours later, before sitting outside a pub clutching a pint of real ale and popping a postcard into a red Royal Mail post box. It really is quite bizarre.

We've visited Gibraltar a few times in our motorhomes, always opting to stay on the Spanish side of the border at La Línea de la Concepción. The main reason for this is the border itself, which can get seriously clogged up with traffic in both directions. Also, there's limited parking on 'The Rock' itself. Because the UK has left the EU, border controls should be removed in 2021 so access will be easier going forwards.

The main attraction for driving into Gibraltar is perhaps to top up with low-cost fuel, or simply for the novelty value. Some motorhomes use the Europa Point car park to the south to stay overnight, reporting few issues but traffic noise.

The Rock had lots to entertain us, like the mischievous Barbary Macaques, high on the mountain, which you can take a taxi to, use the cable car or hike up to see (search www.visitgibraltar.gi for 'nature trails' and expect to pay a small fee for entrance to the nature reserve). If you have a dog, we were advised it's best to leave it in the van to avoid conflict with the macaques.

93

Stop #67: La Línea de la Concepción

Area de Autocaravanas, Alcaidesa Marina (*www.alcaidesamarina.com*) ● GPS: N36.15613, W5.35729 ● Price Guide: ££ ● All Services Except Electricity ● 30-Min Walk to Casemates Square ● **Alternative**: Camping Sureuropa (*www.campingsureuropa.es*), GPS: N36.191804, W5.334733, Price Guide: ££, All Services, Dogs Not Allowed

The parking area by the marina in La Línea is clean, secure and flat, fenced-in with views of the Rock and the pleasure boats in the port. It's popular but has a good number of places and is only a 10-minute walk (or a short cycle ride) to the border between Spain and Gibraltar.

Once you've crossed the border, there's an Eroski supermarket (if you're after supplies) or you can take a bus, taxi or Shanks' Pony (your feet) across the runway, an odd experience in itself. Morrisons is about 3km from the marina, quite a walk when both arms are weighed down with British goodies, keep that in mind when you're gleefully filling your trolley! You can use your Sterling (cash or cards) with the same pound value and without exchanging currency in Gibraltar. Euros may be accepted, but the exchange rate might be poor.

We really enjoyed the Mediterranean Steps hike, a reasonably strenuous walk uphill from the Pillars of Hercules up to O'Hara's Battery (with fabulous sea views across to Morocco) and finally to the area the macaques inhabit, which was packed with taxis and fellow tourists. From the top we opted to walk back down, but the cable car is another option, as is a visit to the Siege Tunnels if you have the energy!

On other occasions we've been unable to resist the opportunity to tuck into some English grub, eating fish and chips, being regaled with a story about the owner loaning a car to Prince Charles and Diana when they visited Gibraltar on honeymoon in 1981. Was it true? Who knows?

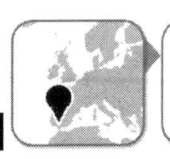

GREECE

QUICK FACTS ● **EU**: Yes ● **Schengen**: Yes ● **Language**: Greek ● **Currency**: Euro (EUR, £1=€1.1) ● **Speed Limits ≤3.5t**: Urban/Single/Expressway/Motorway: 50, 90, 110, 130kph ● **Speed Limits >3.5t**: Urban/Single/Expressway/Motorway: 50, 80, 80, 85kph ● **Tolls**: Yes on Motorways, Rio-Antirrio Bridge and Aktio-Preveza Tunnel, Pay Per Use With Cash or Card ● **LEZs**: Central Athens ● **IDP**: Not Needed ● **Docs**: Driving Licence, Insurance, Passport, V5C ● **Kit**: Headlamp Deflectors, Warning Triangle, Fire Extinguisher, First Aid Kit ● **LPG**: Good Availability, Dish Adapter ● **Time**: UK+2 Hours ● **Daytime Dipped Headlights**: No ● **Overnighting**: Campsites, Parking at Restaurants & Widely Tolerated Freedom Parking, Only a Few Aires Available

Whenever we're asked what our favourite motorhome countries are in Europe, Greece always features in the answer. Its attractions are many: calm and pure blue seas, end-of-the world feel, friendly locals, laid-back attitudes to life, delicious and well-priced options to eat out, historical sights and varied opportunities for freedom parking.

Most motorhome travellers reach Greece from the UK via Italy, taking a ferry across the Adriatic Sea from Venice and Ancona in the north or Brindisi or Bari in the south to Igoumenitsa, Corfu or Patras. Some summer ferries even allow 'camping on board' where you can stay in your van on an open deck for the crossing, hooked-up to electricity supplied by the boat, especially helpful if you have pets.

Alternatively, you can travel overland across Hungary, Romania and Bulgaria, all EU countries making insurance easier to obtain. We've done both routes and encountered no problems. Another option is to travel south through Croatia and across Montenegro and Albania, a more adventurous route requiring insurance to be bought at the borders, but one which lots of motorhome travellers have safely used.

Greece is a mountainous country, so any tour is likely to involve hair pin bends here and there. Be ready for using your gears to engine brake and do your research on snow conditions in winter.

Ferries connect Greece's network of islands, but for motorhomes may be expensive, infrequent and awkward to disembark on smaller islands (*www.ferries.gr*). Some tourers opt to store their van in Athens and fly to the islands instead.

Stop #68: Acrocorinth

Car Park ● GPS: N37.88992, E22.86828 ● Price Guide: Free ● Overnight Possible ● Good, Paved Access Road ● No Services ● Great Views over Gulf of Corinth ● **Alternative**: Camper Stop in Corinth, GPS: N37.911489, E22.878244, Price Guide: ££, All Services

Like many of the very best places we've been able to stay in our motorhome, the sun-scorched parking area high up above the ancient Greek city of Acrocorinth was gifted to us by a fellow motorhomer. A friendly chap showed us it in his copy of *Mit Dem Whonmobile*, a popular series of motorhome guides in his native Germany (*verlagshaus24.de/bruckmann*).

Just a gravel car park, but what a view, it's stunning! From the van windscreen we could see right out across the Gulf of Corinth. Adjacent stood the triple walls of Acrocorinth (Upper Corinth), wrapped around an imposing 575m-high rock. This stronghold gave the ancients control over the Isthmus of Corinth, the thin strip of land giving access to the Peloponnese which has been cut through since 1893 by the Corinth Canal and its amazing submersible bridges.

The ruins are free to enter, and we spent hours wandering them and taking photos, imagining the lives of the successive waves of defenders throughout the centuries, Ancient Greeks, Macedonians, Romans, Byzantines, Frankish Crusaders, Venetians, Ottomans, the Hellenes and even the Nazis from 1941.

Take drinking water when you visit the ruins, we were forced to take refuge under a tree for shade, even in May! Decent footwear makes sense too, as the paths are earthen and there are occasional uneven old steps to navigate. There are more ruins below at Ancient Corinth, an old city state, one-time ally of Sparta and one of the most important cities in Greece around 400BC with a population of 90,000. The modern city is built 3 miles north-east of the ruins. The main settlement moved from Corinth up to Acrocorinth in the 7th Century AD to avoid incursions by barbarian invaders.

Stop #69: Athens

Camping Athens (*campingathens.gr*) ● GPS: N38.00920, E23.67271 ● Price Guide: £££ ● All Services ● Take Bus (Stop Opposite Campsite) to Metaxourghiou Metro Station ● **Alternative**: Parkopolis Parking, GPS: N37.947574, E23.645997, Price Guide: ££, No Black or Grey Water Disposal, Book In At Least 24 Hrs Before Arrival (Phone +30 210 412 1626)

City campsites tend to be a little functional and expensive. Camping Athens fitted that description, but had the benefits of gifting us shade (it was getting very warm even in late May), of being located outside the city so required less manic city driving and the bus to the metro was just a two-minute walk away. It felt a good place for a few nights of secure parking.

Athens proved well worth the effort to visit. The city sprawls across the landscape, the population sadly swelled by an enforced population exchange with Turkey in 1923, retold in *Bird Without Wings* by Louis de Bernières. We got a great view of the cityscape from Mount Lycabettus, taken there by a kind Greek couple we'd met earlier on our tour of Greece, who then showed us around the Palaio Faliro sea-front district with its mega yachts and high-end restaurants.

The following day we took to the city without our chaperones, excited to be stood on the famous Acropolis rock, with the incredible Parthenon, Odeon of Herodes Atticus and Propylaea plus various other ancient buildings, and more breath-taking views of the city.

Sharing the rock with a huge number of tourists was a little testing at times, with the site guards constantly blowing whistles and shouting at people touching or walking where they shouldn't, and we were glad to eventually retreat to the cool of the nearby Acropolis Museum to see the remaining Parthenon Marbles, those which survived Lord Elgin's attempts to move them to Britain.

Stop #70: Diakofto

Beach Parking ● GPS: N38.20196, E22.19415 ● Price Guide: Free ● No Services ● 1.5km Walk to Odontotos Rack Railway ● **Alternative**: Beach Café Camper Stop, GPS: N38.223904, E22.147098, Price Guide: £, All Services, 20-Min Drive to Odontotos Rack Railway Parking

Apparently to satisfy the ego of Mussolini, Italy chose to invade Greece in 1940, being humiliated and pushed back into Albania by the Greeks before German re-enforcements were dispatched. The resulting occupation resulted in numerous heart-breaking atrocities. Some have been made widely known, like the German invasion of Cephalonia depicted in *Captain Corelli's Mandolin*.

Other shocking acts of barbarity directed against the local population are lesser known. We only came across the terribly sad story of Kalavryta in the hills of the northern Peloponnese, when we heard of the Odontotos Rack Railway, which runs from Diakofto up to the village.

The railway itself is a delight, sweeping up 22km into the Vouraikos Gorge through tunnels, across bridges and under sections cut from the cliff-face, eventually reaching the end of the track at Kalavryta.

The village's museum tells its story. In reprisal for the killing of German soldiers by the Greek resistance, 438 men and boys over 13 were massacred and the village was burnt house by house. A statue outside the museum depicts the aftermath, a mother dragging her dead husband, her children stood by her. We wept at the sight.

Parked alongside a beach that evening, we enjoyed a more light-hearted chat with fellow British motorhome travellers about their underwater metal detecting hobby (they did it mainly in Spain, not in Greece as it's illegal there without a permit).

Stop #71: Diros

Beach Parking ● GPS: N36.64122, E22.38325 ● Price Guide: Free ● No Services ● 5km Walk to Shops and Restaurants at Areopoli ● **Alternative**: Sea-Front Parking near Limeni, GPS: N36.680176, E22.374140, Price Guide: Free, No Services, Max 6m Length Due to Tight Access

This parking area at Diros stands alongside a pristine white pebble beach upon which lap pure turquoise waters with only the sounds of waves and the bells of a goat herd cutting through the background roar of cicadas. It seems unbelievable out in the bright sun that just a few hundred metres away lies the cold and dark of an enormous complex of lakes and caverns, the Diros Caves. Although only part of the huge underground area is accessible to the public, it was enough to leave a lasting impression on us.

Access to the caves is by wooden boats, carefully pushed by hand by a guide who requests that you duck from time to time where the cave roof lowers. If you're anything like us, you'll be keen to try and photograph the beauty of the stalagmites and stalactites, but it proved a difficult task in the low light on a moving boat.

Bring a coat if you plan to visit the caves as they are a little cool.

From the beach it's a 6-mile round trip walk to Areopoli, named after the Greek god of war Ares, because the Greek War of Independence against 350 years of Turkish occupation started here, the beginning of a 7-year struggle. While walking we were ushered along by three dogs, faithfully protecting their goat family. After recovering from the uphill effort with a drink in the town's main square, we wandered around the stone-paved streets, standing quietly to one side while a local played his *bouzouki*, a type of lute, waving our appreciation when he finished.

We walked back down to our motorhome snapping photos of lizards, bright-coloured beetles, a hoopoe bird, a jumping spider, a donkey and lots of huge grasshoppers!

Stop #72: Galaxidi

Informal Beach Parking ● GPS: N38.351552, E22.379898 ● Price Guide: Free ● No Services ●
Alternative: Delphi Camping (*www.delphicamping.com*), GPS: N38.478599, E22.474993, Price Guide: ££, All Services, 1.5km from Entrance to Delphi Archaeological Site

Greece felt to us like a land which should no longer exist. Undeveloped stretches of coastline, where we could just park up for the night right alongside the pure blue sea, seemed to be everywhere we travelled. In remote areas (and in many towns), no-one paid us any attention. There were no signs indicating parking charges, hours or lists of restrictions. The sensation of freedom has been matched only in the Baltic States and Scandinavia.

This spot was 3km from the small town of Galaxidi and a 40-minute drive from the archaeological site at Delphi. After a quiet afternoon's swimming, cooking, dog walking and recording a video about how we felt to be going back to find work in the UK after almost two years off (answer: not great, but we needed the money!), we slept like logs.

The following morning, we took the road to Delphi, parking outside the site entrance, having driven up early to avoid the midday heat. The ancient Greeks saw Delphi as the centre of the world, the location of the Oracle, a lady chosen from the locals who'd breathe in fumes from a fissure in the earth and issue prophesies, possibly in gibberish which was interpreted by priests.

Delphi was once massively rich, the location of the pre-Olympic Pythian Games, and hammered by earthquakes before finally being abandoned until the French Archaeological School of Athens was allowed to excavate it in 1892, moving a modern village from the site.

We found Delphi absolutely beautiful on a perfect blue-sky day in May, captivating with a backdrop of pristine wooded hills.

Stop #73: Katakolo

Mixed Parking ● GPS: N37.64765, E21.31770 ● Price Guide: £ ● Water Available ● 40km Drive to Olympia ● **Alternative**: Camping Alfios, GPS: N37.643241, E21.619575, Price Guide: £££, All Services, 30-Min Walk to Archaeological Site of Olympia

After arriving in Patras on a ferry from Italy, our plan was to drive south into the Peloponnese, a route which took us almost straight past the ancient site of Olympia, location of the original Olympic Games. There was no way we'd pass up the opportunity to visit the site. While there are a couple of campsites in Olympia, neither is cheap. Instead we opted to stay a 50-minute drive away at the port of Katakolo, where cruise ships dock for excursions to the site.

With no ships in port, the line of restaurants built to serve them were quiet, the huddle of coaches which usually do the Olympia transfer stood patiently still. From our spot at the port we watched the bearded incarnation of the Ancient Mariner angle-grinding paint and rust from his battered boat. In other places across Greece we'd buy freshly caught fish direct from fishermen like him. His compatriots worked carefully fixing nets or on other inscrutable tasks.

Olympia itself didn't disappoint. After being exposed to a lifetime of stories, copies and images of Greek antiquity, being stood in among the ruins of the real deal was quite a buzz. Armed with our Rough Guide and a map from the ticket office, we deciphered the various parts of the ancient sanctuary as we walked around.

The on-site archaeological museum was a highlight for us, showcasing the original statues from the Temple of Zeus, depicting chariot races and *Lapiths*, a legendary people from Greek mythology. Sadly, the giant statue of Zeus, one of the seven wonders of the world, was lost in the 5th Century BC.

Stop #74: Meteora

Parking at Hotel Arsenis (*www.arsenis-meteora.gr*) ● GPS: N39.70857, E21.65424 ● Price Guide: Free (In Return for Eating in the Hotel) ● Fresh Water, Paid Electricity ● **Alternative**: Camping Kastraki (*www.campingkastraki.com*), GPS: N39.713245, E21.615975, Price Guide: ££, All Services

Meteora's an extra-ordinary place, columns of sandstone abruptly interrupting the mind-numbing drive across the Thessalian Plain, topped off with Byzantine monasteries built in the most unbelievable, vertiginous places.

The story goes that over a thousand years ago hermit monks opted to escape the world by finding niches in which they could live high up on the smooth-sided pinnacles of rock, deterring all but the most dedicated of visitors. Around 500 years ago, increasing Turkish attacks on Greece forced the monks into building the monasteries on the pinnacles of the columns. Access was initially via ladders which could be withdrawn by the monks, or windlass and rope (a type of winch). Steps have since been constructed, allowing easier access to the heights. The monasteries are still active places of worship, requiring modest dress covering knees and upper arms.

The roads around the monasteries are well kept and wide enough for coaches, so were easy to drive, and we enjoyed a quiet visit to one of the smaller monasteries.

Afterwards we drove to the Hotel Arsenis, a short distance away, having to restrain our dog from hunting down a tortoise as it ambled past our parking spot. Like many restaurants in Greece, overnight parking outside the hotel was free on the basis we ate a meal. The choice was simple, chicken or pork, but the food was good value and delicious.

Stop #75: Methoni

Beach Car Park ● GPS: N36.81769, E21.70777 ● Price Guide: Free ● No Services ●
Alternative: Camping Methoni (*www.campingmethoni.gr*), GPS: N36.817320, E21.715162, Price Guide: ££, All Services, 1km from Methoni Castle

A quick aside: while in Greece expect to come across lots of the Greek alphabet! Road signs are often given in both Greek and Latin alphabets, but sometimes not and it's handy to be able to make a guess at the local letters. For example, Methoni is written Μεθώνη in Greek, or ΜΕΘΩΝΗ in upper case. When we arrived in Greece, we spent hours writing out the letters on the sand of a beach, learning the alphabet like kids again.

The mixed parking at Methoni is right alongside the beach, so it can be busy with locals during the day. It's also just a couple of minutes' stroll from *tavernas* (small restaurants), shops, bank and bars and the town's remains of a Venetian fortified castle, marked with the winged lion of St Mark.

The area, like many parts of the eastern Mediterranean, was controlled by Venice for around 300 years, a commercial port and financial centre on the route to the eastern markets in the Levant and a staging post for pilgrims on their way to the Holy Land. The castle was taken by the Ottomans in 1500 who built the *Bourtzi*, an octagonal defensive tower accessed via a causeway, which was also used as a prison and torture chamber. During the Greek War of Independence, the Turks held the fortress before surrendering it to French forces who handed it back to the Greeks.

The castle walls extend right up to the sea, and we enjoyed the unique experience of snorkelling beneath them for a couple of hours, spotting our first Bearded Fireworm. The bright orange centipede-like creature, about 20cm long, walked across the rocks below, harmless unless touched when they inflict a painful sting (we've long learned not to touch anything we don't recognise).

Stop #76: Mezapos

Port Car Park ● GPS: N36.54220, E22.39079 ● Price Guide: Free ● No Services ● Tight Access, OK for 6m Motorhome ● **Alternative**: Car Park in Yerolimenas, 10km South of Mezapos, GPS: N36.48258, E22.39989, Price Guide: Free, No Services

Our first impression of Mezapos was rendered into a stream of panicked expletives when we saw how tight the access road to the port parking was. We came to a halt until a chap appeared and silently pointed down the road. Taking this to mean we'd fit, we took a deep breath and squeezed down the road. After losing concentration in relief and almost reversing into a stone wall, a well-tanned chap appeared who we later found was Stavros. He smiled and pointed at his taverna, the cue for one of the most simple but memorable meals of our lives.

After swimming in the bay, we headed up to the taverna, stepping through the door into what felt like someone's front room. It was packed full of stuff, a map of Europe in Greek, photos of family, crates of drinks, a fishing net, scales, ornaments, you name it. We sat on the only table not occupied by a stripped boat engine. The menu consisted of three questions: "fish?", "two fish?", "Greek salad?". We opted for half a litre of *retsina* too, a white wine flavoured with tree resin, an acquired taste!

Julie not being a big fan of fish, especially with the heads attached, managed to keep a straight face when the deep-fried collection of whole specimens arrived, just the fish, bread, olive oil and salad, simple!

As we picked over the bones Stavros reappeared and turned the TV on to show a Spiderman movie (in English subtitled in Greek), and we all watched for a while before waving him goodbye and retreating a few metres to the van.

Stop #77: Monemvasia

Port Car Park ● GPS: N36.682398, E23.038591 ● Price Guide: Free ● No Services ● 2km Walk to Gate into Monemvasia ● **Alternative**: Free Parking on Grass By Sea, GPS: N36.659522, E23.025827, Price Guide: Free, No Services, 3km from Monemvasia Port Parking

Monemvasia is one of those places which must be seen to be believed. It's a fortified town built on an island which was formed by a strong earthquake in 375 AD. The buildings are huddled around the base of cliffs with a second town occupying the mile-long plateau of rock on the cliffs above.

Neither the upper nor lower towns are visible from the 200m causeway which connects the huge rock to the mainland. It's only when you walk 1km from the causeway around the southern end of the island that you come across stone walls sloping down into the sea, and the single gated entrance through which lies the lower town. This single access route gives the town its name. *moni emvasi* means "single entrance".

The gate calls a halt to the cars, only pedestrians, donkeys and motorised wheelbarrows shall pass. The gate itself is a zig-zag tunnel, leading to the narrow, cobbled Byzantine streets of the lower town, the houses well preserved as boutique hotels and restaurants by the steady flow of tourists. Entrance is free, and you'll have plenty of opportunity to pick up a Monemvasia fridge magnet if you opt to walk the main path into town (the steps leading down to the right just after the gate bypass the shops).

From the lower town a series of hair-pin steps take you to the out-of-this-world views from the upper town. There are far fewer remaining buildings up there, but it's well worth the climb.

We stayed a night in a parking area on the island side of the causeway, but that's off limits to motorhomes now and the town asks you park at the small nearby port. It's still a great place to overnight, where we were lucky enough to spot a sea turtle swimming around the port when we walked that way.

105

Stop #78: Porto Káyio

Taverna Parking ● GPS: N36.428206, E22.486939 ● Price Guide: Free ● No Services ● Buying a Meal at a Taverna is Required ● **Alternative**: Small Sea-Front Parking near Giali (2km East of Gerolimenas), GPS: N36.474985, E22.413689, Price Guide: Free, No Services

A short steep descent and a quick stretch of beach driving popped us into a small car park alongside new friends' motorhome at Porto Káyio, a tiny string of houses and tavernas out on a limb at the southern tip of the Mani Peninsular.

We'd spent the day walking from the car park at Kokkinogia (a few miles to the south of Porto Káyio) down to the Tenaro Lighthouse, a 4km round trip. The trail crosses gentle rocky slopes covered in low scrub which dip down to the ocean, a beautiful place to take a fairly effortless hike. An injection of adrenaline came our way at one point though when we spotted a snake curled on the path, possibly a highly toxic Nose-Horned Viper. We jumped backwards and it left in a hurry before we had chance to get brave and take a photo!

The evening passed quickly, eating a meal at the taverna, with a backdrop of idyllic sea, followed by a few hours of over-indulging with our neighbours in their motorhome (at least one of us did!). Several *Fix* beers were followed by a bottle of Greek Ouzo, a dry anise-flavoured liquor, which was rather badly regretted the following morning!

Hangovers aside, meeting new people on the road is, one of the very best parts of long-term travel. There's something about being so far removed from our day-to-day experiences which makes conversation flow that much more easily. Topics which might normally take weeks, months or even years to touch on are approached more or less immediately, forging long-lasting friendships on fast-forwards.

Stop #79: Vergina

Official Overnight Parking ● GPS: N40.484926, E22.320202 ● Price Guide: £ ● Water Available ● 5-Min Walk to Royal Tombs ● **Alternative**: Tour Bus Parking, GPS: N40.484534, E22.321664, Price Guide: Free, No Services, 5-Min Walk to Royal Tombs

Greece is awash with famous historical monuments: Olympia, Delphi, The Acropolis, Epidaurus, Mycenae, Mystras and more. We'd never heard of Vergina though, a small modern town, founded in 1922. It was accidentally built on the location of Aigai, the first capital of Macedon, where Alexander the Great's father Philip II was assassinated in 336 BC, allegedly by a spurned lover.

In 1977 Philip II's tomb was discovered in the town, along with those of several other kings of Macedon by Dr. Andronikos, a professor of archaeology who'd been searching in the area since 1937. Thieves hadn't accessed the tombs, and they were packed with incredible grave goods.

In his book about the find, Dr. Andronikos wrote *"Inside the sarcophagus there was a golden shrine. On top of its cover there was an imposing relief star with sixteen rays, and a rosette in the center. With much care and more emotion, I lifted the cover with the star by grasping it from the two corners. We all expected to see in it the burnt bones of the dead. But what we saw opening it left us breathless, with teary eyes and filled with awe: indeed there were burnt bones in the urn"*.

We opted for the paid parking, just a few euros, and walked through the plain town to the entrance of the UNESCO-listed Great Tombs of the Royal Tumulus. After being excavated, the tombs were carefully recovered with a grass mound, giving away nothing of the secrets beneath.

In the surrounding area more tombs are being slowly uncovered, with new secrets waiting to be revealed. We chatted alongside a tomb with an archaeologist about his hopes for future funding.

HUNGARY

QUICK FACTS ● **EU**: Yes ● **Schengen**: Yes ● **Language**: Hungarian ● **Currency**: Forint (HUF, £1=400Ft) ● **Speed Limits ≤3.5t**: Urban/Single/Expressway/Motorway: 50, 90, 110, 130kph ● **Speed Limits >3.5t**: Urban/Single/Expressway/Motorway: 50, 70, 80, 80kph ● **Tolls**: Vignette or eVignette for ≤3.5t (*ematrica.nemzetiutdij.hu*), Electronic Tag for >3.5t (*www.hu-go.hu*) ● **LEZs**: None, But Budapest Has Weight-Based Access Restrictions ● **IDP**: Not Needed ● **Docs**: Driving Licence, Insurance, Passport, V5C ● **Kit**: Headlamp Deflectors, Warning Triangle, Reflective Jackets, First Aid Kit ● **LPG**: Good Availability, Dish Adapter ● **Time**: UK+1 Hour ● **Daytime Dipped Headlights**: Yes ● **Overnighting**: Campsites, Wild Camping Illegal but Tolerated in Rural Areas, Some Private Businesses Allow Paid Stopovers

Hungary's famous for its thermal springs, and there are plenty of great-quality campsites attached to spas to allow you to easily give them a try. On our visit spas were off the menu due to the heat. The weather had been slow cooking us in our motorhome for a few weeks, to the point tempers finally flared and we found ourselves driving at speed towards the Austrian border seeking the cool of the mountains. Thankfully calm was restored before we missed half the country, and we pulled a U-turn once we'd cooled off and calmed down.

Hungary doesn't formally allow wild camping, but we didn't know that when we parked alongside the country's enormous Lake Balaton for a couple of nights, enjoying splashing around in the shallow warm waters, retreating into the van before a black mass of tiny bugs invaded each evening.

We were also a little clueless about the toll road system, failing in our attempts to avoid the paid sections and finally buying a vignette to reduce our stress levels (these can now be bought electronically for vans under 3500Kg).

Although Hungary was behind the Iron Curtain until 1989, we didn't see much evidence of communist rule but for the odd Trabant car, until we visited Momento Park (*www.mementopark.hu*) on the southern outskirts of Budapest. As well as statues of Lenin and Marx, there are enormous statues of workers, martyrs and soldiers. It's a sight to see, an eye-opening glimpse into the country's past and the mindset of socialist idealism.

Stop #80: Balatonberény

Free Camping ● GPS: N46.71554, E17.3280 ● Price Guide: Free ● No Services, Toilets Only ● Direct Access to Beach at Lake Balaton ● **Alternative**: Carina Camping Balatongyörök (*www.carinacamping.hu*), GPS: N46.751017, E17.350818, Price Guide: ££, All Services

Stuck for topics of conversation, we once asked a Hungarian if they knew of Lake Balaton. He replied: "yes, of course, everyone in Hungary knows Lake Balaton". Ah, yes, they would since it's huge, the largest lake in Central Europe, a 100km drive from the eastern to western ends!

The lake's shallow and the waters are warm in the summer, as we can attest having waded around in them in search of parts deep enough to swim in. The parking area near to a beach was popular with locals out sunbathing during the day, but we had it almost to ourselves in the evening with a fellow motorhome parked a little distance away, a Belgian family who'd been there a week thanks to the availability of a nearby toilet block.

The lake is a major tourist attraction, with resort towns built from the 18th Century onwards to attract Hungary's new middle classes, and later it was a Mecca for East German tourists before the wall came down. The village of Balatonberény where we stayed is quite small. It has a naturist campsite and beach but otherwise there's not too much to distract you. The village is part of the Balatonboglár wine region, producing white and Concord grapes, if you're looking for an excuse to try out some of the local vino.

If you have bikes, there's also easy access to the 200km-long cycle route around the lake (*www.balatontourism.com*), giving access to the nearest town, Keszthely, with its parks, restaurants, museums and Festetics Palace (*helikonkastely.hu*). It's a 14km ride in each direction or a 20-minute train ride with a few minute's walking either end.

Stop #81: Budapest

Camping Haller (*hallercamping.hu*) ● GPS: N47.47574, E19.08428 ● Price Guide: ££ ● All Services ● 10-Min Walk to M3 Subway, Tickets Sold at Campsite ● **Alternative**: Secure 24Hr Stellplatz, GPS: N47.518263, E19.089665, Price Guide: £, All Services, Near Metro Stop

Camping Haller in Budapest is a melting pot of nations, all gathered in a small friendly patch of earth just five metro stations from the city centre. To one side of us was a young couple in an aged Hymer motorhome like ours, touring before starting their careers. Opposite, a group of recent graduates were taking a break from an epic two-month Mongol Rally journey, travelling in two ambulances they later donated on arrival in Ulaanbaatar.

The site electrics were a snake's wedding of extension cables, reminding us we weren't in Western Europe, as did the low cost of metro tickets, camping and eating at the site's good-quality restaurant.

Our dog's short nose wasn't conducive to it, but we'd read a muzzle was mandatory for dogs on the underground. With the muzzle in our pocket we risked it, finding the staff were more interested in fussing him than ejecting him back above ground.

The city itself, formed by merging Pest, Buda and Óbuda in the 19th Century, is UNESCO-listed and described as "one of the world's outstanding urban landscapes". We found the centre compact enough to explore on foot, taking in St. Stephen's Basilica, the Parliament Building and the Gothic Buda Castle. Other travellers recommend the House of Terror museum to learn the impact of the fascist and communist regimes. Or, for a lighter afternoon maybe, visit a ruin bar or two in the city's old Jewish district, drinking establishments built in abandoned houses or shops (*Szimpla Kert* is reputed to be one of the best).

ITALY

QUICK FACTS ● **EU**: Yes ● **Schengen**: Yes ● **Language**: Italian ● **Currency**: Euro (EUR, £1=€1.1) ● **Speed Limits ≤3.5t**: Urban/Single/Expressway/Motorway: 50, 90, 130, 130kph ● **Speed Limits >3.5t**: Urban/Single/Expressway/Motorway: 50, 80, 100, 100kph ● **Tolls**: Pay Per Use on the Autostrada With Cash/Card (*www.autostrade.it*) ● **LEZs**: Over 100, No National Scheme, Italy Also Has ZTLs – Inner-City Zones Where Non-Local Traffic Cannot Enter ● **IDP**: Not Needed ● **Docs**: Driving Licence, Insurance, Passport, V5C ● **Kit**: Headlamp Deflectors, Warning Triangle, Signal Board on Bike Rack, Reflective Jackets, First Aid Kit ● **LPG**: Good Availability, Dish Adapter ● **Time**: UK+1 Hour ● **Daytime Dipped Headlights**: No ● **Overnighting**: Campsites, Official Sostas, Off-Site Overnight Parking Widely Tolerated, Some Businesses Allow Paid Stopovers

Bella Italia!!! It would be hard for anyone touring Italy to argue with its natural beauty, from the serene mountain lakes and jagged snow-capped Dolomites in the north, to the rolling vineyards of Tuscany, the simple untouched beaches of the south to the raw power and majesty of Sicily's Etna, and that's without even taking a ferry over to the rugged landscapes of Sardinia, sitting out in the Mediterranean Sea.

Alongside nature stands human culture. The Italian passion shines through in their art, architecture, food, motorsports, and frantic football supporting. It's normal to be sat behind an Italian driver who appears to be going quite mad at their passenger, their arms waving around as they express themselves, hands hardly touching the wheel!

With all this passion comes a healthy dollop of gritty reality. The drivers can be a little too keen to overtake. Traffic and parking can be insane around the towns and cities. Urban sprawl and graffiti are everywhere. Many beaches have been spoiled with uncontrolled development.

Whenever we tour Italy, we find ourselves leaving with both a hint of relief, and of regret. Trying to work out where it's OK to park for the night kind of sums Italy up: even where there are signs saying 'No Motorhomes', the police tell us it's fine, as long as it's not in season (when most of the campsites are closed). If you come to Italy, bring an open mind, the country is wonderful to tour by motorhome, but it has its own way of working, which we still haven't quite grasped!

Stop #82: Alberobello

Official Sosta ● GPS: N40.78052, E17.24509 ● Price Guide: £ ● No Services ● 1km Walk to Trulli Houses ● **Alternative**: Official Sosta "Camper Service Nel Verde", GPS: N40.783046, E17.233230, Price Guide: ££, All Services

Alberobello lies in the Apulia region, Italy's 'heel' in the *Mezzogiorno*, the Italian word for the southern half of the country in reference to the intensity of the sun at midday down here. Like the UK, Italy has a north-south wealth divide, but here the money resides mostly in the north. Some fellow travellers we met took this as cue to avoid the south, but we found it an easy-going, relaxed place to travel, and came across some of our most memorable stops down here.

Alberobello has attracted tourists since the 1970s with its collection of *trullo* houses (collectively called *trulli*). We spotted a few of these conical, dry stone shelters out in the fields, historically built without mortar to avoid housing taxes and back when the cost of labour was so low it was economical to move the hundreds of tons of stone needed for a single dwelling.

Here in Alberbello the trulli are permanent dwellings, whole districts of photogenic white-washed homes, some with relatively recent symbols painted on the roofs, some representing Catholic saints or icons. The town even has a trullo church, and there are trulli to rent if you fancy a break from your motorhome (albeit perhaps with less room)!

We parked in one of the town's official camper sostas, arriving on a blue-skied Easter Monday to find it heaving busy, the small streets between the trulli packed with local and foreign tourists. The following morning the town and sosta were all-but deserted and the skies were dark, ushering us on towards Trani on the Adriatic, and then Bari for a ferry to Greece.

112

Stop #83: Castiglione Falletto

Official Sosta ● GPS: N44.623593, E7.974839 ● Price Guide: Free ● All Services Except Electricity ● 5-Min Walk to Village ● **Alternative:** Sosta at Grinzane Cavour, GPS: N44.655243, E7.989543, Price Guide: Free, All Services Except Electricity, Noise from School Traffic

Welcome to Barolo country! If you, like us, know practically nothing about viticulture then this 'wine of kings, king of wines' is likely to be a big unknown. All the more reason to come and explore this UNESCO-listed region. Even if the wine isn't ultimately to your liking, the location of these free official sostas in the Piedmont region is special, set among spectacular vistas of rolling vineyards with a backdrop of the snow-capped Alps.

During our visit in March, snow lay in patches where it had piled during the winter. The vines were naked, devoid of leaves and the small *nebbiolo* grapes which make Italy's (arguably) finest red wine. Workers made their way slowly across the hillsides (the vines must be grown on slopes), expertly clipping away.

Eleven villages make up the Barolo DOCG, the area in which the wine can be formally grown, including Barolo itself. The Barolo wines must be aged at least three years, 18 months of which has to be in wood.

Walks set among the valleys carry you between the medieval hilltop villages, past estates and farmhouses, building thirst for a wine tasting in a *cantina* (cellar) or an appetite for an informal *osteria* or *trattoria* lunch.

The Borolo-producing region is also set just to the south of Alba, the birthplace of the hazelnut-infused Nutella chocolate spread, invented in thriftier times when cocoa was expensive after WW2, but the nuts were everywhere. Alba is also famous for white truffles, a type of fungus highly prized for their flavour, selling for around £2,000 to £4,000 per kg.

Stop #84: Florence

Camper Sosta "Florence Scandicci" ● GPS: N43.76236, E11.20930 ● Price Guide: ££ ● All Services ● 250m Walk to Bus Stop ● **Alternative**: Area Sosta Camper Firenze, GPS: N43.751754, E11.244093, Price Guide: ££, All Services Except Electricity

Florence is served by a couple of sostas, basic but secure parking areas set a couple of miles from the centre of the city, in walking distance of public transport. Unusually for a sosta, ours had a small cabin with a receptionist, who gave us a map and pointed us in the direction of the nearby bus stop.

Walking along the banks of the River Arno we had a great view of Ponte Vecchio, the only bridge not mined by the retreating Nazis in 1944. It's loaded with shops, overhanging sides propped up by wooden supports. In the past they were butchers, fishmongers and tanners until in 1593 when Ferdinando I had enough of the smell and only allowed goldsmiths to occupy the premises!

Next, we tried our luck at the world-famous Galleria Degli Uffizi art gallery, being very fortunate to find there were no queues. We worked our way through time taking in works by Giotto, Botticelli, Leonardo da Vinci, Michelangelo, Rubens, Van Dyck, Goya and Rembrandt.

Making it back into the street we headed to the Piazza Della Signoria to see Michelangelo's David about to strike down Goliath (a replica, the real statue was moved to the city's Galleria dell'Accademia in 1873 and is still there) before being wowed by the Duomo (the cathedral), its Campanile (bell tower) and Romanesque Battistero (baptistry).

The following day we drove along narrow roads to the large parking area at Piazzale Michelangelo (GPS: N43.762684, E11.264567) for a wonderful view of the city, before setting the satnav for a taste of wine in the Chianti Mountains.

Stop #85: Giardini-Naxos

Eden Parking Camper Sosta (*www.edenparking.it*) ● GPS: N37.82224, E15.26699 ● Price Guide: ££ ● All Services ● **Alternative**: Parking Lagani (*www.parkinglagani.it*), GPS: N37.820909, E15.267501, Price Guide: ££ (Reduced for Longer Stays), All Services

Giardini-Naxos lies on the coast in North-East Sicily, on a similar latitude to Murcia in Spain. The town has two motorhome sostas, both popular with Italians from further north over-wintering with average highs of 15°C in January and February (and average lows of 10°C), and low costs for long-term stays.

We spent our Christmas one year at Giardini-Naxos, being treated to blue skies and sunshine, the company of fellow British tourers, and gifts of delicious food and *limoncello* (a lemon liqueur) from our Italian neighbours.

Giardini-Naxos has a long history, but more recently was a quiet fishing port up until the 1970s when tourism arrived, although it still proved very quiet out-of-season when we stayed in December and again in March. The beaches were empty, and the restaurants and pizzerias were similarly devoid of people.

Piaggio Apes brought local sellers to the sosta, tiny-engine vans with space for a driver and, on the larger models, a passenger squeezed into a minuscule cab. We'd nip out curious to see what they had, scoring some freshly caught fish which we cooked with the lemons our Italian neighbours gave us. One evening more dramatic excitement came in the form of an exploding Mount Etna, launching lava high into the sky and causing the ground on the sosta to tremor.

We also enjoyed the 8km walk to the up-market resort at Taormina, visiting the impressive Greek-Roman theatre with its backdrop of Etna and the Ionian Sea to the south, quite an incredible place to sit and rest a while.

115

Stop #86: La Spezia

Sosta Managed by Paramedics ● GPS: N44.104155, E9.859072 ● Price Guide: ££ ● All Services ● 10-Min Walk to Boat or Train for Cinque Terre ● **Alternative:** Sosta "Il Poggio", GPS: N44.155010, E9.659276, Price Guide: £££, All Services, Free Bus to Train Station at Monterosso

North of Pisa in the Liguria region of Italy, La Spezia's main attraction for us was the train to the world-renown Cinque Terre. Five pastel-coloured villages dating back to Roman times cling to the rock as it dips into the sea. The villages were originally supported by olives and grapes, the steep slopes around them shaped into terraces, while income more latterly comes from tourism. The villages have been on the UNESCO World Heritage list since 1997.

Maps of the area resemble a Jackson Pollock painting, roads twisting like spaghetti. Only the E80 motorway, which forces its way across the landscape with viaducts and tunnels offers respite for the frazzled motorhome driver.

From La Spezia, or from the sosta at Monterosso (details above), you can take a train which runs along the coast through a series of tunnels, linking up each village (dogs are allowed on the train, we bought a ticket for ours which the inspector laughed at when he saw how small our dog was). Alternatively, you can take a boat from La Spezia (from May to Oct), giving a dramatic view of the villages from the sea.

There's also a 12km coastal path called the Azure Trail linking up each village, a five-hour hike one way which you need to buy a ticket for. The path is sometimes closed, so it's worth checking the current conditions if this is something you plan to do (*www.parconazionale5terre.it*).

Stop #87: Lake Orta

Official Sosta ● GPS: N45.796777, E8.412124 ● Price Guide: Free ● No Services ● **Alternative**: Official Sosta "Omegna", GPS: N45.863572, E8.399018, Price Guide: ££, Landscaped Area with Some Shade, All Services, 2km to Centre of Omegna

The Italian Lakes rest in the foothills of the Alps where they rise up to meet Switzerland. While the larger lakes of Como, Garda, Iseo and Maggiore tend to grab the headlines, we found the smaller Lago d'Orta to be a truly memorable and welcoming place to visit in a motorhome.

The locals have even provided a sosta, where you can stay for free for 48 hours up in the Parco Sacro Monte di'Orta, on the western shore of the lake. This small reserve contains a collection of twenty Roman Catholic chapels built in various styles in the woods atop the San Nicolao hill (*www.sacrimonti.org*).

From the sosta it's a short walk to the chapels, from where you get great views of the lake, the small San Giulio island (which you can take a boat to) and the mountains behind.

A mile walk brings you to the lakeside town of Orta San Giulio, where you're able to reward yourself with *gelato* (Italian ice cream), or a meal sat looking out over the water. Or if you're feeling hot, take a dip in the lake perhaps? Donning snorkel and mask, one of us leapt in just long enough to spot a metre-long freshwater snake, which ushered us out and back onto dry land sharpish.

Showered and dried off in the van, we grabbed a bottle of red wine and two glasses, ambled down to the lakeside and sat without feet dangling over the edge of an old wooden jetty. Sat chinking glasses, warmed by the sun reflected from the calm waters of the lake, this was perhaps the most relaxed, romantic spot we've ever been.

Stop #88: Marina di Ragusa

Rough Land by Sea (Now a Car Park) ● GPS: N36.780016, E14.570253 ● Price Guide: Free ● Public Toilet, No Other Services ● **Alternative**: Official Marina di Ragusa Sosta, GPS: N36.788148, E14.547021, Price Guide: £, All Services Except Electricity

Marina di Ragusa lies on the southern Sicilian coast, an ex-fishing town and now a modern beach resort with sea-facing parking and a sosta.

Parking-aside, the attraction of this area for us were the towns of Modica and Ragusa, a 30-min drive inland and about 20-min apart. We'd visited them earlier in the day, steeling ourselves to drive the Sicilian towns with their narrow streets and cars parked everywhere, like a bucket of huge randomly-thrown dice.

Both towns are UNESCO-listed, along with Noto and many others in the Val di Noto, the south-eastern third of Sicily. Modica, Ragusa, Noto and around 70 other towns and cities in this area were destroyed in the 1693 *terremoto*. This devastating earthquake was the most powerful in recorded Italian history and killed around 60,000 people, unleashing tsunamis which wrecked coastal villages, reaching almost a mile inland in places.

Sicily has been occupied time and again by different foreign powers, and at the time was ruled by the Kings of Spain who rebuilt the towns in Baroque style, some in their original locations and some transplanted to new areas nearby. They covered the buildings in ornamental carved stone, like cake decoration, incredibly beautiful and photogenic. We spent hours walking the streets, staring at the carvings and wondering how on earth any human could create them.

Modica produces a grainy-textured speciality chocolate called *cioccolata modicana*. While peering at delicious-looking samples in shop windows we spotted a sign on an adjacent bar, indicating it had been closed by anti-mafia authorities, reminding us we were in the home of these underworld criminals.

Stop #89: Montepulciano

Official Sosta ● GPS: N43.095661, E11.787646 ● Price Guide: ££ ● All Services Except Electricity ● Unavailable Thursday Morning Due to Market ● **Alternative:** Sosta at Grinzane Cavour, GPS: N44.655243, E7.989543, Price Guide: Free, All Services Except Electricity

Anyone who's read Frances Mayes' *Under the Tuscan Sun* will come to Tuscany with certain expectations: there'll be sunshine (obviously), hilltop medieval villages, delicious slow Mediterranean lunches, unreliable tradesmen, flowing red wine and pre-Roman Etruscan tombs. Builders-aside, we got to experience all of this and more on our tour.

There are a ton of places to stay across the region, but we picked Montepulciano for this book because the sosta's in a great place next to the town, which itself has world-renowned wine, beautiful medieval and Renaissance streets and buildings and wonderful views out over the surrounding countryside.

If you arrive on a Thursday morning, you'll need to park below the town as the sosta is used by the local *mercato*. Italian markets are a sight to see, especially when they're setting up or closing, as powered awnings swing out above vans like giant insect wings, and the sides of custom-built bus-sized vehicles smoothly slide open (with just the occasional kick).

After eyeballing the colourful fruits, fiddling with chainsaws and pondering buying a stove-top espresso maker, we indulged in a chunk of delicious salted *porchetta* and a *cinghiale* (wild boar) cured sausage, much to the delight of our ever-hungry pooch.

If you happen to arrive in August, you might get to witness the *Bravio Delle Botti* race, where local teams compete, rolling 80kg wine barrels through the streets of the town.

119

Stop #90: Mount Etna

Cable Car Parking at Rifugio Sapienza (*www.funiviaetna.com*) ● GPS: N37.79708, E15.04155 ● Price Guide: ££ ● No Services ● Great Views Over Ionian Sea ● **Alternative**: Piano Provenzana Ski Station Parking, GPS: N37.79708 E15.04155, Price Guide: £, On North Slopes, No Services

Viewed from the north-east Sicilian coast, Mount Etna rises snow-capped, like a lone Alpine mountain, coughing out smoke according to its mood. The idea that you can drive a motorhome over a vertical mile up the side of it, and sleep up there, seems downright bonkers. And yet plenty of people do, and there are even special overnight camper rates for the car parks around 1,800m above sea level.

The roads on Etna itself were good quality and easy to drive when we headed up the southern side of the volcano. The towns on the lower slopes can be tight and busy with parked cars though, so it's worth planning your route up and back down again. The roads and rooftops were clear of snow at the end of December but were dusted with black ash ejected from the volcano a few days beforehand.

The landscapes around the car park are other-worldly, lava fields of varying ages, fascinating to walk around and photograph. To get closer to the craters you can take a cable car up to 2,500m, and from there ride in a Unimog 4x4 all the way to the summit at 3,350m (*www.go-etna.com*). Hikes are possible too, but a guide is legally required above 2,900m.

On our second trip up Etna some weeks later we first stayed at Piano Provenzana on the northern slopes (details above). The volcano was in between a series of *paroxysms* (eruptions) at the time, spaced a few days apart. Although we were some miles from the craters, our car park was built on a decade old lava flow which looked fresh, as though it had solidified over the previous tourist complex just the day before. It was unnerving, but we felt magnificently alive to be parked up there as the wind buffeted the van and the column of smoke billowed out far above.

Stop #91: Palermo

Sosta "Idea Vacanze" (*www.ideavacanzepa.it*) ● GPS: N38.14817, E13.35231 ● Price Guide: ££
● All Services ● 25-Min Bus or Train to Centre ● **Alternative**: Official Sosta, GPS: N38.109701, E13.342423, Price Guide: £££, 10-Min Walk to Centre, All Services

When we looked for advice on visiting Palermo, the universal advice was: don't drive there! As we were taking a ferry from Palermo to Tunisia, we didn't have much choice, so we steeled ourselves and headed for the Idea Vacanze sosta on the northern edge of the city.

The traffic was pretty much as expected, perhaps best described as 'manic'! On the dual carriageway into the city cars drove along the hard shoulder like a third lane, including a police car, making it clear we were far from home and our 'normal' rules of the road. We just tried not to crash into anyone and were relieved to park up at the sosta in one piece.

Having read Tobias Jones' *The Dark Heart of Italy*, we knew mafia exploitation had led to rampant development of the suburbs with little thought for car parks. Even so, as we headed into the city by train, we were astonished at the way cars were double and triple parked.

The streets of the city were a fascination, crumbling and characterful, chaotic, some beautifully decorated and others mere concrete blocks. Open air markets sold fresh fruit and vegetables, spilling into the street, huge chunks of tuna, octopus and salted cod. Locals sat on mopeds in animated hand-waving conversion, tipping back an espresso, running a thumb along their cheek in appreciation. We visited a tile museum recommended on Trip Advisor, rendered fascinating by the knowledge and passion of the curator. Later we found the *Catacombe dei Cappuccini* a thought-provoking place, brought face-to-face with the dead, preserved in their burial clothes.

121

Stop #92: Pisa

Official Sosta "Parcheggio Camper Via di Pratale" ● GPS: N43.72155, E10.42074 ● Price Guide: ££ ● All Services ● 2.5km Walk to Tower ● **Alternative**: Camping Village Torre Pendente, GPS: N43.723946, E10.383188, Price Guide: ££, Open Apr-Nov, 1.5km Walk to Tower

Having seen images of iconic buildings like the Tower of Pisa so many times before, it's a strange, disjointing feeling to be stood before them after walking through the outskirts of the city from the Via di Pratale sosta (which is run by a local motorhome club).

The tower is the bell tower of the city's adjacent cathedral in the beautiful Piazza dei Miracoli, the Square of Miracles. Next to them lies the Campo Santo, the cemetery holding soil brought back from the Holy Land by returning crusaders in 1203, and the Baptistery. These buildings were funded by raiding Muslim-held Sicily in 1063. Their white and black marble faces rise from a short-cropped grass carpet, largely devoid of tourists during our visit on a Tuesday in November. The tower leans as it stands on shallow silt foundations, causing it to slowly topple over, a process which started even while it was being built.

Like most of Europe, Pisa was bombed in WW2 by the Allies (53 times in total). The single biggest raid was in August 1943, just three days before the Italian government signed an armistice. Sadly 953 people lost their lives that day, and a stray bomb intended for an industrial target found the roof of the Campo Santo, setting it alight and causing the timber-lead roof to collapse in a three-day fire.

During a walk we came across Mike on an old motorbike piled high with bags. He was trying to drive to Australia, navigating with a paper map, no GPS and no spares and seemed the happiest man alive.

Stop #93: Rome

Campsite "Campeggio Flaminio" (*www.villageflaminio.com*) ● GPS: N41.956136, E12.482430 ● Price Guide: ££ ● All Services ● 5-Min Walk to Train + 15-Min Train to Centre ● **Alternative**: Official Sosta "LGP" (*lgproma.com*), GPS: N41.875806, E12.555546, Price Guide: ££, 50m to Metro, All Services

Cities take more energy to access and enjoy in your motorhome than smaller towns and countryside locations. Traffic, security and ease of access to the centre are our main concerns, all of which are amplified when it's an iconic capital city like Rome, attracting millions of tourists.

Over the years we've been pleasantly surprised just how easy and inexpensive it is to access Europe's capitals though, usually requiring just a little research into good parking spots and the public transport system (or simply asking at campsite receptions).

In Rome we found the Campeggio Flaminio campsite, five miles to the north of the centre, to be great value with the CampingCard ACSI. The site was quiet and the shower block one of the very finest we've seen, heated with piped music and fountains! It's on the edge of the city, so there's no need to tackle the crazy driving conditions in the centre.

The train station is a short walk from the campsite, and it dropped us off at Flaminio, close to the *Terrazza del Pincio* for rooftop city views before we took to the metro and explored the Vatican City. Back across the border we crossed the Tiber over the Pont San Angelo, heading across the Piazza Navona to the Vittorio Emanuele Monument, built to celebrate the first king of the united Italy.

From there we took in the might of the Colosseum, peered across the Roman Forum, and looked around the Pantheon and the Trevi Fountain. Bushed by this point, darkness had long fallen when we got the train back to the campsite. We did all of that with our dog. There's enough to keep anyone busy in Rome for weeks, never mind a day!

123

Stop #94: Syracuse

Car Park ● GPS: N37.066750, E15.291606 ● Price Guide: ££ ● Free WiFi, No Other Services ● Central, Access Via Ponte Umbertino to Avoid ZTL ● **Alternative**: Sosta Camper Siracusa, GPS: N37.070538, E15.261264, Price Guide: ££, All Services, Shuttle to Centre 5km Away

Our first New Year's Eve on our two-year tour was spent at Évora in Portugal, where we discovered nothing was taking place in public celebration, slinking back to the van at midnight with some beer bought at a petrol station, the only place open. Keen to avoid this the second time around, we found a parking area close to the centre of the ancient Sicilian port of Syracuse, and we weren't disappointed.

Syracuse was once the largest port in the ancient world and is known for its archaeological park, with remains of an ancient Greek theatre and Roman amphitheatre. The parking area we used is located on the island of Ortigia, also known as *Città Vecchia* (Old City).

As the evening fell on the 30th of December, we were intrigued by a large van whose side started to open up in the car park. Delighted to find it was selling *paninis*, we joined the locals picking up delicious mozzarella and porchetta evening meals for the two of us.

The following day we walked the medieval town, the sun shining on the twisting streets of the partly abandoned Jewish quarter, playing with our dog on a beach, investigating a fascinating seafood market, and trying and failing to catch a crab. Later we found a stage being set up for the evening's celebrations in the Piazzo del Duomo, alongside the 7th Century ornate cathedral which was used as a mosque for 200 years before being retaken by the Christians in 1085.

Being Italy, nothing happens until late and it wasn't until around 11pm that people started to stream from restaurants out into the square. Radio Italia's fast-flowing dialogue from the stage was lost on us but we understood and loved the atmosphere, music and the shower of wine from a hundred bottles of *spumante* at midnight!

Stop #95: The Giau Pass

Roadside Ground ● GPS: N46.48752, E12.03758 ● Price Guide: Free ● No Services ●
Alternative: Roadside Parking Area Near Top of Giau Pass, GPS: N46.481719, E12.057600, Price Guide: Free, No Services, Incredible Views at 2,200m Above Sea Level

The *Passo Giau* crosses a section of the Dolomite Mountains to the north of Venice, climbing up to 2,236m on good quality roads with expansive views of high jagged mountain peaks and rolling pastures. The route is kept open in winter, but make sure you're running on winter tyres, even in May we were dusted with snow.

The spot we slept in was just above the 23rd hairpin on the (at times) 1st gear ascent from Posalz, squeezed between the edge of the road and the steep drop-off down the mountain. Even with ramps we slept 'on a wonk', unable to get level. Why? Because the Giro d'Italia world-class cycle race was due (*giroditalia.it*) and the better parking areas at the top of the pass were taken by official vehicles.

We'd been lucky to grab that spot too, a friendly Italian motorhomer had encouraged us further up the mountain and into place. That was the start of a memorable 24 hours up in the cold thin air with our Italian hosts.

Surrounded by the league of nations of frenetic cycling fans, we were complete amateurs, knowing only Mark Cavendish, who the Italians knew as 'The Cannonball'. The atmosphere was wonderful, with partying groups cooking up food, a laughing chap sliding his tricycle down the mountain road, cyclists riding down and back up, buckets of beer being drunk, and music hammering out into the thin air.

We spent the evening with a cycling-mad Welsh chap before watching the race pass the following day, with lots more partying before the entire mountain emptied, leaving us all-but-alone that night to recover.

Stop #96: Turin

Sosta "Parcheggio Caio Mario" ● GPS: N45.028965, E7.639058 ● Price Guide: ££ ● All Services Except Electricity ● 1-Min Walk to Tram Stop ● **Alternative**: Sosta "Grinto" (*grinto.it*), GPS: N45.009722, E7.671486, Price Guide: £££, All Services, 30-Min Cycle to Centre, or Bus & Tram

The sosta we used in Turin is located near the famous Fiat Mirafiori factory, and the road there was so bumpy we lost a wheel trim, even though it had been tie-wrapped on! Italian roads might not be as smooth as we'd like, but the sosta proved a good stop over, very convenient for the tram into the city. Except for being a meeting point for evening dog walkers, it was quiet considering it was in a busy city.

Cities attract people for different reasons, and one of ours was the movie *The Italian Job*. Filmed in the city, three minis famously escaped with stolen gold through an engineered traffic jam. We did our research beforehand and tracked down some of the scenes, the Palazzo Carignano (where the minis were unloaded), the Gran Madre di Dio (where the cars came crashing down the church steps), the Galleria San Federico (where the police motorcyclist skids and falls) and the Palazzo Madama (where the cars drive down the Baroque marble staircase). At one point we sneaked past a receptionist to get a foot onto the banked test track on the old Fiat factory roof (hey, a bit cheeky maybe, but this is Italy!).

Rejuvenated with *gelato*, the next day we spent several hours investigating the Egyptian Museum (*museoegizio.it*). It seemed an odd place to come across such a huge collection of African artefacts in Italy (over 30,000 of them), the collection first started by Italian kings.

For free views of the city, head up to the Santa Maria church on Monte dei Cappuccini (GPS: N45.059861, E7.697184).

Stop #97: Venice

Campsite "Al Batéo Agricampeggio" (*www.albateo.it*) ● GPS: N45.442345, E12.422548 ● Price Guide: ££ ● All Services ● On Punta Sabbioni, 30-Min Boat to Venice ● **Alternative**: Official Sosta "San Giuliano" (*www.sangiulianovenice.com*), GPS: N45.467226, E12.279161, Price Guide: ££, All Services, Bus or Boat to Venice

Around 1,450 years ago, after the fall of the Western Roman Empire, invaders forced local fishermen and salt workers onto islands in the Venice lagoon. 118 of these make up the modern-day Venice, linked together by 400 bridges, all-but-hidden beneath centuries of building and rebuilding. The money came from trade and financial services, cleverly managed by the ruling *doges*, effectively the prime ministers of the day. For an eloquent, fascinating history of the city, we can highly recommend the book *Venice* by Jan Morris.

These days Venice attracts huge numbers of tourists, roughly 30 million a year. How easy and costly it would be to visit by motorhome were unknowns for us, but we couldn't pass up the opportunity to visit somewhere so unique.

The Al Batéo Agricampeggio campsite is located on Punta Sabbioni. It's more of a basic sosta than a full campsite, but the pitches are on grass, there's a clean shower block and the receptionist was friendly and helpful, plus the costs are very reasonable too.

From the campsite we walked a few minutes to the *vaporetto* (water taxi) stop, buying tickets for 12 hours of unlimited travel, and our dog was allowed on board too. The boats proved a wonderful way to arrive in St Mark's Square and explore the various islands in the city. One evening we were treated to a display of lightning across the Veneto and were shook by a minor earthquake, unforgettable days.

127

Stop #98: Vesuvius

Parking by Bar de Gregorio ● GPS: N40.819626, E14.412400 ● Price Guide: Free (Bar Purchase Appreciated) ● No Services ● **Alternative**: Roadside Parking, GPS: N40.824489, E14.412585, Price Guide: £, No Services, 2.5km to Vesuvio National Park Entrance

Full-sized coaches drive up Vesuvius, all the way to the start of the walk to the volcano's rim, so getting a motorhome up there shouldn't be too much trouble. We found the most stressful part of the drive was on the lower slopes, the parts populated with villas and restaurants, where the already-narrow roads are further pinched with parked vehicles. Further up the road through the lava fields and trees, with a handful of hairpins, is good quality and proved easier to drive.

We visited the volcano in December and there were few visitors, enabling us to drive all the way to the top car park. At busier times of the year cars are parked alongside the access road lower on the slopes and a shuttle bus runs to the top, or you can walk.

From the top car park there's a ticket office from where you can hike the remaining 1km to the rim, peering inside the volcano and out across utterly mesmerising views of the Bay of Naples, down towards Pompeii and the islands of Capri, Ischia and Procida.

Vesuvius is an active volcano. It last erupted in 1945 destroying several villages and around 80 US Air Force planes in the process. An estimated 600,000 people living in the area might be affected by a future eruption. That said, the volcano is mostly dormant and it's possible to sleep high on the sides. We parked near Bar de Gregorio and a disused cable car station and stayed the night with a fantastic night-time view of Naples far below us.

LATVIA

QUICK FACTS ● **EU**: Yes ● **Schengen**: Yes ● **Language**: Latvian ● **Currency**: Euro (EUR, £1=€1.1) ● **Speed Limits ≤3.5t**: Urban/Non-Urban: 50, 90kph ● **Speed Limits >7.5t**: Urban/Non-Urban: 50, 80kph ● **Tolls**: Yes, But Only for Commercial Vehicles ● **LEZs**: None ● **IDP**: Not Needed ● **Docs**: Driving Licence, Insurance, Passport, V5C ● **Kit**: Headlamp Deflectors, Two Warning Triangles, Reflective Jackets, First Aid Kit, Fire Extinguisher, Winter Tyres 1 December to 1 March ● **LPG**: Good Availability, Dish Adapter ● **Time**: UK+2 Hours ● **Daytime Dipped Headlights**: Yes ● **Overnighting**: Campsites, Business Parking, Marinas, Off-Site Overnight Parking Allowed in Law

Latvia is one of Europe's least populated countries, with only two million inhabitants. The country is 50% forest and outside the big tourist attractions like Riga, there's plenty of space available to park for the night without issues.

Wild camping in rural areas is allowed in law, encouraged even, assuming you avoid nature reserves, dunes, military areas and places close to people's homes (and of course, leave no trace). Latvian State Forest Management provides a website (*www.mammadaba.lv*) showing hundreds of locations across the country. Be aware many of these are accessed via unsealed roads and some may only be suitable for tents, pull up Google Maps and do your research unless you know that the site is accessible to a big heavy lumbering moho.

Some locations even have fire pits, water and dry (long-drop) toilets, which are only suitable for non-chemical waste) so consider fitting a SOG Unit (*soguk.co.uk*).

For access to full services Latvia has a good network of campsites. None are in the CampingCard ACSI scheme, but probably because they're already low-cost, mostly less than £25 a night. We only used a single 'full campsite' in Latvia but found it to be great quality, with lots of space, fire pits with endless wood, swimming in a lake and a general feeling of being welcome and close to nature.

A relic of the Soviet era, the Līgatne secret bunker is open to visitors (*www.bunkurs.lv*). Completed in 1982 and only declassified in 2003, the underground facility was hidden beneath a rehabilitation centre. The bunker could support 250 people, all of Latvia's Soviet leadership, for up to three months in the event of a nuclear attack.

Stop #99: Jūrmala

Beach Car Park ● GPS: N56.97127, E23.77167 ● Price Guide: Free ● No Services ● City Has a €2 Per Day Entrance Charge from Apr to Sep ● **Alternative:** Neptūns Restaurant Camping (*www.restoransneptuns.lv*), GPS: N56.975136, E23.556979, Price Guide: ££, All Services

Jūrmala (Latvian for *seaside*) is made up of a series of beach resorts set alongside a 21-mile stretch of white-sand beach on the Bay of Riga. Once a holiday retreat for the elite of the USSR, it's a fascinating place, a disjointed mix of Western high street shops, leafy streets filled with widely spaced, faded art nouveau wooden houses and concrete hotels and apartment blocks.

With the demise of the Soviet Union, Jūrmala lost many of its Russian patrons, leaving it struggling to attract new visitors. These days a third of the city's residents are still Russian, and houses advertised in estate agents are often described only in Russian. On the main shopping street, full of familiar brands such as Superdry, Baskin Robbins and Vision Express, we found ourselves staring at a small child being driven down the pavement by his father, in a remote-control BMW car. Anyone able to buy a €250k property in Latvia can get a Golden Visa, providing a way for wealthier Russians to obtain EU residence permits.

To drive into Jūrmala you need to stop at road-side toll machines and buy an entrance ticket for your vehicle (*www.visitjurmala.lv*). It's not expensive, and there are plenty of free car parks to stay in near the beach. The Neptūns Restaurant Camping 7km north-west of Jūrmala looks a good official site to stay with direct access to the forest and an endless white sand beach (details above).

Stop #100: Klapkalnciems

Official Baltic Sea Camping Area ● GPS: N57.03836, E23.40254 ● Price Guide: £ ● Black Waste Disposal, Electricity and Firepits Available ● **Alternative:** Camping Roņiši in Klapkalnciems (*www.rtu.lv/lv/ronisi*), GPS: N57.042868, E23.366333, Price Guide: ££, All Services

Having left Lithuania in the morning, the promise of getting some sand under our feet drew us all the way across Latvia to the Baltic Sea for our first night's stay in the country. We'd bounced our way along some long stretches of poorly repaired Latvian B roads, resolving to stick to main routes in future.

We weren't disappointed when we arrived though! Having first reached Jūrmala, we opted to head east and find somewhere quieter to stay on the coast, coming across this parking area and pulling in, finding it in great condition and a just couple of minutes' walk to the sea through the pines and dunes, wonderful!

During the week the area was free, although a charge came in at the weekend. We stayed two nights, and just before we left we realised the area is split in two, with a car park on one side (where we'd slept) and a camping area with motorhome-sized spaces, electricity and fire pits on the other.

Like much of the Baltic States, this parking spot is set in an area of unspoiled nature. The pines run for miles along the dunes. The beach is equally endless, a pure white sand, squeaking beneath our bare feet. The sea is shallow here, warmed in the early June sunshine.

Small memorials near Klapkalnciems commemorate Finnish and German soldiers killed fighting the Russians in WW1 (GPS: N57.042900, E23.370405). To the south of the area lies the Ķemeri National Park, with bogs and forests to explore (*www.kemerunacionalaisparks.lv*).

Stop #101: Raiskums

Kempings Apaļkalns (*www.apalkalns.lv*) ● GPS: N57.317641, E25.148415 ● Price Guide: ££ ● All Services ● Firepits with Grills ● **Alternative:** Camping Jaunzāģeri (*www.jaunzageri.lv*), GPS: N57.229017, E24.906006, Price Guide: ££, All Services, Access via Unsealed Road

In our early tours, we switched location on average every one and a half days, for two years, there was just so much to see and do! As a result, long-term travel can start to feel like hard work after a while.

We'd been on the road for four months when we arrived in Raiskums, and we were ready for a short break away from visiting museums, cathedrals, castles and cities. The site proved ideal, a back-to-nature place with the option to choose your own spot on the cropped grass, or to take a stabilised, levelled-off pitch. The site owners were laid back and friendly, lending us a wheelbarrow so we could take as much free wood as we wanted down to the fire pit nearest to our van. They also provide boats for use on the adjacent lake.

The rule book consisted of a single sign with a picture of a radio and a cross through it, and the same sentence in Latvian, Russian, German and English: "Please Do What I Ask You To". That's our kind of rule book, especially as he didn't ask us to do anything!

A couple we'd met earlier in the Baltics arrived on the site after us and we all enjoyed a smoky BBQ before shooting the breeze sat with Latvian beers in hand, warmed by the fire and with a view of Lake Raiskuma.

The Gauja National Park lies 40km to the south east of this campsite (*www.entergauja.com*) and provides opportunities for hiking and kayaking.

Stop #102: Rīga

CCTV-Monitored Paid Parking ● GPS: N56.95399, E24.08127 ● Price Guide: £ ● No Services ● 2km Walk into City **Alternative:** Riverside Camping (*riversidecamping.lv*), GPS: N56.965938, E24.080482, Price Guide: ££, All Services, 3.5km Walk into City

Through a helpful suggestion from the *europebycamper.com* motorhome touring bloggers, we found a low-cost CCTV-monitored car park 2km from the centre of Rīga on an island in the Daugava River. The same couple had made a bet with us that we couldn't finish a pint of garlic beer at the city's Garlic Pub restaurant, a quirky place where we not only supped the ale but also enjoyed garlic-infused ice cream.

Our waitress at the Garlic Pub confirmed it was mainly frequented by tourists and told us many young Latvians had left the country seeking better opportunities elsewhere in Europe. We found the city's old centre of Rīga was also busy with fellow tourists, and on a first visit we found ourselves a little burned out, like we were on a conveyor belt from photo opportunity to photo opportunity.

We had a crack at some of the less touristy areas of the city the next day, spotting *The World*, a luxury live-aboard cruise ship moored on the river (*aboardtheworld.com*). Next, we visited the huge Soviet Revolution Monument, commemorating the 1905 revolution, a reminder of Latvia's ex-USSR past. After that we wandered the huge Rīgas Centrāltirgus (Central Market) packed with locals, located in five giant halls under Zeppelin hangers left by the Germans after WW1. The arches and contours of the Nativity of Christ Cathedral also drew our interest, converted into a planetarium by the Soviets but back again into a place of worship following independence.

LIECHTENSTEIN

QUICK FACTS ● **EU**: No, EEA ● **Schengen**: Yes ● **Language**: German ● **Currency**: Swiss Franc (CHF, £1=1.2CHF) ● **Speed Limits**: Urban/Non-Urban: 50, 80kph ● **Tolls**: No ● **LEZs**: None ● **IDP**: Not Needed ● **Docs**: Driving Licence, Insurance, Passport, V5C ● **Kit**: Headlamp Deflectors, Warning Triangle ● **LPG**: Not Available ● **Time**: UK+1 Hour ● **Daytime Dipped Headlights**: Yes ● **Overnighting**: One Campsite in Triesen, Overnight Parking Allowed at Stadium Near Vaduz

Liechtenstein's tiny at just 62 square miles of mountains and meadows. Officially, it's a microstate, the 4th smallest country in Europe behind the Vatican City, Monaco and San Marino. We were drawn to it by fascination: how did it come into being, and what does such a tiny independent state look like?

The principality was created in 1719 by the House of Liechtenstein, the land being bought for political reasons, and no member of the House visited it until 1842. In WW1 the principality was tied to the Austro-Hungarian empire and after its defeat was forced into a customs and monetary union with Switzerland. The country remained neutral in WW2, like neighbouring Switzerland, but was in a dire financial situation by the end of the war, being forced to sell off family treasures. Since then the principality has used a low corporation tax to draw in companies, eventually making it one of the wealthiest in the world. According to the CIA, Liechtenstein residents have the highest standard of living anywhere in the world.

Liechtenstein is easy to access from Switzerland, we just drove across one of the bridges over the Rhine, failing to spot any sign we were crossing into another country (there have been no border controls here since 1923). The border from Austria has an immigration and customs post but should also be easy to pass through.

The country has a single campsite, Camping Mittagspitze (*www.campingtriesen.li*), 7km south of the capital, Zaduz. If you don't need the full services of a site, *park4night.com* lists several parking areas, including the overnight stadium parking we used near Vaduz (see the next page).

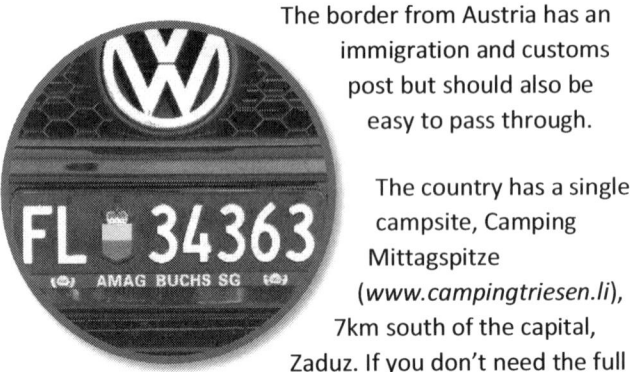

Stop #103: Vaduz

Stadium Parking • GPS: N47.13804, E9.51161 • Price Guide: £ • Black Water Disposal and Fresh Water Available • **Alternative:** Camping Mittagspitze (*www.campingtriesen.li*), GPS: N47.086778, E9.527110, Price Guide: £££, All Services

As we drove towards Liechtenstein from Lake Constance, the snow-capped Alps rose in the distance, a seemingly impregnable barrier to a big, lumbering motorhome. The road followed the Rhine valley, staying low as it approached Liechtenstein, leaving the mountain driving for another day.

Crossing the Rhine, Liechtenstein looked as perfect, rugged and vine-clad as Switzerland, a seamless border, as though we were driving into another Swiss canton. Vaduz (Liechtenstein's capital) was just a 2km drive away, the seat of the country's parliament and home to fewer than 6,000 people, 42% of whom are foreigners. The centre is a 1km walk from the parking area at the Rheinpark Stadium, with a further 1km to the 12th Century Vaduz Castle, the official residence of the Prince of Liechtenstein.

Wandering the pristine streets, we peered into the estate agent windows, laughing and shaking our heads in wonder at the enormous cost of the places advertised. Prices in the shops elicited a similar response, on average 50% more than those at home, and but for a single bottle of locally brewed Liechtensteiner Brauhaus beer, we kept the purse shut!

Once we'd captured a few photos of Vaduz Castle, with a rugged snowy mountain as a dramatic backdrop, we had a wander around the surrounding vineyards and over to the castle at nearby Balzers before retreating to the van for tea and to hide from the wind.

135

LITHUANIA

QUICK FACTS ● **EU**: Yes ● **Schengen**: Yes ● **Language**: Lithuanian ● **Currency**: Euro (EUR, £1=€1.1) ● **Speed Limits** ≤3.5t: Urban/Single/Expressway: 50, 70, 110kph ● **Speed Limits** >3.5t: Urban/Single/Expressway: 50, 70, 90kph ● **Tolls**: Yes, But Only for Commercial Vehicles ● **LEZs**: None ● **IDP**: Not Needed ● **Docs**: Driving Licence, Insurance, Passport, V5C ● **Kit**: Headlamp Deflectors, Warning Triangle, Reflective Jackets, First Aid Kit, Fire Extinguisher ● **LPG**: Good Availability, Dish Adapter ● **Time**: UK+2 Hours ● **Daytime Dipped Headlights**: Yes ● **Overnighting**: Campsites, Some Aires, Off-Site Overnight Parking Allowed in Law

Lithuania is easy to access from Poland, avoiding the potential difficulties of driving across Kaliningrad (Russia) or Belarus. Our old copy of Lonely Planet advised us we might have to wait an hour or two at the border, but times have changed around here, and we drove straight across and into the Baltics. Lithuania was the first Baltic country to declare independence from the USSR in 1990 (a year later, the Soviet Union was dissolved) and has since joined the Euro and 'borderless' Schengen Area.

Like the other Baltic states, overnight parking outside official areas is legal, and we found the car parks for businesses were happy for us to stay overnight for a few euros. To avoid attracting the attention of the local *policija*, avoid overnight camping at non-designated places in regional or national parks, beaches and nature reserves, including all the Curonian Spit.

If you're looking for official campsites, the tourist board has a map of them, along with some example itineraries taking in the country's towns and rural attractions:

lithuania.travel/en/news/campsites

We found Lithuania to be an easy-going, charming country to visit with some fascinating if troubled history, particularly from the World War 2 and USSR eras. The country feels relatively untouched by mass tourism. The capital Vilnius is one of the most compact in Europe, an easy-going city which we could easily explore it on foot from our parking space outside a lively youth hostel.

Outside Vilnius the main attractions for us were the Hill of Crosses, Trakai Island Castle, Grūtas Park and the landscapes of wetlands, beaches, lakes and forests.

Stop #104: Druskininkai

Car Park to Grūtas Park (*grutoparkas.lt*) ● GPS: N54.02469, E24.07854 ● Price Guide: £ ● No Services ● **Alternative:** Druskininkai Camping (*druskininkai.lt*), GPS: N54.008754, E23.978088, Price Guide: ££, All Services, 10km from Grūtas Park

Grūtas Park is a curious, controversial place in Lithuania. The park plays host to Lithuania's collection of Soviet-era statues, brought here by the park's owner after they were removed from their locations in towns and cities across the country following the country's independence from the USSR. The statues themselves don't seem to be the problem, but more the mock-*gulag* style barbed wire, watch towers and piped music which accompanies your visit.

Lithuania suffered repeated invasions during WW2, first by Russia, then Germany and again by Russia. The Red Army committed widespread, horrific atrocities during the occupation. Following the war all Lithuanians lost their property, except for personal belongings. Farms were collectivised, despite the fact the Soviets had tried this before in the 1920s, resulting in massive loss of life to famine as production plummeted. Tens of thousands of Lithuanians were deported. Exhibitions in the park get this message across.

Standing beneath trees out in the open air, the monumental statues of Lenin, Stalin, Marx and other heroes of the Soviet ideology provoked thought. We've met people who loved life under the Soviets, and others who despised it enough to leave their loved ones and risk their lives escaping to the West. Grūtas Park served to get us thinking again about the past, not a bad thing.

After our stay the car park guardian allowed us to stay overnight alongside a New Zealand couple in another motorhome, for just a few euros.

Stop #105: Jurgaičiai

Car Park to Hill of Crosses (*www.kryziukalnas.lt*) ● GPS: N56.01450, E23.40861 ● Price Guide: £ ● No Services ● **Alternative:** Parking for Guesthouse Girele (*sodybagirele.lt*), GPS: N55.998609, E23.385077, Price Guide: ££, Electricity, Showers, Toilets Available, 3km to Hill

The Hill of Crosses, 12km to the north east of Šiauliai (pronounced *shoo-lay*), is a place of pilgrimage set on the location of a former hill fort. In the 19th Century, Lithuania was part of the (pre-Soviet) Russian Empire. During uprisings against the Russians, locals placed crosses on the hill as memorials, when they couldn't locate the bodies of rebels who'd been killed in fighting.

During the later Soviet occupation, the hill took on a deeper meaning, representing the Lithuanian identity, religion and heritage. Lithuanians came and placed hundreds of crosses on the hill, irritating the Soviets who officially refused to accept any form of religion. In 1961 they destroyed over 5,000 crosses, but they continued to re-appear. Even under guard, with a ditch dug around the site a further 1,200 were added, before being removed again in 1973 and 1975. Pope John Paul II prayed on the hill in 1993, declaring it a place for hope, peace, love and sacrifice.

A visitor's centre at the entrance sells crosses of various sizes, and anyone can place a cross less than 3m high without a permit. Today there are maybe 200,000 crucifixes, completely filling the hill and spreading off along pathways.

The visitor's centre is also well used to motorhomes staying in the car park and charges a small overnight fee. It's located among fields and is a quiet spot to spend the night.

Stop #106: Vilnius

Downtown Hotel Forest and Camping (*downtownforest.lt*) ● GPS: N54.67793, E25.30221 ● Price Guide: ££ ● Electricity, Showers, Washing Machine and Toilets ● Limited Space, Book Before Arrival ● **Alternative:** Vilnius City Camping (*www.vilnius-camping.lt*), GPS: N54.674444, E25.227935, Price Guide: ££, No Services (It's a Pop-Up Secure Parking Area), Open May to Sep

Vilnius, the capital of Lithuania is a bohemian place full of artists, parks, bars and Baroque architecture.

Downtown Camping is a youth hostel which allows motorhomes to stay in its parking area. With a younger clientele, it has a vibrant, relaxed feel while being less than a mile walk to the centre of *Senamiestis* (Vilnius old town). The hostel is in a somewhat run-down area though. Bricks crumbled behind a layer of graffiti and window ledges were made from bent sheet metal. The pavement was a worn sand-earth path. While it wasn't pretty, it didn't feel in any way dangerous. The area is called *Užupis* and is unofficially not part of the city. The locals have comically proclaimed it, just a few backstreets, an Independent Republic, with a tiny army and a comical constitution stating: "everyone has the right to die, but this is not an obligation".

We walked the Bernardine Garden before heading up the steps to the Three Crosses viewpoint for an expansive view across the city. The path down from the hill brought us out at the stunning white cathedral outside of which sits the miracle tile (the *Stebuklas*). The tile is the end point where two million people joined hands to form the Baltic Way across Lithuania, Latvia and Estonia in support of independence from the USSR. Located in ex-KGB offices, the Museum of Occupations and Freedom Fights in Vilnius tells the story of Lithuania's repression and fight for independence (*www.genocid.lt/muziejus*).

139

LUXEMBOURG

QUICK FACTS ● **EU**: Yes ● **Schengen**: Yes ● **Languages**: Luxembourgish, French, German ● **Currency**: Euro (EUR, £1=€1.1) ● **Speed Limits ≤3.5t**: Urban/Single/Expressway/Motorway: 50, 90, 130, 130kph ● **Speed Limits >3.5t**: Urban/Single/Expressway/Motorway: 50, 75, 90, 90kph ● **Tolls**: None ● **LEZs**: None ● **IDP**: Not Needed ● **Docs**: Driving Licence, Insurance, Passport, V5C ● **Kit**: Headlamp Deflectors, Reflective Jackets, Winter Tyres in Ice/Snow Conditions ● **LPG**: Good Availability, ACME Adapter ● **Time**: UK+1 Hour ● **Daytime Dipped Headlights**: No ● **Overnighting**: Campsites, Small Number of Aires, Car Parks

We've transited Luxembourg several times, but only stayed once, something we plan to remedy in future as this small country is often on our route through Europe with good quality toll-free motorways and a network of aires and campsites. Also, the maximum price of petrol, diesel and LPG is set by the government at a national level, below that of the surrounding countries. Tobacco and alcohol are also relatively cheap in Luxembourg.

Luxembourg City is accessible to motorhomes via a large car park in the centre of the city, or campsites within easy public transport reach of the centre.

Three miles east of the city lies the moving Luxembourg American Cemetery, near Hamm, the final resting place of General George S. Patton and over 5,000 of his fellow service men and women. There's also a museum to the general at Ettelbruck (*www.patton.lu*). For those travelling with children, Le Parc Merveilleux (*parc-merveilleux.lu*) has a zoo, rides and play areas at Bettemburg, 12km south of the city.

Luxembourg has many pretty towns and villages to explore. To the southern end of the Moselle, where it reaches France, lies Mondorf-les-Bains, a thermal spa town with a free aire. To the east, the town of Echternach, has pastel-coloured medieval buildings on the banks of the River Sûre, with a central campsite. Clervaux in the north has a castle, an abbey and a popular campsite (*www.camping-clervaux.lu*). To the north-east, the Schiessentümpel waterfalls near Müllerthal have a beautiful forest walk from Camping La Pinède (in the CampingCard ACSI scheme), plus the town has a museum to the Echternach Abbey, where beautiful manuscripts were hand-written.

Stop #107: Luxembourg City

Car Park • GPS: N49.61661, E6.12367 • Price Guide: £ • No Services • **Alternative:** Campsite Kockelscheuer (*www.ccclv.lu*), GPS: N49.572394, E6.108465, Price Guide: ££, All Services, 15-Min Bus Ride into Luxembourg City, Open April to October

When we arrived at the large car park in central Luxembourg City were pleased to find it guarded, although the city ranks as one of the safest in the world. We were amazed to find we could stay right in the very centre of the city. It wasn't the quietest of spots overnight, with traffic starting to flow early in the morning, but we got a good night's sleep nevertheless.

Our spirits were dampened a little when we headed out to look around the city under grey clouds. At least there weren't many other tourists knocking about! The city's Notre-Dame Cathedral, the National Museum of History and Art, Lëtzebuerg City Museum, and the Museum of Modern Art Grand-Duc Jean are all top-quality indoor attractions in wet weather (*www.visitluxembourg.com*).

Most of the outdoor sights are found in the old town, split across two levels, the upper and lower old towns, known as the *Grund*. We stayed in the old quarter, the previous location of the Fortress of Luxembourg, giving the city the impregnable-sounding title of *Gibraltar of the North*, but it was demolished as part of a treaty to prevent conflict between the French Empire and Prussia in the late 19th Century. The Bock Cliff remains, with 21km of casemates, tunnels initially bored during Spanish rule and expanded twice since, intended for hiding soldiers, horses and equipment.

MOROCCO

QUICK FACTS ● **EU**: No ● **Schengen**: No ● **Languages**: Arabic, French ● **Currency**: Moroccan Dirham (MAD, £1=12MAD) ● **Speed Limits**: Urban/Single/Motorway: 60, 100, 120kph ● **Tolls**: On Motorways, Pay in Cash ● **LEZs**: None ● **IDP**: 1968 (Not Needed for Europeans) ● **Docs**: Driving Licence, Insurance, Passport, V5C ● **Kit**: Headlamp Deflectors, Reflective Jackets ● **LPG**: No Refill Stations ● **Time**: UK+1 Hour ● **Daytime Dipped Headlights**: No ● **Overnighting**: Campsites, Guardian Parking, Limited Free (Wild) Camping Options

Morocco proved more accessible for motorhome tourists than we could have ever imagined. Thousands of motorhomes over-winter across the country, taking advantage of friendly locals, a wide campsite network, s great climate, low prices and exotic landscapes.

You'll need to either choose a UK insurer who'll provide a Green Card for Morocco, or buy 3rd party insurance when you arrive at Tanger Med port. Most people buy their ferry tickets from the same office in Algerciras (*www.viajesnormandie.net*), before stocking up on food and alcohol at the adjacent supermarkets. There is no national breakdown service in Morocco, so you might want to make sure your van is well serviced, and brim off any refillable LPG bottles in Spain before you go, as there are no refill stations in Morocco. Diesel is cheap over there though, so hold off filling your fuel tank!

Stick to daylight hours, and you'll find driving in Morocco isn't as scary as you might imagine. The motorways and roads are generally good quality and the police enforce speed limits everywhere, often with mobile detectors. Expect a fine if you're stopped, but otherwise the police don't bother tourists and wave motorhomes through the spot-checks they often set up around the perimeter of towns. You'll need to be patient though, and allow lots of time for non-motorway journeys, especially through towns on market day.

Morocco's a short ferry hop across the Straight of Gibraltar, geographically close to Europe but separated by a wide cultural gulf. Life in Morocco is tightly integrated with the state religion of Islam, so alcohol and pork products aren't widely available.

For a detailed description of getting into Morocco, using campsites, avoiding problems and ideas for more fantastic places to visit, have a look at our book *Motorhome Morocco* on *amazon.co.uk*.

Stop #108: Aït Mansour

Guardian Parking ● GPS: N29.547902, W8.877461 ● Price Guide: £ ● No Services ●
Alternative: Camping Vallée Tarsaoute (*campinglavalleedet.wixsite.com*), GPS: N29.577759, W9.022791, Price Guide: ££, All Services, An Hour (35km) from Aït Mansour

Many of the very best places we've stayed have been gifted to us from fellow travellers. A French couple who'd spent many years living in Morocco suggested a detour to the Aït Mansour Gorge was worth the effort. How right they were! Little-visited, the gorge cuts through the layered red rock in the other-worldly Anti-Atlas Mountains and was filled with a thick forest of palms being trimmed and harvested for their crop of dates.

The route to the gorge is impressive, tarmac all the way if a little rough in places, skirting the edge of a shallow gorge of barren black rock. Arriving in the oasis, palm fronds brushed the side of the van as we drove to the parking spot at the northern end of the gorge. Spotting a few French vans, we were guided into place by Mustapha, the parking guardian who emerged from the trees, lifting his faded badge to show he was an official and taking payment for our stay.

Using our combined French vocabulary, we managed to gather from Mustapha that we could drive through the gorge, if we wanted, and that a road emerges from the other side carrying us back west through the mountains to the R107. There was no road on our map, he drew it on, henceforth to be known as the *biro road*.

We cycled and walked the gorge that afternoon, meeting some local schoolkids, amazed at how life continues in such remote places on Earth. After a night's sleep listening to the croak of a thousand frogs, we steeled ourselves and drove the narrow road of the gorge in the morning, a simply unforgettable experience.

143

Stop #109: Azrou

Emirates Euro Camping (*www.morocamping.com*) ● GPS: N33.444944, W5.190865 ● Price Guide: ££ ● All Services ● **Alternative:** Camping Amazigh (*www.camping-amazigh.com*), GPS: N33.449549, W5.170715, Price Guide: ££, All Services, 7km East of Azrou

Azrou is written ⵄⵋⵆ in the alphabet of the Berbers, the descendants of the pre-Arab inhabitants of North Africa. This Berber town sits on a crossroads, with most travellers opting to use the N13 to link up with Erg Chebbi to the south.

Emirates Euro Camping lies a 4km walk or cycle from Azrou, where the main attraction for us was the Tuesday weekly souk. Get there early if you want to witness the sale of livestock, complete with some unlikely loading of animals onto the tops of trucks and vans. Alongside the owners of food stalls slice chunks from fresh carcasses hanging next to your table in their tents, throwing them into mincers with onions and spices and BBQing them as you sup your mint tea. If this is something you'd prefer not to see, make sure you also stay well clear of the chicken stalls in the main market area. Elsewhere in the souk there are handmade mule saddles, tools, kitchenware, clothes, sheepskins and colourful displays of fruits and vegetables to choose from, among selections of dates and caramelised nuts. We came away with a bag of fruit, some tools and a length of colourful fabric, which now adorns the cushions in our van.

A short drive from the town brings you to a cedar forest, the home of wild Barbary macaques, the only African monkeys in the cold climate north of the Sahara (puddles were frozen solid on our visit). It was quite a privilege to be among these wonderful animals as they trooped around the dirt road and surrounding trees.

Stop #110: Chefchaouen

Camping Azilan ● GPS: N35.175603, W5.267009 ● Price Guide: £ ● All Services (No Grey Drain, Normal in Morocco) ● **Alternative:** Overnight Mixed Guardian Parking, GPS: N35.165829, W5.262224, Price Guide: £, No Services

Photogenic Chefchaouen lies 130km south of the Tanger Med port, so Camping Azilan could be your first night's stop and your first taste of Moroccan campsites. How to describe the site? Well, it sits just above the town, which is accessed via a footpath past the Hôtel Atlas and down through the cemetery. Being in the Rif Mountains, where much of Europe's cannabis is reputed to be grown, you'll likely be offered the drug via various code names but the dealers were a friendly lot when we told them *la shrukran* (no thanks in Arabic).

We've been to the site a couple of times and once we'd gotten over the culture shock of being in Morocco, it felt very safe. You may want to keep clear of the ablutions block though! While not the worst we've seen, there are far better facilities on other Moroccan campsites.

Chefchaouen was originally created as a small fortress by a descendant of the Islamic Prophet Muhammad, defending the area from attacks by the Portuguese. The city's now known as *The Blue Town*, for obvious reasons when you arrive in the old part. All the walls and doors are painted shades of blue. No-one knows why, although there's some speculation Jews who settled here after fleeing persecution started the practice. Others think the blue colour repels mosquitoes, or to helps keep homes cooler.

Street markets are held on Mondays and Thursday and we can recommend the delicious fish and chips, cooked on outdoor stoves (with gas bottles resting in buckets of hot water). Beware the 'ketchup', it's actually a hot spicy sauce!

145

Stop #111: Erg Chebbi

Haven Auberge La Chance (*desert-hotel.com*) ● GPS: N31.133677, W4.018880 ● Price Guide: £ ● All Services ● Right Alongside the Dunes ● Restaurant and Pool Available ● **Alternative:** Camping Océan des Dunes (*www.aubergeoceandesdunes.com*), GPS: N31.142694, W4.025749, Price Guide: £, All Services

Erg Chebbi is the most accessible of Morocco's two sand dune seas, the other famous one is Erg Chigaga near M'hamid, which needs a 4x4 to access it. Both ergs are in the Pre-Saharan Steppes, technically not part of the Sahara Desert proper, but it really feels like you're there when you're parked besides the huge butter-coloured dunes with camels being led past the windscreen!

On our first visit to Erg Chebbi we had to rumble over a couple of kilometres of unsealed road to get to the sand from the main N13 south of Rissani. A few years later a new road had been built, and we could drive from the UK all the way to the erg on sealed roads, a journey of around 4,000km across France and Spain.

There's a row of 70 or so *auberges* alongside the erg, hotels with good-quality restaurants catering for tourists bussed in to enjoy the sands. Many have areas for motorhomes to park, some more formal than others, some walled with better protection from the wind but with poorer views as a result. The auberges are set around 4km north of Merzouga which has shops for supplies.

The dunes rise to 150m and there are numerous options to explore them, either on foot, by camel, quad bike or 4x4. Several companies offer overnight trips out towards Algeria to camps miles into the sands, out of sight of the hotels. We enjoyed a sunset camel ride one evening, being offered the opportunity to buy from the guide's array of polished fossils retrieved from the *hamada*, the stony desert which covers large areas of Morocco.

Stop #112: Fez

Camping Diamant Vert ● GPS: N33.987284, W5.021136 ● Price Guide: ££ ● All Services ● 11km Taxi to Fes el Bali ● **Alternative:** Camping de Fes, GPS: N34.000293, W4.969661, Price Guide: ££, All Services, 8km Taxi to Fes el Bali

Morocco was a French Protectorate between 1912 and 1956, which resulted in modern towns being built alongside the *medinas*, the historic old towns. The French colonialists largely left the medinas intact, and perhaps the greatest of these in Morocco is Fes el Bali (the walled Fes Medina), a UNESCO World Heritage site.

Fes has two campsites a few miles south of the old town. Like everything in Morocco, this is subject to change and at the time of writing Camping Diamant Vert was closed but hoping to re-open soon. As you drive into the city you may find yourself being waved down by a moped rider, paid by one of the sites to bring you to them. It's up to you whether you choose to follow them!

We've visited the Fes medina a few times, and it never fails to amaze us. The best way to experience this incredible car-free place is to pay for a guide, the campsite reception will call one for you. They will pick you up in a car or minibus and take you to various sights around and inside the old town depending on what contacts they have and who is taking visitors: the tannery, schools, a *hammam* (a kind of sauna), workshops, bakery and, of course, a carpet shop or two. Moroccans are wonderful salespeople, but always remember there's no obligation to buy.

Guides aren't expensive and should speak at least some English. Don't forget to agree the price before you agree to use them and a tip when you're dropped off at the campsite is appreciated too, if the tour has been good.

Stop #113: Marrakech

Camping Ourika ● GPS: N31.526367, W7.959907 ● Price Guide: ££ ● All Services ● 12km Taxi to Jemaa el-Fna Square ● **Alternative:** Guardian Parking near Koutoubia Mosque, GPS: N31.624161, W7.994569, Price Guide: ££, All Services (No Drive-Over Grey Disposal), 5-Min Walk to Jemaa el-Fna Square

Marrakech has great-quality campsites on the outskirts, plus a guardian parking located right next to the famous Koutoubia Mosque, if you're feeling brave enough to drive into the centre (the traffic isn't that bad, just take your time).

Marrakech's lush gardens, exotic medina and most memorable of all, the famous *Jemaa el-Fna* square, have all long been the gathering place of travellers, touts, tourists and entertainers.

Perhaps the most relaxing place to get a view of the action in the square is from the terrace of one of the cafés along the eastern edge, like Café de France. From up here you're free of the incessant sales tactics going on below and can do some wonderful people watching as you sup your sugary mint tea. Come the evening there's no other option but to dive in, as the food stalls go up and the charcoal fires are lit. Trying to walk through the lanes between the eateries is nigh-on impossible without being accosted by a tout or three, all throwing humorous one-liners into the fray. It's quite an experience, keep an eye out for the sheep heads too, a local delicacy.

Away from the square, we enjoyed an hour in the *Maison de la Photographie*, with its atmospheric photos of old Marrakech, before taking in the modern rooftop vista from the terrace.

The *Jardin Majorelle* is a big draw for anyone interested in gardens, or just wanting a break from the speed of the city. The *Palácio da Bahia* is also very popular for its architecture and Moorish decoration.

Stop #114: Meski

Camping Source Bleue de Meski ● GPS: N31.857759, W4.283627 ● Price Guide: £ ● All Services ● **Alternative:** Auberge du Vieux Ksar, GPS: N31.857698, W4.283012, Price Guide: £, All Services (No Grey Drain, Normal in Morocco), Located Outside Source Bleue Campsite

The small village of Meski lies south of the High Atlas, just off the N13, a great resting point on the way to or from Merzouga and the Erg Chebbi. Friends who'd passed this way a few days earlier advised us we'd get an interesting reception if we came to this site, and they weren't wrong.

The Source Bleue de Meski campsite is in an oasis which runs along a water course, dramatically sunk into a valley below the surrounding desert. The locals use the water to irrigate and farm the land beneath the date palms. The Source itself is where the Ziz River bubbles up from the ground, into a swimming pool built by French Legionnaires, used by tourists and locals but far too cold for anyone to brave when we visited in January.

The site has a few shops targeting tourist traffic, and if you come this way, you'll be certain to be invited to swap some of your things for theirs! It was a new, nerve-wracking experience for us, sitting in the shop, entering into protracted negotiations to swap an old bike we'd brought with us but rarely used, for a silk blanket, a coat and necklace. Drums were beaten and mint tea drunk to celebrate the conclusion!

One of the owner's children took us through the oasis and up to the plateau to look around the crumbling fortified village, a *ksar*, with the Middle Atlas Mountains as a dramatic backdrop. As we walked back towards the site, we passed a cemetery, almost invisible on the rocky surface, each gravestone a simple upturned rock.

Stop #115: Tafraoute

Municipal Parking Area ● GPS: N29.723201, W8.985595 ● Price Guide: £ ● Service Point Available Here: N29.721599, W8.977133 ● **Alternative:** Camping Granite Rose, GPS: N29.717351, W8.984745, Price Guide: ££, All Services (No Grey Drain, Normal in Morocco)

Tafraoute sits in a valley deep in the Anti-Atlas Mountains, a place like nowhere we've ever seen, endless hills eroded into shelves appearing as though a giant comb has been dragged across them. House-sized boulders lie around, like a scene from The Flintstones, popular challenges for visiting climbers.

The town has three walled campsites, but an official open area parking is the attraction for many, bringing in hundreds of over-wintering motorhomes and giving Tafraoute the informal name of *The Valley of the Vans*. A service point has been built in the town, allowing black and grey water to be disposed of correctly and fresh water to be taken on board (GPS: N29.721558, W8.977201).

Tafraoute is an easy-going Berber town, well used to European tourists, with a weekly market for fresh fruit and vegetables, restaurants, cafés, shoe shops (some offer a made-to-measure service which we took advantage of) and motorhome repair garages. Around the end of February, the town holds the Almond Blossom Festival featuring music, dancing and Berber cuisine.

Around six miles south of the town lie The Painted Rocks, a series of huge boulders covered in colourful paint, originally in 1984 by Belgian artist Jean Verame, and repainted since. We cycled to the rocks and later returned in the van, driving a mile of dirt road to a spot above the rocks where we free-camped alongside a few other motorhomes, the only 'wild camping' we've done in Morocco and a spectacular place at that (GPS: N29.664898, W8.972959).

Stop #116: Tata

Camping Hayat ● GPS: N29.7384469, W7.9776043 ● Price Guide: £ ● All Services ●
Alternative: Camping Palmier, GPS: N29.752807, W7.974702, Price Guide: £, All Services

After staying at the Aït Mansour mountain oasis, we travelled south down the R107 to Icht, a bonkers but unforgettable drive of roughly 20km of dirt road (at some points we were driving across rocks and sands in a dry riverbed). After recovering at Icht we picked up the famous N12, an amazing desert drive running parallel to the Algerian border a few miles away.

Tata (beautifully written as طاطا in Arabic or ⴰⴰ in Berber) means 'take a break'. It was once a resting place for caravans crossing the Sahara and is a modern-day garrison, with four types of police and military stationed in the town. Tata has several campsites for us modern-day travellers. We chose the Hayat site with pleasant views of the river, just a short walk from the town. Often locals will walk or drive through campsites in Morocco selling anything and everything and saying "no, thank you" endlessly can be draining. It wasn't a problem on this site as the traders expected you to go to them in their shops, perfect. The town itself proved easy going too, with no touts or shouts, a pleasure to wander.

We spent our days watching kids splash around, brightly dressed local ladies carefully crossing the river, and goats being herded with a donkey in tow. The 6am *muezzin's* call to prayer didn't wake us, but the van pinged as it stretched in the sun a short time later. Each evening we'd crane our necks to stare at the star-packed skies.

Paths lead through the forest of date palms, offering the occasional surprise like a five-a-side pitch, an oasis of sport in the surrounding desert. We had fun poking around the atmospheric crumbing old town, another quite incredible place to be.

NETHERLANDS

QUICK FACTS ● **EU:** Yes ● **Schengen:** Yes ● **Language:** Dutch ● **Currency:** Euro (EUR, £1=€1.1) ● **Speed Limits ≤3.5t:** Urban/Single/Expressway/Motorway: 50, 90, 100, 130kph ● **Speed Limits >3.5t:** Urban/Single/Expressway/Motorway: 50, 80, 80, 80kph ● **Tolls:** No ● **LEZs:** Yes in Centres of Several Cities, See *www.milieuzones.nl* ● **IDP:** Not Needed ● **Docs:** Driving Licence, Insurance, Passport, V5C ● **Kit:** Headlamp Deflectors ● **LPG:** Good Availability, Bayonet Adapter ● **Time:** UK+1 Hour ● **Daytime Dipped Headlights:** Yes ● **Overnighting:** Campsites, Official Aires, Some Private Businesses Allow Paid Stopovers

The Netherlands is one of Europe's great camping nations, *campercontact.com* lists almost 1,500 campsites. Despite being one of the most densely populated countries in Europe, the Dutch have also made space for over 750 low-cost or free motorhome stopovers at aires and businesses across the country.

When it comes to communicating, you'll have no problem with English, around 90% of the population speak it, and we've always found the Dutch to be welcoming, easy-going people to be around.

Amsterdam has a selection of well-reviewed campsites, accessible with public transport, making this fascinating canal-crossed capital easy to explore. Rotterdam's City Camping (*www.stadscamping-rotterdam.nl*) makes this historical port city easy to access too.

The motorways are in great condition and free of charge, so it's easy to get around. They do occasionally lift up vertically though, a stunning sight as they allow ships to pass beneath, while three lanes of traffic wait either side. At the Gouwe Aqueduct near Gouda this delay's been removed by engineering the river to flow over the top of the A12, quite incredible.

Somewhat older Dutch engineering's also on proud display at Kinderdijk, a UNESCO-listed series of photogenic windmills, dykes and reservoirs used to manage flooding in the low-lying land (*www.kinderdijk.com*).

When it comes to culinary exploration, cheese is an obvious candidate! Keep an eye out for other Dutch favourites too: *AVG'tje, snert, hutspot, stamppot, hachee* and *huzarensalade*. If you've a sweet tooth, try the *stroopwafels*, two thin waffles stuck together with sweet syrup, popped on top of a hot coffee to soften before eating.

Stop #117: Den Helder

Official Aire ● GPS: N52.96250, E4.77058 ● Price Guide: ££ ● All Services ● Next to Maritime Museum, 1.2km Walk to Centre of Town ● **Alternative:** Camping de Donker Duinen (*www.donkereduinen.nl*), GPS: N52.936861, E4.734126, Price Guide: ££ (With CampingCard ACSI), All Services, 3km from Centre of Den Helder, 1.5km to Beach

The history of the Dutch navy is brought to life in style at Marinemuseum Den Helder (*www.marinemuseum.nl/en*), which has a popular aire adjacent. The area also happens to be patrolled at night by the Dutch navy, so must be one of the most secure places we've stayed too!

The museum started off a little staid, with a display of historical navy uniforms and text descriptions of old wars against the English. From there, things picked up though and we eventually stayed for over five hours.

Walking out a side door we found ourselves stood on top of a million kilograms of cold-war era submarine, HNLMS Tonijn. Inside felt surprisingly spacious, until we thought about a crew of 60 odd in there. Two ex-submariners sat inside, one pointing out which of the fold down beds had been his, and we played around with the periscopes (there are two, one with two lenses for navigation and one for a single eye for attack).

The Abraham Crijnssen minesweeper floats in the adjacent harbour, part of the same museum. When the Japanese invaded the Dutch East Indies in WW2, the skipper camouflaged the boat using foliage from the tropical islands. During the day he anchored off the nearest island, and crept along at night, managing to sneak all the way to Australia! Two actors hilariously pranced around telling the story on deck, interjecting English so we could understand.

153

Stop #118: Gouda

Official Aire ● GPS: N52.01086, E4.71712 ● Price Guide: £ (Free on Sundays) ● All Services ● 700m Walk to Market Square ● **Alternative:** Camping Streefland, GPS: N52.000939, E4.755522, Price Guide: ££, All Services, 4km from Gouda (Cycle Paths Available)

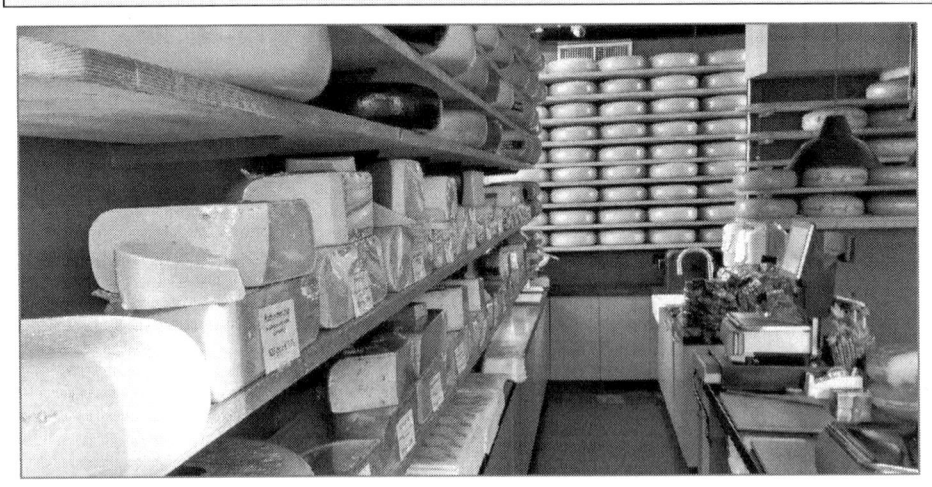

On long tours we can run out of steam researching places to stay and will sometimes be drawn to a place simply because it has a low-cost, well-reviewed aire or campsite. That was the case in Gouda (pronounced 'how-da', with a guttural 'h'), when we visited at the end of a 10-month trip having toured over 10,000 miles through 19 countries, as far south as Croatia and as far north as Norway's North Cape. The aire turned out to be even better than expected when we discovered it was free on Sundays, the day we'd arrived.

A 700m walk took us right into the centre of the city, up alongside the dramatic 15th Century *Oude Stadhuys* (town hall), originally surrounded by water but now located in a wide marketplace surrounded by old buildings and interesting shops.

We popped into one of these shops to pick up some Gouda cheese. The shopkeeper explained that some Goudas are made locally by small farm producers using unpasteurised cow's milk, while others are made in factories with pasteurised milk. The older it is, the stronger the taste. We opted for the *Boerenkaas Overjarig*, a farm-produced mature variant, like a strong mature cheddar, delicious.

Between April and August, a weekly cheese market is held in Gouda (Thursday morning), with the produce being transported to *De Gouden Waag* (the former cheese-weighing house) by horse-drawn wagon.

154

Stop #119: Kinderdijk

Aire at Alblasserdam Marina ● GPS: N51.860307, E4.657668 ● Price Guide: ££ ● All Services ● 4km South of Kinderdijk ● **Alternative:** Camping Landhoeve (*www.landhoeve.com*), GPS: N51.895610, E4.722064, Price Guide: ££, All Services, 6km from Kinderdijk

About one third of the Netherlands lies below sea level, only the ongoing efforts of the Netherlanders prevents this whole area being gradually submerged. An ingenious system of banks (called *dykes*), pumps and sand dunes along the coast keeps the country relatively dry. As the saying goes: "God created the world, but the Dutch created the Netherlands".

The low-lying areas of the country are made up from a series of *polders*, parcels of land contained by dykes, which lie lower than the surrounding water. Pumps are needed to keep them dry, and at Kinderdijk the most spectacular array of 19 windmills was built around 1740 to fulfil this function. These would pump water from the Alblasserwaard polders into a reservoir which could then be emptied into the adjacent tidal river whenever it was low enough.

These days some of the windmills still function, supported by a couple of diesel-powered pumping stations with Archimedes Screws. The windmills, or *molens* in Dutch, are UNESCO-listed and a highly photogenic scene.

There is no on-site motorhome parking (huge signs make this clear) but free daytime parking is available around 2.4km from the site (GPS: N51.883595, E4.661474). Alternatively, you can walk or cycle from the aire or campsite or take a bus from further afield.

Access to the area is free, but you can pay to look inside the mills, a pumping station and the museum or take a boat tour of the site from the jetty at the visitor's centre (*kinderdijk.com*).

NORWAY

> **QUICK FACTS** ● **EU**: No ● **Schengen**: Yes ● **Languages**: Norwegian, Sámi ● **Currency**: Norwegian Krone (NOK, £1=NOK12) ● **Speed Limits ≤3.5t**: Urban/Single/Expressway/Motorway: 50, 80, 100, 100kph ● **Speed Limits >3.5t**: Urban/Single/Expressway/Motorway: 50, 80, 80, 80kph ● **Tolls**: Yes, Register Before Arrival (*www.autopass.no*) ● **LEZs**: Yes in Bergen and Oslo ● **IDP**: Not Needed ● **Docs**: Driving Licence, Insurance, Passport, V5C ● **Kit**: Headlamp Deflectors, Warning Triangle ● **LPG**: Limited Availability, Dish or Bayonet Adapters ● **Time**: UK+1 Hour ● **Daytime Dipped Headlights**: Yes ● **Overnighting**: Campsites, Official Aires, Free Camping Legally Allowed with Restrictions Under Everyman's Right (*Norwegian Allemannsretten*)

Norway's a magnificent country to tour by motorhome. The landscapes are outstanding, with giant fjords, gleaming blue glaciers, jagged mountains, thundering waterfalls and rolling meadows. We particularly enjoyed visiting the North Cape, touring the Lofoten Islands and the fjords in the south.

The northern part of the country is inside the Arctic Circle, so if you head up in there in summer you'll be treated to the otherworldly experience of seeing the sun low on the horizon at midnight. Bring eye masks for a good night's sleep! In the winter, the Northern Lights also play out across the sky. We got lucky on our 10-week tour, seeing both phenomenon on one trip.

Norway's Everyman's Right makes it possible to legally sleep in some quite incredible off-site locations, especially towards the less-populated north of the country. There's also a good network of campsites and service points, although LPG stations are limited, so you'll need to plan refills.

One thing Norway's not great for is fast roads. The combination of narrow routes, frequent tunnels, ferries, reindeer and elk in the road and mountains will frustrate anyone wanting to move around quickly. One tip is to use Sweden's quicker roads as a backdoor into Norway. Also, budget for ferries. You don't need to book these to cross fjords, but be aware costs increase significantly for every metre over 6m. Also, Norway is expensive for food, stock up accordingly but be aware there are restrictions on what you can import. If you plan to bring a pet dog, you'll need them wormed by a vet before arrival.

Stop #120: Aurlandsfjorden

Patch of Land by Aurlandsfjorden • GPS: N60.88406, E7.15484 • Price Guide: Free • No Services • **Alternative:** Flåm Camping (*www.flaam-camping.no*), GPS: N60.862832, E7.109649, Price Guide: £££, All Services, 10-Min Walk to Flåm Railway Station

This was a beautiful, free spot to stay the night, recovering from an epic driving day, with a cold can of Norwegian beer and a great view. While working out a route through the Western fjords towards Bergen we saw we'd a choice: take the 25km Lærdalstunnelen, the longest road tunnel in the world, or head up and over the mountains along the 'snow road', the 48km Aurlandsfjellet National Tourist Route. Both would have made for an interesting drive, but since the mountain road was free of snow (it closes in winter), we opted to use it and to take in the scenery all the way up to 1,306m.

The Aurlandsfjellet road was first opened in 1967 and runs between Lærdal and Aurland. It's normally open from the 1st of June to mid-October, weather depending. The road crosses magnificent scenery, past waterfalls and mountain lakes, across stony wastelands with old icy snow still on the ground for our dog to play in, even though it was September.

The road is in good condition, but has steep sections with hairpins, and stretches of single-width road with passing places. We found the last few miles where the road zigzags down to Aurlandsvangen to need the most concentration, but we didn't have any issues in our 2.2m wide, 3.5 tonne motorhome.

Just before this descent starts, you'll find parking space at the Stegastein, one of Norway's stupendous viewing platforms, completed in 2006. It reaches out 30m into the air, 650m above Aurlandsfjord. A cruise ship was making its way along the fjord while we were there, its wake smoothly playing out behind like the train of an elegant dress, a picture-perfect image.

Stop #121: Bergen

Midttun Motell & Camping (*mmcamp.no*) ● GPS: N60.32086, E5.36483 ● Price Guide: £££ ● All Services ● 10-Min Walk to Tram into City Centre ● Open All Year ● **Alternative:** Bergenshallen Motorhome Aire, GPS: N60.354636, E5.358231, Price Guide: ££, All Services, 15-Min Tram to City Centre, Open May to October

Midttun Motell & Camping was an odd place to stay, an official 'campsite' which was just the car park for the motel. Our parking spot was next to the fence for someone's garden, but it was safe and friendly and just a 10-minute walk to the tram.

Arriving in Bergen the city felt lovely. It was warm and sunny, and we had been dropped off right in the centre next to a small garden, a flowering bandstand and a fountain. Knowing that the city is small enough not to get lost, we just wandered freely, first heading up to Johanneskirken, an 1894 red brick church set on a hill among the city's wooden houses.

Afterwards we wandered around the cobbled streets with wooden houses. Looking out over the port we saw the Hurtigruten, Norway's 'postal ferry', docked ready to take passengers up to the Arctic. We were on the edge of the harbour opposite the UNESCO-listed *Bryggen* (wharf), harking back to the days when Bergen was part of the Hanseatic Trading League. The multicoloured wooden houses looked like the miniatures you buy in the souvenir shops. The famous Fish Market was a glitzy affair as far as seafood goes, all glass and shine, no shouting fish mongers or white-tiled walls in sight. Outside we shared a fish and chip lunch, treating ourselves as eating and drinking out in Norway, even takeaway, is very expensive. Mount Fløyen offers great views over the city, which you can either hike up (3km each way) or let the Fløibanen funicular do the hard work (*www.floyen.no*).

Stop #122: Dalsnibba Plateau

Car Park (*www.dalsnibba.no*) ● GPS: N62.04894, E7.26941 ● Price Guide: Free, But Access via Toll Road (££) ● No Services ● **Alternative:** Camping Dalen Gaard (*www.dalengaard.no*), GPS: N62.069186, E7.254835, Price Guide: ££, All Services, 7km from Geiranger

Norway does viewpoints on a grand scale, with stylish constructions of concrete, steel and glass offering incredible, vertigo-inducing vantage points across the landscape below. Sometimes you can park at them and spend the night, like you can on Mount Dalsnibba, where you've the opportunity to stand alone in the evening or early morning, clutching a hot cup of tea and gazing out at the magic nature has created.

Most of the viewpoints are free, but to get to Dalsnibba you first need to drive the 4.7km toll Nibbevegen road, a dramatic hairpin route, built in 1939, many of the workers coming from the newly completed Trollstigen. The road was paved in 2013 and now attracts over 200,000 visitors a year. It's normally open May to October and has some steep sections over 12% but was built for coaches and easily accommodated our 6m, 3.5 tonne motorhome (just remember to engine-brake on your descent).

At the top you're 1476m above the level of the sea in Geirangerfjord below, with views over the fjord, Blåbreen Glacier and Lake Djupvatnet. The road offers a unique way to get high into the mountains without a long hike.

At the top you'll find the visitor's centre and the Geiranger Skywalk. There's a good-sized parking area but it's mostly not level. The spots closest to the skywalk are reasonably flat and should free up once cars leave in the evening. There are also a couple of parking areas lower down on the road, again with outstanding views. Staying overnight is no problem.

159

Stop #123: Eggum

Official *Bobil* (Motorhome) Parking ● GPS: N68.30728, E13.65127 ● Price Guide: ££ ● Fresh Water and Toilets ● **Alternative:** Car Park for Lofotr Viking Museum (*www.lofotr.no*), GPS: N68.244770, E13.756419, Price Guide: Free, No Services

Eggum is a fishing village on the island of Vestvågøy, in the Lofoten archipelago. The attraction for us was the official parking area, facing the sea with a backdrop of dramatic cliffs. A nearby trail takes you into a pristine landscape, with wonderful views out over the ocean, past artist Markus Raetz's clever sculpture, a head which appears upright from one angle and upside down from another. Near the car park lie the rusting remains of a German WW2 radar installation behind stone walls known locally as "the Fort". Adjacent there's a small amphitheatre-style picnic spot.

After a quiet night at Eggum we drove 10km inland to visit the Lofotr Viking Museum at Borg (*lofotr.no*). A Viking Age longhouse was discovered here in 1981, having laid untouched for 1,000 years. A full-scale replica of the Iron Age chieftain's longhouse has been built nearby, 83m long, and inside you get a great sensation of what it might have been like back when the original was in use.

Low lighting shone on wood, fur, textiles and leather. Dried cod hung from poles, as they still do today on racks around the Lofotens. A craftsman carefully picked out details on a carving. A cooking pot hung over a fire, the only metal to be seen besides armour and weapons: chain mail shirts and long swords. A couple of helmets and swords were laid out behind a heavy wooden table, allowing big kids like us to pop them on and get a photo! Out in the grounds we had a crack at throwing axes and firing arrows, before making a ham-fisted attempt to row a replica Viking ship around the lake.

Stop #124: Holmvassdammen

Free Camping Below a Dam ● GPS: N66.75260, E14.09990 ● Price Guide: Free ● No Services ● Access Via an 'At Own Risk' Unlit Construction Tunnel ● **Alternative:** Free Camping, GPS: N66.775721, E14.152746, Price Guide: Free, No Services, Unlit 'At Own Risk' Construction Tunnels and Some Unsealed Road to Access

Norway's packed with off-site places to pitch up for a night in nature, but this one, about 10km southeast of Glomfjord, stays with us as being one of the most remote we'd ventured to. Without a 4x4 vehicle, this location sited below a stone dam can only be accessed via a long, unlit and pot-holed tunnel, bored through the mountain so heavy construction traffic could pass to build the dam. Signs made it clear using the tunnel was at our own risk, and we felt a real sense of adventure as we drove slowly through the gloom.

The small parking area is set in a rugged landscape of mountains and lakes. A short hike up onto the dam brings glaciers into view as you stand alongside the Storglomvatnet Lake. The lake holds around 3.5 billion cubic metres of water, 500l for every inhabitant on earth. The water feeds the Svartisen Hydroelectric Power Station, which generates the most hydro power of any site in Norway. A second uphill tunnel brings you to an even more remote spot at the on the same lake at Storglomvassdammen (see 'alternative' above).

The evening before we'd had a clear night with a wonderful early autumn showing of the Northern Lights at a parking spot by the coast (GPS: N66.89598, E13.64913). The clouds rolled in for our night at the dam though, so we didn't get a repeat performance. While you're in Norway, keep an eye on an Aurora forecaster (like *www.aurora-service.eu*) to get an idea when the lights are likely to be visible.

161

Stop #125: Nordkapp

Nordkapp Visitor's Centre Car Park (*www.visitnordkapp.net*) ● GPS: N71.16863, E25.78141 ● Price Guide: £££ ● Toilets, No Other Services ● **Alternative:** BaseCamp North Cape Camping (*www.basecampnorthcape.com*), GPS: N71.107833, E25.813957, Price Guide: £££, All Services, 14km from the North Cape Visitor's Centre, Near Skarsvåg

Nordkapp (the North Cape in English) is a 'topping out' point in many a tour of Europe. It's the name of a region in the far north of Norway, but for most travellers it refers to the plateau above the sea on which a visitor's centre and large parking area has been built. Large numbers of motorhomes stay overnight, in the very expensive but uniquely located car park.

Nordkapp is the furthest north you can drive on mainland Europe (if you ignore the fact it's on the island of Magerøya, accessed via a toll-free undersea tunnel). Part of Magerøya extends almost a mile further north to Knivskjelodden, but it's only accessible via an 18km hiking trail from a small car park near the E69 (GPS: N71.121902, E25.708516). Nordkapp has a reputation for being an over-priced tourist trap, and while that seems a fair description, it does miss some of the magical appeal of the place. It has a symbolic nature, attracting all kinds of people, and has a feel of joy and success about it. It's where cyclists, motorbikers, hitch-hikers, and motorhomers all 'complete' a goal in life, and are in a collective good mood, even when the weather closes in, fogging the view from the 300m cliffs and blasting us all with wind and ice-cold rain!

We enjoyed succulent reindeer steaks with friends while the wind blew outside. The next morning, we awoke at 5am to the van pinging with the heat of the sun. Heading outside we spotted groups of boats in the Barents Sea, realising they were whale-watchers as we saw tiny spurts of water being blown from the backs of the animals far below.

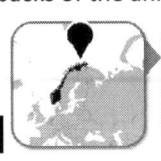

Stop #126: Oldedalen

Campsite Melkevoll Bretun (*www.melkevoll.com*) ● GPS: N61.665006, E6.816361 ● Price Guide: £££ ● All Services and Saunas ● **Alternative:** Gryta Camping (*www.gryta.no*), GPS: N61.741152, E6.790689, Price Guide: £££, All Services, Free Use of Rowing Boats

We loved the Melkevoll Bretun campsite at Oldedalen, even going so far as to say on our blog that this might be the best campsite in the world!

What made it so special? A combination of things, but mostly the spectacular location. The site's mixed between camping and grass-roofed log cabins. Over 6,000 years ago a stone avalanche fall left giant rocks spread across the site, and the free-format pitches are set among them.

Above you roars the 300m Volefossen waterfall, sounding for all the world like a never ending rock fall. A 45-minute stroll along the river brings you to the lake at the base of the Briksdal Glacier, which feels almost within touching distance of its rugged blue tongue of ice.

The site's facilities are top-notch too. As well as a wonderful shower block, with free saunas, there is a large wood-glass-and-stone indoor BBQ barn, where we sat with a glass of red and cooked corn-on-the-cob and fish we caught in a fjord. There's also a kitchen where we had fun baking bread and biscuits. If you're into climbing, there are over 100 bouldering challenges available. For serious, experienced hikers, the Kattanakken (cat's neck) path leads from the parking area at Briksdal up to 700m with views down onto the glacier. It's a 4 hour and 5.5km hike each way.

At night the stars grew until we could see the Milky Way and (proven with our camera on long exposure!) the dim green glow of the Northern Lights was just visible. This is a simply fantastic place for anyone who likes nature.

Stop #127: Oslo

Bogstad Camping (*bogstadcamping.no*) ● GPS: N59.96516, E10.64168 ● Price Guide: £££ ● All Services ● 40-Min Bus Ride into City Centre ● Only Official Location in Oslo Open All Year ● **Alternative:** Oslo Marina Aire, GPS: N59.920039, E10.675616, Price Guide: ££, All Services, 5km from City Centre, Open June to September

We arrived in Oslo in late September, finding that the marina aire had just closed so we had to use the city's Bogstad Camping, more expensive and further away, but a good campsite. Our initial impression of the city came at the campsite gates, where we saw a series of electric cars quietly slide past (a novelty at the time), and several people Nordic skiing on 'skis' fitted with wheels, a fit-looking bunch. We bought 24-hour transport passes from the campsite reception, which proved a good buy as we found several attractions were a few miles apart.

On the bus into the city we got chatting with a New Zealand couple who'd experienced the 2010 Christchurch earthquake first-hand, terrifying and fascinating. They later showed us their luxurious fifth-wheel caravan, towed by a pickup truck (theirs was made in the UK by *fifthwheelco.com*).

Once in the city we walked the sloping roof of the half billion-pound opera house before heading to the incredible Fram Museum, which houses the wooden ship which took Amundsen and his crew to Antarctica for his successful assault on the South Pole. Our hairs stood on end as we held the ship's wheel. The city has a ton more major sights to explore: the Kon-Tiki Museum, the Nobel Peace Centre, the Viking Ship Museum and the Vigeland Sculpture Park to name a few.

Stop #128: Saltstraumen

Car Park ● GPS: N67.22506, E14.61560 ● Price Guide: Free ● No Services ● Overnighting Now Forbidden ● **Alternative:** Camp Saltstraumen-Elvegård (*campsaltstraumen-elvegard.no*), GPS: N67.234689, E14.597955, Price Guide: £££, All Services

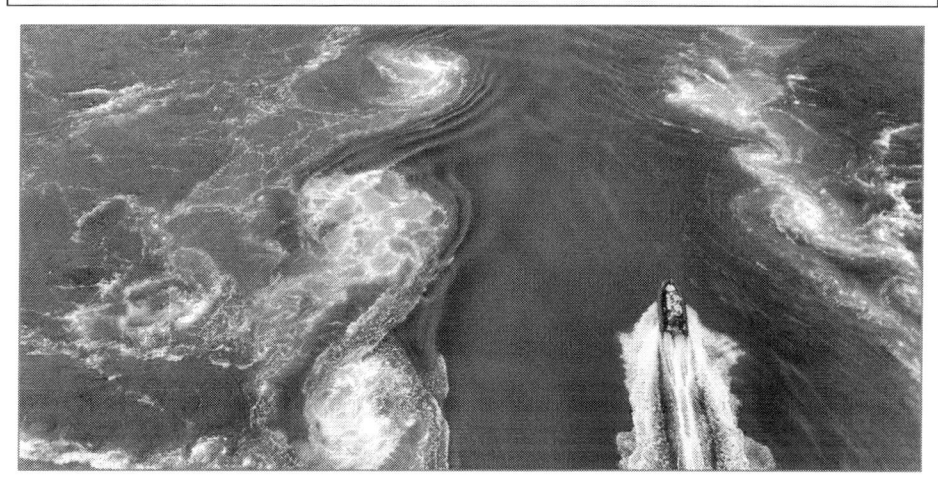

Just south of Bodø, a narrow sea channel called Saltstraumen connects the Saltfjorden to the Skjerstad Fjord. A road bridge offers a great view of what happens when hundreds of millions of cubic metres of seawater are forced through the straight every six hours. The current is one of the strongest in the world, producing a series of awe-inspiring vortices, each measuring 10m across.

The enormous flood of water creates another phenomenon too, filling the fjord with large numbers of Coalfish, Cod, Halibut, Pollack and Halibut. The world record for the largest Coalfish ever caught was set here, with a 22.7kg fish, and there are plenty of stories online of fishermen pulling out 10kg cod.

We're fishing amateurs, armed only with a telescopic rod and some spinners we'd bought on the way to Norway. That didn't seem to matter much though once the current started to pick up. Almost as soon as the spinner hit the water a fish would grab it. It was completely bonkers! Small fish were leaping onto the shore at our feet, presumably to escape a frenzy of larger predators in the green swirling waters. Within half an hour we had a bucket full of good-sized Pollack which we'd clean, freeze, and eat in the coming weeks.

We slept alongside the fjord at a free camping spot, but that's no longer possible. There are parking spots about 100m from the sea, or a couple of campsites. Camp Saltstraumen-Elvegård looks a great choice, just 700m from the water. They can arrange sea eagle and moose spotting expeditions too.

Stop #129: Sand

Motorhome Parking by Sandsfjorden ● GPS: N59.48504, E6.24717 ● Price Guide: £ ● No Services ● Popular, Arrive Early ● **Alternative:** Designated Motorhome Parking in Sand, GPS: N59.482152, E6.257713, Price Guide: £, No Services, Alongside Salmon River

When we parked up at Sand the campervan next to us had all its doors open but no one was around. Eventually a chap arrived on a bicycle and introduced himself. Tijmen from Amsterdam was the owner of the van and was happy to leave it all open while he cycled around. We were surprised, but Norway did feel very safe to us too.

The tourist office next to the parking had a 'Welcome Motorhome' leaflet which listed things to see and do as well as doctors, dentists, garages for repairs, and a service point. It felt as if Sand had rolled out the red carpet to motorhomes.

Over the course of a couple of days we enjoyed the company of our fellow travellers, fishing in the fjord (catching a mackerel), snorkelling for a bucket of mussels, and jumping from a high board built for the purpose above a deep area of water.

The Suldalslågen salmon river flows into the fjord on other side of the village. A 'salmon ladder' was built here in 1986, to allow fish migrating upstream to more easily pass the Sandsfossen waterfall. Between July and September, you can see the magnificent animals, some over 10kg, leaping above the water. Or you can step down into the studio built below the water to see the fish through glass windows, a unique experience.

Fishing is licensed on the river itself, but not in the fjord, and amazingly one of our fellow vanners caught a huge salmon, sharing it as sushi between us all as another cooked pancakes in a wonderful mini community.

Stop #130: Steinsvik

Beach Parking by the Fv355 ● GPS: N69.876397, E21.120812 ● Price Guide: £ ● Toilets, No Other Services ● **Alternative:** Fosselv Camping Straumfjord, GPS: N69.839631, E21.209327, Price Guide: ££, All Services

Steinsvik lies about half-way between Alta and Tromsø, a tiny village sat on a peninsular below the cliffs of a central grey rock. Being set away from the main E6 route, the peninsular is replete with free camping options, and we stayed in three places in total. This spot was special though, set besides a beautiful sandy beach, facing north for a spectacular view of the midnight sun as it 'bounced' across the sea from east to west, never sinking below the horizon.

We were parked alongside friends and spent the day watching heron and oyster catchers, fishing, snorkelling and swimming in the Arctic Sea (yes, it was cold even in July, bring a thick wetsuit and gloves!). Locals brought deckchairs and picnics to the beach to enjoy the summer sunshine.

Later we gathered tinder-dry driftwood from the beach and got a fire going in one of the stone pits built beside the parking area, cooking fish we'd caught during the day (there is no need for a licence when sea fishing in Norway unless you're fishing for salmon, sea trout or arctic char). The salty liquorice flavoured crisps even made an appearance, a Scandinavian speciality, although they weren't universally appreciated in our crew!

This was a beautifully bucolic spot. Simple living in nature, a Scandinavian speciality. There's no town, no restaurants, no shops or bars, just the sea, the sand, the sun, the rocks, birds and fish. Away from the cities in Norway, it felt like we were really escaping the speed and pressure of modern life through the entire country, but nowhere was quite as wonderfully calm and enjoyable as this little beach, enjoying time with friends on a road to nowhere.

Stop #131: Trollstigen

Visitor's Centre Car Park (Overnight Stays No Longer Allowed) ● GPS: N62.45295, E7.66371 ●
Price Guide: Free ● No Services ● **Alternative:** Trollstigen Camping and Guesthouse, GPS:
N62.500216, E7.672273, Price Guide: ££, All Services, 5km from Trollstigen

The Trollstigen (Troll's Ladder), is a part of one of Norway's best-known tourist drives from Sogge Bru (near Åndalsnes) to Langvatnet. Covering 104km, the overall route has one ferry crossing, is usually clear of snow and is open from May to October.

The Trollstigen first opened in 1939 and is an unforgettable section of road consisting of 11 hairpin bends carved into the side of a deep valley. The route is narrow in places, but the surface is in very good condition and the bends are wide enough for coaches, so we had no problems at all in our 6m motorhome.

The ascent is spectacular, although the driver won't have much opportunity to take it in on the way up (we had the passenger film it so we could both enjoy it afterwards)! There is a small parking area just before the road crosses the dramatic Stigfossen Waterfall, but if it's already full don't worry, the views from the steel vantage point constructed at the top, which leaps high into thin air, are bonkers enough.

There's a visitor's centre at the top with a large car park. We stayed there overnight but that's no longer allowed. There are areas of gravel and parking for trail heads to the south of the main car park, or there's a campsite 5km to the north of the hairpins (details above).

www.nasjonaleturistveger.no describes the route and many others across Norway, providing photos, descriptions and downloadable maps for free.
www.visitnorway.com also offers great inspiration for a tour of Norway.

POLAND

QUICK FACTS ● **EU**: Yes ● **Schengen**: Yes ● **Language**: Polish ● **Currency**: Polish Złoty (PLN, £1=PLN5) ● **Speed Limits ≤3.5t**: Urban/Single/Expressway/Motorway: 50, 90, 120, 140kph ● **Speed Limits >3.5t**: Urban/Single/Expressway/Motorway: 50, 70, 80, 80kph ● **Tolls**: Yes, ≤3.5t Pay with Cash, >3.5t viaBOX Needed (*www.viatoll.pl*) ● **LEZs**: Central Krakow ● **IDP**: Not Needed ● **Docs**: Driving Licence, Insurance, Passport, V5C ● **Kit**: Headlamp Deflectors, Warning Triangle, Fire Extinguisher ● **LPG**: Good Availability, Dish Adapter ● **Time**: UK+1 Hour ● **Daytime Dipped Headlights**: Yes ● **Overnighting**: Campsites, Paid Mixed Parking, Free Camping Not Allowed (Enforced on Coast and Nature Reserves)

We were pleasantly surprised by Poland as a motorhome destination the first time we crossed the country. Having just left Ukraine, we were doubly appreciative of the smooth roads, easy availability of paid overnight parking and good quality campsites. The towns and cities had fascinating (if turbulent) histories, with interesting architecture, new foods to try and a general safe feel to them. A few sections of Polish motorway are toll, but we found them to be well worth the money to quickly cross large swathes of countryside.

We visited some of the country's main tourist draws, finding we could access them easily in our motorhome, including being able to stay within easy walking distance of central Warsaw.

We've visited Kraków twice, staying a short bus ride away, once at an aire provided by a motorhome dealer and once for a few nights in the paid parking at the famous Wieliczka Salt Mine. We've also used a few Polish campsites, finding them to be a mixture between cosy, friendly 'am I in someone's garden here?' sites and larger affairs indistinguishable from those in Western Europe.

Poland hasn't had an easy history, and everyone touring will have to choose whether they want to visit the sites of atrocities inflicted on the country, including the infamous Auschwitz-Birkenau concentration camp at Oświęcim. We decided to go and pay our respects. Able to stay overnight in one of the parking areas, we found the site to be one of the most moving experiences of our lives.

169

Stop #132: Kazimierz Dolny

Camping Pielaka (*www.campingpielaka.pl*) ● GPS: N51.3313, E21.9585 ● Price Guide: ££ ● All Services ● **Alternative:** Marina Camping (*www.portkazimierzdolny.pl*), GPS: N51.322970, E21.941723, Price Guide: ££, All Services

Kazimierz Dolny gave us a taste of small-scale Polish camping, effectively staying on the short-cropped grass of a family home at Camping Pielaka. We were given a friendly welcome in German so we could exchange a few words, since we only know *dziękuję* (thank you) and *dzień dobry* (good morning) in Polish.

Kazimierz Dolny is a small, picturesque town set alongside the Vistula River, which was used by the residents to transport grain in the 16th and 17th Centuries. Prior to WW2 around half of the population were Jewish, but almost all of them had been murdered by the Nazis by 1942.

It's a beautiful place to wander these days, especially on a sunny day. The river path was full of strolling families, and the cobbled streets and old market square were alive with tourists. The town has long attracted artists, some of whom had displayed their pieces on fences or along the ground, some great quality, some a little more mediocre! A large folk music festival also takes places here each summer.

The town's square, the *rynek*, is the focal point. At one end stand the intricately carved pale stone facades of the Mikołaj and Krzysztof Przybył brother's townhouses. An old well stands in the centre of the square, still providing water to thirsty tourists. The town's synagogue was destroyed by the Nazis but rebuilt in the 1950s as a cinema, and now displays photos of the city's Jewish history.

We spent a lovely couple of hours in a restaurant along the square with a few drinks, people-watching in the shade before retreating to the garden campsite to relax under our awning.

Stop #133: Oświęcim

Auschwitz-Birkenau Car Park (*auschwitz.org*) ● GPS: N50.02886, E19.20039 ● Price Guide: Free (Separate Payment for Entrance to Site) ● No Services ● **Alternative:** Auschwitz Dialogue and Prayer Center Camping, GPS: N50.023712, E19.198964, Price Guide: ££, All Services

Nazi Germany started operating concentration camps in the 1930s, building up to more than 1,000 camps during WW2, holding political prisoners, Jews, criminals and anyone they deemed a threat of any kind, for any reason.

Auschwitz was originally built in 1940 when local prisons were unable to contain the volume of Poles being arrested by the Nazis. In 1944 a second part of the camp was built, Auschwitz II, or Birkenau. This latter part of the camp was where most of the ensuing extermination took place, with an estimated 1.1 million victims.

We knew all of this before we arrived, so why visit? We debated it between ourselves. We didn't want to see the place as a 'tourist attraction', that would clearly be very wrong. We knew it would be an upsetting experience. But the site was on our route and we felt to pass it by would be an act of cowardice. On arriving at Auschwitz I, where the tours start, we found the parking area where we knew we could stay overnight, gave our dog a walk and headed for the entrance.

Laughing teenagers in the queue were soon replaced with the sombre voice of our guide, as she walked our group through the buildings and described the terrible, inhuman conditions. Tears flowed. Later we were bussed to Birkenau, past the infamous Death Gate where the transport trains arrived. The sight of the partially destroyed gas chambers was impossible to absorb, from our position of freedom and safety, under a blue sky.

Fewer than 15% of Auschwitz staff ever stood trial for their crimes, although camp commandant Rudolf Höss was hanged in 1947 having evaded arrest until 1946.

Stop #134: The Wolf's Lair

Wolf's Lair Car Park (*wilczyszaniec.olsztyn.lasy.gov.pl*) ● GPS: N54.078785, E21.493129 ● Price Guide: £ ● Electricity and Fresh Water, No Waste Disposal ● **Alternative:** Camping Echo (*campingecho.pl*), GPS: N53.966773, E21.776213, Price Guide: ££, All Services, 45-Min Drive East of Wolf's Lair

The Wolf's Lair was Hitler's top secret, high security headquarters from which the invasion of the Soviet Union was orchestrated during WW2. Hitler spent over 800 days at the site (the *Wolfsschanze* in German), a self-contained town built in the forests of what was the German state of Prussia. The site was destroyed in January 1945 using huge amounts of explosive only two days before the Russian Army discovered the enormous concrete bunkers in varying states of collapse.

The Wolf's Lair was the location of Colonel Claus von Stauffenberg's assassination attempt on Hitler in July 1944, and the remains of the conference room where the suitcase bomb exploded are still visible.

We drove to the Wolf's Lair on the day of Corpus Christi, finding ourselves slowly following a religious procession for a mile along the road, driving over rose petals. After some rumbling across rough-surfaced roads, we found the site and paid our entrance fee, parking beneath the trees where we were welcome to stay overnight. Two huge slabs of concrete sat alongside us, where they'd landed in 1945.

Site guides are available, or you can simply walk around in awe at the sheer scale of the bunkers and of the power which must have been required to destroy them. Orders were issued here which resulted in millions of deaths, so it's a sombre place to contemplate last century's story.

Stop #135: Warsaw

Guarded Car Park "Parking ZTM Bugaj" ● GPS: N52.25070, E21.01568 ● Price Guide: ££ ● 10-Minute Walk to Market Square ● Noisy ● **Alternative:** Camping SUM, GPS: N52.213826, E21.101700, Price Guide: ££, All Services, Use Nearby Bus Route to Access City Metro

The drive into Warsaw along the S17 tested us, a single carriageway road with dashed paint along either side creating two half-width lanes which the locals drove on to create a sort of impromptu three-lane highway, playing chicken to decide who got to use the middle lane at any one time. By the time we reached the guarded parking in the centre of the city we were worn out, very pleased to finally get safely parked up for the night.

We were rewarded with the easiest access to a city centre of any capital city we've visited by motorhome. As we were travelling with our pet dog, and daytime temperatures were climbing, the ability to walk only 10 minutes to the city's old square was just wonderful.

The original square was medieval, but it was systematically destroyed by the German Army along with 85% of the surrounding city in retribution for the 1944 Warsaw Uprising when the Home Army tried to liberate the city. It was rebuilt in the 1950s.

It was too hot to leave our dog in the van, so we simply walked the city admiring the recreated architecture, quite an incredible, mind-bending achievement on such a monumental scale. In the evening, with the temperature cooled off, we headed into the city for a couple of drinks in one of the many bars. Warsaw also has a great range of museums from serious inspections of war and communism to the World of Illusion and the Vodka museum. See *warsawtour.pl* for information on the museums, vantage points and suggested itineraries.

173

Stop #136: Wieliczka

Wieliczka Salt Mine Car Park (*www.wieliczka-saltmine.com*) ● GPS: N49.98494, E20.05279 ● Price Guide: ££ ● No Services ● **Alternative:** Camping Adam in Kraków (*www.campingadam.pl*), GPS: N50.046135, E19.902956, Price Guide: ££, All Services

The Salt Mine at Wieliczka has been on the UNESCO World Heritage list since 1978 and attracts over 1.2 million visitors a year. Wieliczka is located a 30-minute drive south-west of Kraków and there are several car parks around the town which allow overnight motorhome parking. When we visited in 2013 the main car park for the mine was cheap to stay in. We opted to sleep there for three nights, visiting the mines and later heading to Kraków on the bus.

Looking at reviews of the Wieliczka parking areas in later years the prices have been increased significantly, so staying at a campsite in Kraków and taking the bus to the mine probably makes more sense now.

The mine itself proved to be a wonder, like walking into something from a J. R. R. Tolkien fantasy novel. The mine is on nine levels which are between 64 and 327 metres underground. There are over 2,400 chambers connected by corridors with a total length of 178 miles! We got to walk about four kilometres of it and visited over 20 chambers, peering around chapels, underground lakes, carvings made by the miners and mile after mile of supporting wood, it gets so impregnated with salt that it doesn't rot.

Our guidebook tipped us off to the fact the tour is split in two, with the second part optional. We opted to do it along with a handful of others, although the guides told us it was 'just for geologists'. We found the underground museum they took us into to be fascinating.

PORTUGAL

QUICK FACTS ● **EU**: Yes ● **Schengen**: Yes ● **Language**: Portuguese ● **Currency**: Euro (EUR, £1=€1.1) ● **Speed Limits ≤3.5t**: Urban/Single/Expressway/Motorway: 50, 90, 100, 120kph ● **Speed Limits >3.5t**: Urban/Single/Expressway/Motorway: 50, 80, 80, 90kph ● **Tolls**: Yes, Pre-Pay With Credit Card at Border, or Sign Up at *www.portugaltolls.com* ● **LEZs**: Central Lisbon ● **IDP**: Not Needed ● **Docs**: Driving Licence, Insurance, Passport, V5C, MOT Certificate ● **Kit**: GB Sticker, Headlamp Deflectors, Warning Triangle, Reflective Jackets, Spare Bulbs ● **LPG**: Good Availability, Dish or Euroconnector Adapters ● **Time**: Same as UK ● **Daytime Dipped Headlights**: No ● **Overnighting**: Campsites, Aires, Paid Mixed Parking, Free Parking Used to Be Overlooked Away from the Coast and Tourist Hotspots But New Legislation Might Prevent This

Portugal is a major motorhome destination in Europe, particularly the Algarve region which runs along the southern Atlantic coast. This area has a great climate and is popular for over-wintering, with daytime highs averaging 16°C in January. The Algarve is also packed with campsites and aires.

Portugal has more to offer than Algarve's beaches though. In our trips we've visited a ruined Roman town (Conimbriga), the headquarters citadel of the Knights Templar (Tomar), one of the oldest universities in the world (Coimbra), a surf town (Nazaré) and the city which ships out fortified wine to the world (Porto).

We've barely scratched the surface and have much more to explore. Lisbon has a large city campsite and a popular aire, making it easy to visit by public transport. The inland route along the Douro River from Porto is reputed to have wonderful scenery, and there are some very popular vineyard aires to enjoy en-route. We've also only stayed at one of Portugal's dams (*barragens*), many of which have free parking.

Portugal's roads aren't always as flat as we might be used to but on the flip slide the cost of living is low, with some aires costing just a few pounds a night within walking distance of restaurants serving Portuguese specialities like salt cod (*bacalhau*), sardines (*sardinhas*), custard tarts (*pasteis de nata*), spicy chicken (*frango peri-peri*), vegetable soup (*caldo verde*) and roasted piglet (*leitão*).

Stop #137: Alvor

Aire (Estacionamento de Caravanas) Alvor ● GPS: N37.124841, W8.595128 ● Price Guide: £ ● Muddy When Wet ● All Services ● **Alternative:** Camping Alvor (*www.campingalvor.com*), GPS: N37.134961, W8.590315, Price Guide: ££, All Services

Alvor remains a fishing village despite the encroach of tourism into this corner of the Algarve region. It was originally inhabited in 436BC by the Carthaginians, whose capital was in Tunis in North Africa. It was later absorbed into the Roman Empire before being taken again by the North Africans, this time the Moors, who named it *Al-bur*. Sadly, most of the old architecture was destroyed in the infamous 1755 Lisbon Earthquake, whose epicentre was in the Atlantic, south of Algarve.

The village is set by an estuary on one side, the Ria de Alvor, and fronted by a two-mile sandy beach to the south. Wooden boardwalks run through a network of sand dunes between the river and the Atlantic, offering relaxing routes to walk, cycle or run.

The aire at Alvor is a haphazard affair, set on a large area of sandy earth, unsealed except for the service point, and reputed to be very muddy in wet weather. It's low cost, and some motorhomes spend months at a time here enjoying the climate, the beach, the company of fellow motorhomers and nearby restaurants and bars which remain open all-year.

We stayed at Alvor one Christmas with friends before heading to Morocco with them. A small multi-national community had built up on the aire, and we all received an invite to a Christmas Day meal at an out-of-town family-run restaurant. After numerous courses of delicious food, and a large volume of beer and wine, we were given a frankly miniscule bill, leaving a decent tip to try and say *obrigado* and *obrigada* (thank you, ending in an *o* if you're male and an *a* if you're female).

176

Stop #138: Braga

Car Park at Bom Jesus ● GPS: N41.552553, W8.375353 ● Price Guide: Free ● No Services ● Unofficial Spot, May Not Be Accessible ● **Alternative:** Mixed Parking, GPS: N41.552799, W8.381160, Price Guide: Free, No Services

As great a proportion of the Portuguese identify as Roman Catholics as the Italians. Portugal has several Catholic pilgrimage sites, including the UNESCO World Heritage listed Bom Jesus de Monte sanctuary in Tenões, just outside the city of Braga.

While maybe not as famous as the Shrine of Fátima, at Cova da Iria, the monumental Bom Jesus baroque stairway is said to make the church at the top the most photographed in Portugal. The stairway was constructed in three sections over the past 300 years, parts being dedicated to the Passion of Christ, the three virtues (Faith, Hope and Charity) and the five senses. Devotees climb the ziz-zag stairs on their knees.

Our journey to Bom Jesus was one we'll never forget, and one which taught is a valuable lesson: don't trust your satnav! Ours insisted the only route to the top of the hill was up a steep cobbled, narrow street. We doubted this was the way and tried to find a way around, but as the rain fell and the light started to fail, we eventually lost patience and tried to follow its directions. The result was our 3.1 tonne motorhome threatening to slide back down the road we'd climbed, which had become too steep and slippy to drive.

We'll never forget the sight of people coming out of their homes to watch us edging back downhill, inches from their parked cars, trying not to show how panicked we were. When we eventually found the nice wide way up we just parked in the first car park we came to, relieved and ready for a beer!

Stop #139: Cascais

Campsite "Parque De Campismo Orbitur Guincho" (*www.orbitur.pt*) ● GPS: N38.721726, W9.466027 ● Price Guide: ££ ● All Services ● **Alternative:** Guincho Beach Parking, GPS: N38.727739, W9.475673, Price Guide: £, Fresh Water and Paid Showers

Christmas is an introspective time to be on the road, away from family and the rituals at home. We have fond memories of the campsite north of Cascais as the place we spent our first Christmas away, in the company of great friends we met while travelling. We'd never imagined we'd meet so many friendly, interesting and inspirational people as we travelled. We've found over the years that we enjoy mixing up touring alone and with friends.

The campsite we stayed at is 6km from the pleasure port town of Cascais, set in a sandy pine forest a couple of kilometres from a long sandy beach. Long board walks provided access to the beach through a protected area of dunes. Surfers pulled off spectacular stunts out on the waves offshore, even on Christmas Day, as we all messed around being hit by waves in the shallows.

Later we video-called our families at home, feeling a little homesick, before heading back to our friends for a sunny BBQ and pinecone fires in small metal fire pits sold by the site. The beers and wine flowed, and we sat inside a gazebo chatting and laughing late into the evening, with an electric heater to keep the chill off as our dog munched his way through an Xmas bone.

Cascais is around 16km south of Sintra, a town famous for its palaces, estates and gardens. The historic centre of the town is included on the UNESCO World Heritage list (*www.sintraromantica.net*).

Stop #140: Coimbra

Paid Parking ● GPS: N40.199951, W8.423375 ● Price Guide: £ ● No Services ● Noisy ●
Alternative: Municipal Campsite, GPS: N40.188926, W8.399558, Price Guide: ££, All Services, 2.5km Walk or Cycle to Centre of Coimbra

Coimbra used to have a free aire, just next to the Ponte Pedonal Pedro e Inês bridge across the Rio Mondego (or the 'Elton John Bridge', named because the coloured glass sides reminded us of his glasses). The aire appears to no longer be accessible, but the above two locations get good reviews and look like useful alternatives.

On our tour we were lucky to spend our time in Coimbra with a few other couples, some we'd met earlier on our trip and others we got chatting to in the aire. The city is famous for having one of the oldest universities in continuous operation, first established in 1290 and moving to Coimbra in 1537 (*www.uc.pt*). Walking tours of the University are available, taking in the famous Johannine Library.

See *turismodocentro.pt* for more information and itineraries on this region of Portugal.

During an evening meal out with our fellow travellers we were adjacent to a room full of students, wearing black gowns and celebrating the last day of the university year. At a bar later we were entertained by traditional *Fado* singers, a Portuguese genre with songs focussing on loss and mourning.

When we left Coimbra we headed south, seeking the winter sun. En route we visited Conímbriga, the excavated remains of one of many Roman cities in Portugal (*www.patrimoniocultural.gov.pt*). The city evolved over time, including the rushed building of a defensive wall in the 3rd Century AD, which passes right through the centre of a villa.

179

Stop #141: Évora

Campsite "Parque de Campismo Orbitur Évora" (*www.orbitur.pt*) ● GPS: N38.557256, W7.925775 ● Price Guide: ££ ● All Services ● **Alternative:** Évora Aire, GPS: N38.563261, W7.916614, Price Guide: Free, All Services Except Electricity

Évora sits inland, east of Lisbon, easily accessed via the A6 motorway. We headed to the city for New Year's Eve, in the hope we could join in the celebrations. As it turns out, *véspera de ano novo* is more of a family affair for the Portuguese in Évora, celebrated in private, and we ended up welcoming 2012 in our van on the town's campsite, with some beers bought from a local petrol station!

Our sightseeing attempts were more successful, visiting the Roman temple and gardens in the main square (*www.visitevora.net*). Although known as the *Templo de Diana*, it was more likely dedicated to the Roman God Jupiter. In medieval times the building was incorporated into a tower of the Castle of Évora before being turned into a butcher's shop. Restoration of the monument, removing medieval walls, started in the 19th Century.

Another fascinating if macabre attraction of Évora is the *Capela dos Ossos*, the Chapel of Bones. The interior walls of the chapel are lined with the skulls and bones of around 5,000 skeletons exhumed from the city's medieval graveyards by Franciscan monks. The purpose is simple: to force you to reflect on the inevitability of death, and to live a fuller life as a result.

After leaving Évora we drove to the *Cromlech of the Almendres*, a collection of ancient granite standing stones, some with engravings. The site is surrounded by cork oaks, their lower trunks orange where the bark has been harvested.

Stop #142: Faro

Car Park • GPS: N37.01124, W7.93260 • Price Guide: Free • No Services • May Only Be Suitable for Day Parking Now, Check Locally • **Alternative:** Faro Campervan Park (*en.farocampervanpark.com*), GPS: N37.029791, W7.970384, Price Guide: ££, All Services

Faro is the capital of the Algarve region, perhaps best known for being the location of the airport many of us fly into when we're not driving our motorhomes.

The parking spot we used was a car park located a stone's throw from the old town, free to use but alongside a railway line and beneath the flight path. With rain hammering on the roof, it wasn't the quietest night's sleep! A well-reviewed aire has since opened, 5km from the centre of Faro, 4km from Faro Beach and 3km from trails through the Parque Natural da Ria Formosa (*en.farocampervanpark.com*).

Faro was our first experience of using the Poste Restante service, where you can use a post office as a delivery address, and they hold it for you for a small fee. The service operates in many countries around the world but doesn't have the greatest reputation for reliability (both our parcels were found, after we insisted that they keep searching). Other services are starting to come available now for receiving parcels as you travel, like Amazon Locker (you'll need to order from the relevant country's website). Campsites sometimes also accept parcels if you know where you will be in advance, check with reception first.

We enjoyed wandering around the cobbled, white washed streets of old Faro, taking in the fortified cathedral and the Baroque architecture of the Igreja do Carmo church. Rows of orange trees brighten the streets, and we quickly discovered the fruit is a sour variety, explaining why no-one eats them!

Stop #143: Porto

Parking by the Duoro ● GPS: N41.14337, W8.63236 ● Price Guide: Free ● No Services ● Informal, May Not Be Accessible ● **Alternative:** Camping de Canidelo (*www.orbitur.pt*), GPS: N41.124730, W8.666560, Price Guide: £££, All Services, 20-Min Bus or Uber to Porto

Our parking spot in Porto was just a 15-minute walk from the port lodges along the southern side of the Duoro in Vila Nova de Gaia. It was an area of unused land in front of an abandoned house and had a creepy feeling like something from Scooby-Doo. We had no issues there, but we did move the van during the day to a secure paid car park (which we noticed afterwards had a sign saying no motorhomes, but the attendant didn't mention this). Next time we'll use a campsite on the coast and take a bus into the city.

Port wine became very popular in England in the 18th Century, as war with France deprived the nation of French wine and import duty on port was also lowered. The wine is fortified with distilled grape spirits, which helps preserve it, and while in Porto we discovered it's not just the red, sweet wine we were used to, but it also comes in dry and white varieties. The port lodges (or houses) like Cálem, Kopke and Sandeman offer tasting tours, contact them in advance to be sure of an English language one.

We walked across the famous iron-framed Ponte Dom Luis I Bridge, getting great views of the Duoro and the city below us, to Porto's Ribiera district. Historically, Ribiera's quayside would have been busy with cargo being loaded and unloaded, but today it's a tourist destination with eateries and shops facing the port lodges on the opposite bank. We had a wonderful lunch here before exploring the city's medieval streets and alleyways.

Stop #144: Silves

Swimming Pool Parking ● GPS: N37.18465, W8.44231 ● Price Guide: Free ● No Services ● Motorhomes Now Officially Forbidden ● **Alternative:** Algarve Motorhome Park Silves (*algarvemotorhomepark.com*), GPS: N37.187233, W8.451366, Price Guide: £, All Services

We arrived in Silves in January 2012, a few months into our first year-long tour, surprised to find around 100 motorhomes free-parking at the swimming pool spot we'd been tipped off about. This area is off-limits to motorhomes now, but a new low-cost official area has been created nearby, a 15-minute walk into the centre of town.

Silves (pronounced *Sil-vesh*) was once the capital of the Kingdom of Algarve, a sort of honorary area within Portugal created after the Christian re-conquest of the previously Muslim-held lands. Silves castle was taken first in 1160 before the Moors quickly retook it, and again in 1189 by King Sancho I supported by a Crusader army (the Moors took it again in 1191). An oversized statue of Sancho I now stands at the castle gates, taller than the entrance itself, holding an enormous sword.

The castle stands above the town, fashioned from red stone, with great views of the surrounding farmland from within. The town itself is a relaxed affair, with narrow cobbled streets, bars, restaurants, shops and supermarkets.

The town has a municipal market which is open Monday to Saturday, but we came across a street market with beautiful-looking local produce and characterful, cheerful faces of the stallholders. We bought a couple of *malassadas*, Portuguese doughnuts, fresh from the deep fat fryer and coated in sugar and cinnamon. Delicious, if not exactly healthy!

Stop #145: Tomar

Municipal Aire ● GPS: N39.606958, W8.410270 ● Price Guide: Free ● All Services Except Electricity ● Former Municipal Campsite and Very Popular ● **Alternative:** Car Park, GPS: N39.602365, W8.408913, Price Guide: Free, No Services

Tomar's famous for being the one-time seat of the Templar Knights. Around 10% of them were skilled fighters, taking part in the Crusades, while the other members were involved in support and finance, offering an early form of banking across Europe. This was the eventual downfall of the order, brought about by King Philip IV of France to avoid repaying his debts.

Although individual Templars were sworn to poverty and gifted all their assets to the order when they joined, the charity itself was very well financed. This is clear when you're presented with the enormous, beautifully decorated Convent of Christ Castle, originally a 12th Century stronghold against Moroccan Muslims, which successfully repelled the army of caliph Abu Yusuf al-Mansur in 1190.

Over the centuries the fortress and convent have been expanded and adorned with carvings, paintings and sculptures on a grand scale, making the site a wonderful, calm place to spend a few hours wandering, learning about and photographing.

A few towns across Europe have decided to convert their municipal campsites (which are already low-cost) into completely free aires. This tends to create very pleasant overnight locations, as is the case in Tomar, where the ex-campsite is now a very well-reviewed, large and popular aire. You should only need to seek out a car park in Tomar if the aire is closed for some reason or is completely full.

ROMANIA

QUICK FACTS ● **EU**: Yes ● **Schengen**: No, But In Process of Joining ● **Language**: Romanian ● **Currency**: Romanian Leu (RON, £1=5.4 RON) ● **Speed Limits ≤3.5t**: Urban/Single/Expressway/Motorway: 50, 90, 130, 130kph ● **Speed Limits >3.5t**: Urban/Single/Expressway/Motorway: 50, 90, 110, 110kph ● **Tolls**: Yes, Motorways and State Roads, Buy E-vignette at *www.roviniete.ro*. Some Bridges Also Toll ● **LEZs**: None, But Access to Central Bucharest Restricted for Vehicles Over 5 Tonnes ● **IDP**: Not Needed ● **Docs**: Driving Licence, Insurance, Passport, V5C ● **Kit**: GB Sticker, Headlamp Deflectors, Warning Triangle, Fire Extinguisher, Reflective Jackets ● **LPG**: Good Availability, Dish Adapter ● **Time**: UK+2 Hours ● **Daytime Dipped Headlights**: Yes ● **Overnighting**: Campsites, Some Aires, TIR (Lorry) Parking, Car Parks, Free Camping Officially Allowed, Be Aware of Bears in Mountains

Romania offers the best of both worlds for motorhome touring: a good network of campsites while also offering huge potential for free camping.

The country was under communist rule for over 40 years, the latter 24 years as a totalitarian state under Nicolae Ceaușescu. This left Romania a poor country, still visible now with dogs roaming wild, people working the land by hand, some travelling by horse and cart, transporting goods on old bikes and living in dilapidated housing. Times are changing though, and the per-capita GDP has increased seven times over since 2000.

We crossed the country on our way north after spending the spring in Greece, pleasantly surprised at the quality of the road network and how welcoming the country felt.

After crossing the Danube, we travelled first to the capital Bucharest before heading north into the mountains, coming across warning signs for bears as we visited monasteries and palaces on our way to the eye-popping hairpins of the famous Transfăgărășan Pass.

A tip off from a touring motorbiker at the pass led us to a mini-adventure watching the adrenaline-fuelled Red Bull Romaniacs enduro off-road motorcycle race near Sibiu. Further north we stayed in Sighișoara, a medieval town in Transylvania where the father of the man said to inspire Dracula, Vlad Țepeș (Vlad the Impaler), was exiled. Next, we visited painted monasteries before heading north to a new adventure in Ukraine.

Stop #146: Bucharest

Campsite Casa Alba (*www.casaalba.ro*) ● GPS: N44.517348, E26.091950 ● Price Guide: £££ ●
All Services ● Relatively Expensive But Convenient for Bus to City ● **Alternative:** Camping
Bucharest Belvedere (*campingbucuresti.ro*), GPS: N44.375169, E25.966371, Price Guide: ££,
Relatively New Site, All Services, Bus or Uber to Bucharest

When we visited Bucharest in 2013, we didn't have the Eastern Europe map for our satnav. The only campsite available at the time was Casa Alba, to the north of the city. This should have been a simple route around the ring road, but our lack of map had us driving straight into the city centre on a Friday afternoon. After forcing our way through a heaving, horn-blaring mass of angry traffic, it took more than a few beers to recover from the experience!

Casa Alba camping has a simple parking area with motorhomes packed in. That's not unusual for 'city campsites' in eastern Europe, but Bucharest Belvedere Camping (*campingbucuresti.ro*) to the west now looks a much better option with stabilised pitches surrounded by grass.

Casa Abla reception sold us all-day bus tickets into the city, explaining how to electronically 'validate' them on the bus, and the bus stop was just a short walk from the campsite.

Bucharest was a surprise to us, a modern and affluent city with plenty to occupy us. We took an hour-long hop-on, hop-off bus tour to see the main sights, including the enormous Palace of the Parliament (bring your passports if you want to see inside) and the Centrul Vechi (the grand old town).

To learn more about the country's former communist leaders you can visit the Ceaușescu Mansion (*casaceausescu.ro*) and for foodies, the city has several markets, Piața Obor being the largest with terraces selling *mititei* (seasoned meaty sausages) and low-cost beer.

Stop #147: Sibiu

Road Parking Outside a Private House ● GPS: N45.81439, E24.19867 ● Price Guide: Free ● No Services ● **Alternative:** City Aire "Nomad Camp" (*www.nomad-caravan.ro/en/camping-sibiu-nomad*), GPS: N45.793516, E24.117976, Price Guide: £, All Services

Romaniacs is an off-road motorcycle event sponsored by Red Bull which takes place each summer in the region around Sibiu (*www.redbullromaniacs.com*). A biker told us about it in a chance conversation. We decided to attend the final day of the event and headed to where we thought it would take place, driving a few miles of dirt road with no sign of anything happening.

Reaching the end of the road, we parked opposite someone's house and waited nervously. When they returned, we nipped over to check if we were in the right spot and could stay there. That's when the fun began!

"Yes! It's here, of course you can stay, you're welcome!". It turned out the family had spent years working in the USA before returning home and building the house, so they all spoke English. They couldn't have been nicer to us, arranging for a Dacia taxi into Sibiu, a beautiful Saxon town where we enjoyed the old-world ambience and delicious food at the Crama Sibiul Vechi cellar restaurant (*www.sibiulvechi.ro*). Our neighbours even cooked us breakfast a couple of days later when we left.

The Romaniacs event itself was a blast. Industrial diggers arrived and converted a field into an extreme motocross circuit before a crowd gathered, entertained with music, beers and bikers trying to ride up a high, near-vertical wall of earth and skim across a deep pool of water.

187

Stop #148: Sighișoara

Camping Aquaris (*aquariscamp.net*) ● GPS: N46.222918, E24.796507 ● Price Guide: ££ ● All Services ● **Alternative:** Mixed Parking, GPS: N46.218681, E24.788071, Price Guide: £, No Services, Noisy

German Saxon merchants and workers were invited to Sighișoara in Transylvania in the 12th Century and have long co-existed with native Romanians and Hungarians. The medieval fortified city they built is still well-preserved, sprouting stone towers, photogenic with pastel-painted houses and surrounded by wooded hills.

Each summer a medieval festival takes place with fighting knights, musicians, poets, storytellers and craftsmen and women. The town also has an association with Bram Stoker's Dracula as Vlad Dracul was exiled here, father of Vlad Țepeș (Vlad the Impaler), the real-life Romanian prince who served as the inspiration for the fictional count. Bram never actually visited Transylvania, and it's debateable how the locals feel about their national hero being the inspiration for a blood-thirsty vampire.

After a few night's off-site parking we were ready for a campsite. The pitches at Camping Aquaris were a little basic, closer to a grassy aire in nature, but were just a 10-minute walk through the old town to the hill-top citadel and the town's interesting cemetery.

The campsite drew in fellow travellers and we enjoyed an evening eating and drinking with British, German and Dutch motorhome tourers. The German couple had rescued a puppy and were going through the process of obtaining a pet passport so they could take it home.

Stop #149: Transfăgărășan Pass

Car Parking at the Pass ● GPS: N45.60252, E24.61380 ● Price Guide: £ ● No Services ● Typically Accessible June to October ● **Alternative:** Camping Transfăgărășan (*transfagarasan-camping.blogspot.com*), GPS: N45.570076, E24.611433, Price Guide: £, All Services

The BBC TV programme Top Gear visited the serpentine curves of the Transfăgărășan Pass in 2009, raising the question of whether it's the 'best road in the World'? That brought the DN7C highway, as the road is officially known, to international attention and diverted us across the Carpathian Mountains to make an ascent in our aging 3.1 tonne non-turbo motorhome.

We stayed the night before at an informal campsite alongside a stream, south of the Vidaru Dam, with a Polish biker sheltering from the hammering rain (GPS: N45.34511 E24.63483). The following morning, we headed north stopping off to photograph the impressive dam, keeping a close eye on the road ahead for small rocks strewn across the tarmac. Once past the dam we left the trees behind us, the landscape rises as hulking green-flanked mountains. The southern side of the pass is impressive, but the northern side, accessed via a tunnel at the top, is even more photogenic.

There are a few free-camping spots at the very top of the pass, but we opted to pay for parking to feel more relaxed. The pass is popular, busy with cars and bikers and we even spotted a chap on a unicycle. Cabins provided souvenirs and snacks, the owners sleeping in caravans rather than commuting all the way down and up the pass. Although it was July, there was enough snow for locals to snowboard jump over a 'kicker', handing us some of their dad's *țuică* (moonshine) in return for some mid-flight photos.

Stop #150: Vatra Moldoviței

Car Parking at the Moldovita Monastery ● GPS: N47.657336, E25.571756 ● Price Guide: Free
● No Services ● Check If OK With Nuns to Stay ● **Alternative:** Camping Cristal
(*vilacristalsucevita.ro*), GPS: N47.781979, E25.730826, Price Guide: £, All Services

The Moldovita Monastery stands in a peaceful courtyard to the north of Vatra Moldoviței in Moldavia. Like the other four Romanian 'painted monasteries', it's colourfully decorated inside and out in Eastern Orthodox style frescoes of Christian scenes.

The monastery was built in 1532, partly as a defensive structure at a time when Europe's Christians were fighting against Muslims of the Ottoman Empire. The front gate resembles the entrance to a stone castle. The paintings were added a few years later, predominantly in yellow and blue, and considering they're almost 500 years old they're incredibly vivid.

On our way to the Southern Bucovina region which houses the monasteries we passed medieval scenes of locals gathering hay with pitch forks, ready to feed livestock in winter (a single cow might eat a tonne of it). Long grass was heaped high onto carts pulled by horses along the road ahead of us or piled into stacks stood across the rolling fields. Stalls beside the road were selling huge green watermelons, piled in their hundreds.

The nuns charged a small fee to visit the monastery, checking our clothing was suitably modest before admitting us. Depictions of the Last Judgement cover the west wall, with demons ushering sinners into a river of fire, and the dead being given up by the sea. Saints, prophets and scenes from the life of Jesus are painted across the remaining walls.

After our tour a nun confirmed we could stay the night, where we planned our onward journey into Ukraine to the north.

SAN MARINO

QUICK FACTS ● **EU**: No ● **Schengen**: No, Stays Up to 10 Days Don't Require a Permit ● **Language**: Italian ● **Currency**: Euro (EUR, £1=€1.1) ● **Speed Limits**: Urban/Single/Expressway/Motorway: 50, 70, 110, 130kph ● **Tolls**: No ● **LEZs**: None ● **IDP**: 1968 ● **Docs**: Driving Licence, Insurance, Passport, V5C ● **Kit**: GB Sticker, Headlamp Deflectors ● **LPG**: Good Availability, Dish Adapter ● **Time**: UK+1 Hour ● **Daytime Dipped Headlights**: Yes ● **Overnighting**: One Campsite, Aires and Mixed Parking

San Marino is a landlocked microstate, surrounded by Italy, founded by a stonemason from modern-day Croatia who first came to Rimini before heading inland and into the mountains to escape persecution or seek isolation, building a church on Mount Titano. It's not in the Schengen Area, but it has no border controls either, so it's a simple process to enter, you might not even spot the 'RSM - Repubblica Di San Marino' sign as you enter.

The tiny 61km² San Marino shouldn't really exist, it's an odd and interesting place, a city-state in a land where all the city states are long gone. It's not in the Eurozone but uses the Euro, it has two concurrent heads of state chosen from opposing political parties in homage to the old Roman ways, it remained neutral in both WW1 and WW2, it has its own army and it has more vehicles than people (Italians register their cars here to get lower taxes).

The economy is supported by banking, tourism, ceramics, paint, wine, furniture and clothing, with more than 80% being exported to Italy. Oh, and it once scored a world cup goal against England in about 3 seconds flat, remember that?

San Marino has remained autonomous as much by luck as by judgement over the years. When the modern Italian national state was formed 150 years back, merging all but the Vatican and here into a single state, it retained independence as it had supported the *risorgimento* movement.

www.sanmarinoforall.com has details of all the motorhome parking areas and service points available. It also gives several walking routes around the old town, taking in museums, statues, viewpoints, city wall gates and gardens. In among all of this you'll find plenty of duty-free shops selling bags, sunglasses, watches, toys and replica weapons.

Stop #151: City of San Marino

Official Sosta at Parking P10 • GPS: N43.934457, E12.445147 • Price Guide: ££ • Only Electricity, Other Services on Via Gamella, GPS: N43.926063, E12.448142 • **Alternative:** Centro Vacanze San Marino Camping (*www.centrovacanzesanmarino.com*), GPS: N43.959159, E12.461667, Price Guide: ££ with CampingCard ACSI, All Services, Gets Good Reviews

We found San Marino easy to visit by motorhome, driving the SS72 dual carriageway from Rimini on the Italian coast and heading up to the large official overnight sosta at Parking P10 on the Via Napoleone Bonaparte. The roads were great quality, dual carriageway most of the way up into the city and easily accommodated our 2.2m wide motorhome. From Parking P10 it's a 30-minute walk to the panoramic views along the walls leading to the Guaita Tower.

Parking P10 has views west to the Apennines, the mountains which run down the spine of Italy. The parking area is clean and well-presented with large marked-out motorhome spaces, but on a slope so bring your levelling ramps.

For our second night in San Marino we headed down the hill to the free (and flat) Parking P13 (GPS: N43.940869, E12.442211) where we spent a quiet night alone. A nearby cable car (the *Funivia di San Marino*) lifts you up to the heights of the city but wasn't running when we visited in late March.

If you opt for San Marino's Centro Vacanze San Marino Camping, the site reception sells low-cost tickets for the bus which leaves from outside. The on-site restaurant also gets good reviews but if you want to use the swimming pool, remember to bring your bathing cap or you'll have to buy one first!

SLOVAKIA

QUICK FACTS ● **EU**: Yes ● **Schengen**: Yes ● **Language**: Slovak ● **Currency**: Euro (EUR, £1=€1.1) ● **Speed Limits** ≤3.5t: Urban/Single/Expressway/Motorway: 50, 90, 130, 130kph ● **Speed Limits >3.5t**: Urban/Single/Expressway/Motorway: 50, 90, 90, 90kph ● **Tolls**: Yes, ≤3.5t Buy E-Vignette at *eznamka.sk* or Windscreen Sticker at Border, >3.5t Pay per Km with On-Board Electronic Box (*www.emyto.sk*). ● **LEZs**: None ● **IDP**: Not Needed ● **Docs**: Driving Licence, Insurance, Passport, V5C ● **Kit**: GB Sticker, Headlamp Deflectors, Warning Triangle, First Aid Kit ● **LPG**: Good Availability, Dish Adapter ● **Time**: UK+1 Hour ● **Daytime Dipped Headlights**: Yes ● **Overnighting**: Campsites (*camp.cz*), Car Parks, Private Businesses, Free Camping Not Officially Allowed But Widely Tolerated, Especially in the East

Slovakia deserves more entries than the single one we've included in this book, Tatranská Lomnica, a cracking ski resort in the High Tatras mountains to the north of the country near the Polish border. To be fair to us (and Slovakia), the weather when we crossed the country was appalling, so we travelled faster than we normally would.

Bratislava would be included in this book, the country's capital with Camping Zlate Piesky just a tram ride away (GPS: N48.188215, E17.185366), but we'd already visited on a city break before arriving in the country in our motorhome. After arriving from Austria, our first stop in Slovakia was Devin Castle (free car park: GPS: N48.17595, E16.97962), which is a 30-minute bus ride into Bratislava if you want to visit the city.

From there we headed east, enjoying a stop-off in Trnava, staying for a few hours to walk the picturesque cobbled streets, climb the City Tower and enjoy the street market. Trnava has no campsites and feeling like we'd seen what we wanted to see, we opted to carry on east to Trenčín.

Trenčín has a city centre campsite, Autocamping Trenčín na Ostrove (GPS: N48.900110, E18.041042), which we'd probably use these days, but back then we opted to sleep on a residential street by the noisy football stadium, eased to sleep by some strong real ale sold at a small brewery in the town!

Next, we headed for the mountains, staying for a night at a car park in Liptovský Mikuláš, (GPS: N49.07988, E19.61193) before decamping to Tatranská Lomnica, which is described on the next page.

Stop #152: Tatranská Lomnica

Ski Lift Parking ● GPS: N49.167301, E20.271299 ● Price Guide: Free ● Toilets Only, Paid Services at Slnečný Dom Restaurant (GPS: N49.166634, E20.282345) ● **Alternative:** Camping Vysoke Tatry (*www.campingvysoketatry.sk*), GPS: N49.143854, E20.294285, Price Guide: ££, All Services, 4km from Tatranská Lomnica

Lomnický štít (Lomnicky peak) is the second highest mountain in Slovakia's High Tatras, rising to 2,634m above sea level. Since 1940 it's been possible to ride up to the peak from Tatranská Lomnica by cable car, allowing you to wander around the summit taking in the views for 50 minutes. That's if there are any views. Check the weather forecast before buying your tickets, or you may end up with your head in the clouds like us!

The cable car journey up is in three stages from the car park where we stayed for a few nights at Tatranská Lomnica. The final car is only large enough for 15 people, so you must book a timed slot. The weather hadn't been good as we crossed Slovakia, so when the sky cleared, we decided to try our luck. On reaching the final cable car station it was obvious we'd not get the magnificent views the top is famous for, as the tiny car disappeared into cloud. We genuinely enjoyed it up there anyway, an ice and snow-blasted world in mid-May, with occasional glimpses of the surrounding peaks.

Back at base we headed to Restaurant Fiaker, with tables fashioned to resemble horse-drawn coaches. Our starter consisted of a slab of thick, fatty bacon, pickled peppers and paté, followed by cheese and bacon in gnocchi and ravioli.

The cable car has a large free parking area where we stayed for three nights with no problems and it has direct access to hikes in the surrounding hills.

194

SLOVENIA

> **QUICK FACTS** ● **EU:** Yes ● **Schengen:** Yes ● **Language:** Slovene ● **Currency:** Euro (EUR, £1=€1.1) ● **Speed Limits ≤3.5t:** Urban/Single/Expressway/Motorway: 50, 90, 110, 130kph ● **Speed Limits >3.5t:** Urban/Single/Expressway/Motorway: 50, 80, 80, 90kph ● **Tolls:** Yes, ≤3.5t Buy Windscreen Vignette at Border (*dars.si*), >3.5t Pay per Km with On-Board Electronic Box (*darsgo.si*). Karavanke Tunnel to Austria is Toll ● **LEZs:** None ● **IDP:** Not Needed ● **Docs:** Driving Licence, Insurance, Passport, V5C ● **Kit:** GB Sticker, Headlamp Deflectors, Warning Triangle, First Aid Kit, Fire Extinguisher, Spare Bulb Kit, Reflective Jackets ● **LPG:** Good Availability, Dish Adapter ● **Time:** UK+1 Hour ● **Daytime Dipped Headlights:** Yes ● **Overnighting:** Campsites, Aires, Free Camping Not Legal and Likely to Be Enforced In More Visited Locations

Slovenia was the first country we drove into east of the old Iron Curtain. We expected rough road surfaces, run-down towns and cheap prices, none of which were true! Slovenia has long been a tourist destination, along with Croatia to the south, contributing hard currency income to the former Yugoslavia.

Slovenia endured the 'Ten Day War' in 1991 to secure its independence from Yugoslavia, which its citizens had overwhelmingly supported in a referendum. Foreseeing armed resistance to their move, the Slovenian government prepared for war in the lead up to the referendum, secretly mobilising 21,000 troops and police, who took control of the Yugoslav People's Army (JNA) stationed in Slovenia. The Slovenes also wrong-footed the Yugoslav government by declaring independence 24 hours earlier than anyone expected.

These days Slovenia is well and truly on the tourism map, with top-class destinations including Lake Bled, the capital Ljubljana, the magnificent Postojna Cave, the Triglav National Park, and the diminutive but attractive Vintgar Gorge.

Slovenia also has 47km of coast on the Adriatic Sea, with the pretty resort towns of Koper, Izola and Piran. The coast is reputed to be very crowded in the summer season, and the network of aires and campsites are pricey.

The country's Škocjan and Postojna Caves are also very popular attractions (the latter has an adjacent aire at GPS: N45.780430, E14.203598).

Stop #153: Bled & Vintgar Gorge

Camping Bled (*www.sava-camping.com/si/camping-bled*) ● GPS: N46.361616, E14.081812 ● Price Guide: £££ ● All Services ● Lakeside Location ● **Alternative:** Official Aire, GPS: N46.370314, E14.118349, Price Guide: £££, All Services, 1km from Lake Bled

Lake Bled is reputed to be one of the most picturesque spots in Slovenia, a small lake in the Julian Alps with a castle perched on an adjacent hillside, a pretty island to row to, hikes and even a summer toboggan (on rails, we had a go and it was a ton of fun).

The lake's reputation means it draws plenty of international visitors and the staff at the only campsite (on the opposite end of the lake to the town of Bled) all speak perfect English, as does pretty much every Slovenian we met, as well as German, and French for that matter.

The site takes the CampingCard ACSI, and with it is much cheaper to visit out of the main summer season. Since we visited an aire has also opened in Bled itself, although it's the same price as the campsite with the discount. For views over the lake, look out for the hike up the 610m Ojstrica Hill above the campsite.

As well as exploring the lakeside, the area around Lake Bled has some lesser visited but impressive attractions to draw you. A twenty-minute drive to the north brings you to the Vintgar Gorge, a mile-long crack in solid rock above the small pure-green Radovna River, along which you can walk on boardwalks and bridges (GPS: N46.392224, E14.084256).

An hour's drive west of Bled takes you to the famous Vršič Pass, a 1,611m high mountain road in the Julian Alps, built by 10,000 Russian POWs in 1915. We did the drive in our friend's car and it looked testing but possible in a motorhome.

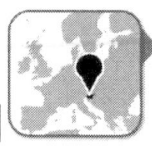

Stop #154: Izola

Mixed Parking with Official 24-Hour Camper Bays ● GPS: N45.538836, E13.664141 ● Price Guide: ££ ● No Services ● **Alternative:** Official Aire, GPS: N45.532843, E13.649136, Price Guide: ££, All Services, Noisy at Weekends

Izola stands on Slovenia's short stretch of Adriatic coastline, originally an island until it's town walls were dismantled and used to fill in the gap with the mainland in the 19th Century. After WW1, the area was assigned to Italy, and almost everyone in the town spoke Italian. With the conclusion of WW2 the town was subsequently incorporated into Slovenia (a part of Yugoslavia at the time), and many of the Italian speaking populace left for Italy, being replaced with Slovenian speakers from surrounding villages.

The town has a sea-facing campsite 1km from the old town (*www.jadranka-avtocamp.si*), an official aire with services and a few mixed parking locations which allow overnight stays. We opted for one of the latter, squeezing into one of the car parking spots as the camper bays were all full in early June.

We didn't plan it, but just happened to arrive the weekend of the town's yearly Olive, Wine and Fish Festival! During the day we watched the locals attempt to wind surf in becalmed conditions, fuelled on with Red Bull and Laško beer. Later that evening we wandered into town, paying for a couple of empty glasses before ambling around the narrow cobbled streets of the old fishing village, busy with fellow revellers, tasting several local wines and snacking on chips while being entertained by musicians.

The town also has an annual beer festival during the Easter holidays (*www.visitizola.com*), and a marathon runs through in April (*istrski-maraton.si*).

Stop #155: Kočevski Rog

Camp 20 Car Park ● GPS: N45.69696, E15.04936 ● Price Guide: Free ● No Services ● Brown Bears, Wolves and Lynx in Surrounding Forest ● **Alternative:** Camperstop Stara Vrtnarija Grm, Novo Mesto, GPS: N45.795390, E15.170545, Price Guide: ££, All Services, Gets Good Reviews

Kočevski Rog is a forested plateau in the Kočevje Highlands to the south-west of Novo Mesto with a violent and terrible history. In late 1945, after WW2 had formally ended in Europe, thousands of pro-Nazi Slovenians attempted to escape the Russian army along with German soldiers by fleeing to British forces in Austria. The British turned them away, repatriating them to Slovenia where over 10,000 men, women and children were bussed into the Rog and shot, their bodies falling into natural pits in the ground which were then sealed with explosives.

After staying in a free aire in Kočevje (GPS: N45.64433, E14.87113), our drive up into the forest was a nerve-wracking experience as the road turned first to gravel and then to mud. At one point a logging truck saw us hesitate and encouraged us onwards. As we approached the site of the pits, carved trees appeared, depicting the fallen and we felt a sense of impending dread. The pits proved a very moving experience, the larger ones marked with signs and one had a memorial, but they were otherwise untouched in the eerily-silent forest.

Further down the road towards Novo Mesto we arrived at the site of Baza 20 (Camp 20), one of several secret bases used by Slovene partisans during WW2. The wooden huts and field hospitals lie in folds in the earth and through clever and determined means (no fires, even in deep winter, raisable walkways used to access the paths to avoid leaving tracks in snow), the Axis forces never located it. When we went to ask the guide how to pay, he told us the visit was free, we were his guests and more than welcome to stay the night in the car park.

Stop #156: Ljubljana

Ljubljana Resort Campsite (*www.ljubljanaresort.si*) ● GPS: N46.09871, E14.51898 ● Price Guide: ££ ● All Services ● **Alternative:** Official Aire at Dolgi Most Park 'n' Ride, GPS: N46.036329, E14.462249, Price Guide: £, All Services, Noisy

Slovenia's capital city Ljubljana is a compact affair, one of Europe's smallest capitals, vibrant and straightforward to explore the centre on foot. It's served by the Ljubljana Resort Campsite 5km to the north, an easy bus journey. The site takes the CampingCard ACSI so is inexpensive out of season, but quite pricey otherwise.

Several official aires and parking spots are also available, some very central and most of them cheaper than the campsite. None get stand-out reviews on *campercontact.com*, with some comments focussed on noisy surroundings and relatively high parking fees (although cities do tend to be noisy and expensive).

Ljubljana was largely flattened by an earthquake in 1895 and has been rebuilt in an impressive, easy-on-the-eye Art Nouveau style. In lists of the top things to do in the city, outside spaces feature highly, focussed on Prešeren Square and the three decorated bridges which lead away from it, the *Tromostovje*. A five-minute walk east brings you to the Dragon Bridge, adorned with the mythical creatures which are an emblem for the city.

Overlooking the city from a hill, you can get up to the 11th Century castle on foot or via a funicular or tourist train. The main courtyard is free to enter. Tivoli Park lies a km from the centre and has 5km² of formal gardens and picnic areas.

The Ljubljana tourist info website has more information on the city's top 10 attractions and upcoming events: *www.visitljubljana.com*.

SPAIN

QUICK FACTS ● **EU**: Yes ● **Schengen**: Yes ● **Languages**: Spanish, Catalan, Aranese, Valencian, Galician, Basque ● **Currency**: Euro (EUR, £1=€1.1) ● **Speed Limits ≤3.5t**: Urban/Single/Expressway/Motorway: 50, 90, 120, 120kph ● **Speed Limits >3.5t**: Urban/Single/Expressway/Motorway: 50, 80, 90, 90kph ● **Tolls**: Yes, On Around 20% of the Motorway Network, Pay in Cash or Cards at Booths ● **LEZs**: Yes, In Barcelona and Madrid ● **IDP**: Not Needed ● **Docs**: Driving Licence, Insurance, Passport, V5C ● **Kit**: GB Sticker, Headlamp Deflectors, Reflective Jackets, Signal Board for Bike Rack ● **LPG**: Good Availability, Bayonet and Euroconnector Adapters ● **Time**: UK+1 Hour (Canary Islands UK Time) ● **Daytime Dipped Headlights**: Yes ● **Overnighting**: Campsites, Aires, Business Parking (*espana-discovery.es*), Free Camping Laws Vary with Region, Widely Tolerated Away from Hotspots

Spain's a magnificent country to tour by motorhome, and large numbers of British, Dutch, German, French and Scandinavian visitors do just that. From the UK you can be in Northern Spain in 24 hours, hardly turning a wheel, by taking an overnight ferry to Santander or Bilboa. Alternatively, cross France and the Pyrenees where they bow to the sea (there are toll motorways or slower toll-free routes in both the east and west). Or finally head up and over the mountains, if snow conditions allow, perhaps taking in Andorra on the way.

Spain is very accommodating to motorhome (*autocaravana*) tourists, with *search4sites.co.uk* listing over 500 touring campsites and 1,500 motorhome stopovers. That's not including many thousands of unofficial 'wild camping' locations.

With only the barest degree of forward planning we've toured Spain several times, enjoying the mountains, Mediterranean and Atlantic coasts, the delicious food and wine, laid-back locals, vibrant cities, historical locations and the white Andalusian *pueblos*, a remnant of Spain's 500 years of North African Muslim rule.

Spain is made up of 'autonomous communities': Madrid, Catalonia, Galacia, Valencia and so on. Each of these has its own culture, climate, landscapes and often even language. We've found the descriptions of each region on the *about-spain.net* website to be useful, as well as the maps of toll-free routes and descriptions of local traffic laws.

Stop #157: Ansó

Village Car Park ● GPS: N42.756176, W0.825546 ● Price Guide: Free ● No Services ●
Alternative: Camping Valle de Ansó (*www.campingvalledeanso.net*), GPS: N42.752422, W0.829393, Price Guide: ££, All Services

Having bought a new (to us) motorhome, we decided to try it by first heading across France to the western end of the Pyrenees. We'd then cross into Spain and travel down to the eastern end of the mountains where they meet the Med, and then back up through France again. All worked out really well, although to experience the mountains we had to make forays up narrow, winding roads, which were rewarding but tiring on the driver, so we'd spend some nights on flatter land on the Spanish side.

At one point we stayed for a couple of nights at the free aire at Sos Del Ray Católico, south-east of Pamplona (GPS: N42.491410, W1.213881), being entertained by a flock of swirling Griffin Vultures, and meeting a young couple spending a year touring Europe. The following day we headed north towards the mountains.

With no planning other than an overnight stop, we were delighted to come across the Foz de Arbayún, taking a detour off the NA-178 to a mirador (viewpoint) with a view of the 100m deep gorge pictured above (GPS: N42.691437, W1.184214).

At Ansó, one of us did a quick recce on foot, to make sure our satnav wasn't trying to get us stuck in the narrow streets. Parked up, we enjoyed a first taste of *migas*, a shepherd's meal made with breadcrumbs, oil, ham and mushrooms. Our handbrake slipped off that afternoon and we rolled backwards into trees, damaging a rear light cluster. These days we always park with the van in gear!

201

Stop #158: Barcelona

Camping 3 Estrellas (*www.tresestrellascampings.com/barcelona*) ● GPS: N41.272280, E2.042874 ● Price Guide: ££ With CampingCard ACSI ● All Services ● 40-Mins Bus Ride to City Centre ● **Alternative**: BSM Bus Garcia Fària Underground Parking, GPS: N41.406726, E2.218624, Price Guide: ££, No Services, Max 7m Long, Reserve Online at *www.aparcamentsbsm.cat/els-aparcaments/per-a-vehicules-de-mides-especials*

Barcelona is Spain's most visited city, the capital of Catalonia set alongside the Mediterranean. It's the fifth largest urban area in Europe, and since 2020 has a permanent low emission zone covering all the central area bounded by the B-10 and B-20 ring roads, plus some areas outside them. The ring roads themselves are exempt, so any vehicle can transit the city.

When we visited Barcelona in 2012, we first used one of the coastal campsites to the south of the city (Camping 3 Estrellas looks like the best option these days). Here we discovered dogs aren't allowed on the Spanish bus system unless they're small enough to fit in a carry on container, so we found a city centre parking area and built up the courage to drive there! Sadly it's since been developed, and would be inside the LEZ anyway, but there's still an underground car park which accepts motorhomes if you want to stay in the city itself (expect to be awake at 7am and for it to be hot below ground at night).

Gaudí's Sagrada Família and Park Güell were highlights for us. We took an open top bus tour to get a look at the wider city, including FC Barcelona's stadium, Parc de Montjuïc for views over the city, the old port and the Olympic Park. In the evening we enjoyed walking the Las Ramblas boulevard and the charming *Barri Gòtic*, the Gothic Quarter.

202

Stop #159: Benarrabá

Official Aire ● GPS: N36.549403, W5.278921 ● Price Guide: £ ● All Services ● **Alternative**: Official Aire at Casares, GPS: N36.446031, W5.278462, Price Guide: Free, All Services Except Electricity

Just a few miles inland from the coast brings you to Andalusia's *pueblos blancos*, the white towns. These tightly-packed clusters of white-washed, red-roofed buildings huddled around a hillside are incredibly picturesque and characterful. Many of them are easy to visit by motorhome, some with low-cost or free aires or mixed parking areas.

We've found the pueblos blancos offer a complete contrast to the resorts along the coast. Quiet and calm, with authentic tapas bars and resturants where you can discretely people-watch the locals or make attempts to converse if your Spanish is up to it! The ones we've visited have offered wonderful vistas of the surrounding mountains, often sun-bathed even in the deep winter.

We've listed the village of Benarrabá, north of Estepona, in this book as we had a memorable stay in the aire there. A couple of other British motorhomes parked up along with a fascinating, eccentric, English-speaking Frenchman who, in his 70s, was living in a tiny Citroën Berlingo van with his dog. He was an easy-going sort, with stories of living with tribes in South America, publishing books and living as a goatherd.

Our mini-community enjoyed shared food and drinks in the evening, walking trails in the surrounding oak forest in the day. A viewpoint above the town has signs showing the migration routes of birds returning across the skies above from Africa.

We also enjoyed the free aire at Casares (GPS: N36.446031, W5.278462) and the mirador parking outside Algatocín (GPS: N36.564698, W5.282219).

Stop #160: Cangas de Onís

Official Aire ● GPS: N43.352201, W5.125484 ● Price Guide: Free ● All Services Except Electricity ● **Alternative**: Camping Picos de Europa (*www.picos-europa.com*) at Avín, GPS: N43.334654, W4.947197, Price Guide: ££, All Services

When we arrived in Northern Spain we'd no idea what to expect. Our idea of Spain was based mainly on the beaches and resorts of the south, the Balearics and the Canary Islands, and we were taken aback when we discovered the rugged Picos de Europa National Park.

We soon found the roads into the park can be a little testing in a motorhome, narrow, sometimes with cliffs on one side and sheer drops on the other. However, the 23km route from our overnight aire in the Asturian town of Cangas de Onís up to the circular walk around the mountain lakes of Enol and Ercina proved easily passable for our 5.5m and our friends' 7m long motorhomes. The car park by the lakes is only suitable for day parking (GPS: N43.276897, W4.986055) so we returned back to Cangas afterwards.

An attempt to reach the southern end of the famous Cares Gorge walk (an old and spectacular hydro-electric maintanance path carved into a cliff face) at Caín wasn't so successful. As the road got tighter and tighter we bottled it, parked up and walked the last couple of miles.

In retrospect (if we'd done our research!) a location like Camping Naranjo de Bulnes (*www.campingnaranjodebulnes.com*) near Las Arenas would have made a better base for the Cares hike (GPS: N43.299865, W4.803056). The start of the hike is at Poncebos (as is the funicular up to the mountain village of Bulnes, the start of more walks), a 20-minute bus ride from Las Arenas.

Stop #161: Córdoba

Official Aire ● GPS: N37.874545, W4.786838 ● Price Guide: ££ ● All Services ● 1km to the Mezquita ● **Alternative**: Campingred Córdoba (*www.campingcordoba.com*), GPS: N37.953460, W4.553898, Price Guide: ££ with CampingCard ACSI, All Services,

Córdoba was once the second-largest city in Europe, a centre of learning and discovery during the Caliphate of Córdoba. We were drawn to the city by the same architectural wonder that attracts around 1.5 million other tourists each year: the Mezquita, a UNESCO World Heritage Site. Built over a period of 200 years during the Islamic rule of Spain, the former mosque is now over 1,000 years old.

After the area was retaken by the Christians, the mosque was used as a church and, around 1500AD, a catholic cathedral was inserted into the middle, sticking up out of the roof of the old mosque, rendering it the oddest hybrid between Islamic and Renassance styles.

Apparently the king who gave permission for the cathedral did so without seeing the work, and was none too impressed when he saw the final result! It's left a magnificient and unique monument for us modern day travellers though, with rank upon rank of red and white Islamic arches standing side to side with images of Jesus on the cross.

Córdoba's official aire is only a 1km walk from the Mezquita, the city's Roman Bridge and the maze-like Jewish area just to the north. The aire appears to be a converted car park, as the entrance barriers are quite tight to get through, the whole area slopes and the spaces are all car-sized. It was calm at night though and felt very safe.

If you fancy a campsite instead, Campingred Córdoba is only a 35-minute bus ride away to the east of the city (details above).

Stop #162: Donostia-San Sebastián

Official Aire • GPS: N43.307428, W2.013752 • Price Guide: £ • All Services Except Electricity • 1km Walk to Beach, 4km Walk or Cycle to Old Town • Popular, Arrive Early • **Alternative:** Camping Igueldo San Sebastián, GPS: N43.304794, W2.045899, Price Guide: ££ with CampingCard ACSI, All Services, Bus to San Sebastián

Set around La Concha Bay, this beach city is one of our favourite places in Northern Spain. The dual carriageways leading into the bay pop in and out of tunnels beneath the surrounding hills, and you need to be on your toes to spot the correct exit as you emerge into the sunlight.

The city has an official aire about 1km from the beach by the university, in a quiet area for a great night's sleep. Despite San Sebastián being one of Spain's most expensive cities, the aire is low cost and allows you to stay for up to three nights. If you have push bikes, off-road cycle paths will take you into the old town in 10 or 15 minutes (or it's a pleasant walk around Concha Bay). Once there you can enjoy the *pinxtos* the city is famous for, pieces of bread with various tasty toppings, held on with a skewer.

The city has two names, Donostia-San Sebastián, as it has two identities, Basque and Spanish. You'll spot the Basque language everywhere, the aire is an *autokarabanak* for example, hello is *kaixo*, pronounced kai-sho and thank you is *eskerrik asko*, es-care-rick ass-co.

For us the university city of Donostia-San Sebastián has a vibrant, orderly, cosmopoliant feel. Locals can pop for their lunch break at 2pm, surf for 90 minutes and be back ready to restart work at 4. Leaving the office at the usual Spanish time of 8pm, they might refresh themselves in their favourite bar with a glass of Rioja before walking or taking the bus home. Work-life balance in action.

Stop #163: Granada

Camping Reina Isabel (*campingreinaisabel.com*) ● GPS: N37.124615, W3.585921 ● Price Guide: ££ with CampingCard ACSI ● All Services ● 15-Min Bus to City ● **Alternative:** Camping Alto de Viñuelas (*campingaltodevinuelas.com*), GPS: N37.224590, W3.488667, Price Guide: ££ with CampingCard ACSI, All Services, 35-Min Bus Ride to City

The biggest tourist draw at Granada is the Alhambra, a 14th Century palace built by the Islamic Moors and later employed as the Royal Court by the Christian re-conquitadors Ferdinand and Isabella. The palace and fortress complex plus the adjacent Generalife gardens are on the UNESCO world heritage list, and require a good few hours to explore, and a lot of space in your camera's memory!

The Alhambra is very popular and buying a ticket in advance makes sense. You can buy them online at *www.alhambra-patronato.es*, or from Camping Reina Isabel, but you may need to stay at least two, probably three nights if you do this. We took a risk and turned up at the Alhambra entrance ticket office on a Friday morning, and were lucky to get access straight away. The site didn't disappoint, with spectacular architecture and decoration which shone a light on the greatness of Spain's Moorish past. The views from the gardens are extraordinary.

For panoramic views of the Alhambra and Generalife head for the Mirador de San Nicolás, in the Albaicín (the old Arab quarter). This small square is accessible on foot about 1km from the cathedral or several bus routes pass nearby (GPS: N37.181041, W3.592662).

With children on board you might also want to take a look at the Parque de las Ciencias (the Science Park), a 15-min walk from the centre of Granada, with a planetarium, butterfly park, interactive museum and viewing platform.

Stop #164: Guadix

Official Aire ● GPS: N37.303682, W3.133730 ● Price Guide: Free ● All Services Except Electricity ● **Alternative**: Camping Alpujarras (*campingalpujarras.es*), GPS: N37.012053, W3.012243, Price Guide: ££, All Services, 50km South of Guadix

Almost half the population of Guadix lives underground, protected from the Andalusian summer heat. Most of the 2,000 caves were dug 500 or 600 years ago, although some are believed to date back 1,000 years, to the time of the Moors who built the Guadix Alcazaba fortress which still stands above the town. Many of the caves were built by refugees from wars, choosing to dig into the soft rock to provide shelter for their families.

We took in the trogolyte district from a couple of purpose-built viewpoints. Standing in the late February sunshine, we peered out at the rocky landscape with chimneys sprouting upwards like whitewashed sentinels under a blue sky. The snow-capped bulk of the Sierra Nevada provided a stunning backdrop, rising high above the desert-like plain.

Afterwards we took a walk through the cave district observing the variety in building styles.

There's no campsite around Guadix, but the town officially allows motorhomes to stay in a large parking area a short walk from the centre. The aire is reputed to be noisy at the weekend (we woke one day to a hot air balloon taking off in front behind our van, not a bad alarm clock!).

If you want the facilities of a site, you could use the aire to park for the day and then head 30 miles south to Camping Alpujarras. This would make a good base for heading west along the A-4130 exploring the Alpujarran mountain villages made famous by Chris Stewart's *Driving Over Lemons*.

Stop #165: La Jarosa Reservoir

Lakeside Car Park ● GPS: N40.670110, W4.127016 ● Price Guide: Free ● No Services ● 12km from Valley of the Fallen ● **Alternative**: Camping Capfun El Escorial (*www.capfun.com*), GPS: N40.626597, W4.099639, Price Guide: ££ with CampingCard ACSI, All Services

The packed earth car park at La Jarosa Reservoir proved a calm stopover for us as we crossed Spain on the way back to France and the UK, located to the north-west of Madrid off the AP-6 motorway. From the parking area we could see the monumental cross of the *Valle de los Caídos*, the Valley of the Fallen, the reason we'd opted to take this route home.

The Valley of the Fallen isn't a tourist attraction, but it is reminder of how Spain tore itself apart in the 1930s. It's the controversial mass grave location of over 40,000 people killed in the Spanish Civil War. Francisco Franco led the victorious Nationalist side in the war and was Spain's subsequent dictator until 1975. He was also buried at the Valley until 2019 when his remains were exhumed and moved.

No-one knows how many were killed in the war, hundreds of thousands of soldiers and civilians died and terrible atrocities were committed by both sides. Franco oversaw the building of a cavernous Catholic basilica afterwards, partly with forced labour, and claimed the location to be a place of conciliation. Many Spaniards don't see it that way however, and the brutal, overpowering architecture such as the huge 150m tall cross are seen as paying homage to fascism and the dictator himself

After Franco died Spain decided to politically 'forget' the civil war and the Franco era, in order to allow the country to move forwards. Subsequent laws have enabled Spain to start formally accepting the past, locating loved ones buried in around 2,000 mass graves across the country, for example.

Stop #166: Madrid

Official Aire at Pinto (*www.ayto-pinto.es/area-de-servicio-de-autocaravanas*) ● GPS: N40.238402, W3.690751 ● Price Guide: £ ● All Services Except Electricity ● 1 Mile Walk to Train Station, 30-Min Train Ride to Centre of City ● CCTV ● **Alternative:** Camping Internacional Aranjuez (*www.campingaranjuez.com*), GPS: N40.042222, W3.599425, Price Guide: ££ with CampingCard ACSI, All Services, 35-Min Fast Train to Madrid

After staying in the aire at Pinto and visiting Madrid we drove south to the campsite at Aranjuez, only realising at that point that the faster trains from the town took only a few minutes longer than the slow trains from Pinto to reach the centre of Madrid! The aire was fine though, clean and low cost, but located next to the Autovía A-4 motorway and a shopping centre, so a little noisy. It was monitored by CCTV, and we had no problems leaving the van all day, but it didn't feel as secure as the Aranjuez campsite.

Madrid's a fairly compact city, although with the walk to the train station in Pinto we covered about eight miles on foot each day. The city has a metro system if you're not able to do that, and plenty of taxis.

The Puerta de Atocha train station is convenient for the Prado and Museo Reina Sofía, with the excellent Museo Arqueológico Nacional a 2km walk to the north. The Puerta de Sol station is best used for the Royal Palace, Gran Vía and Mercado de San Miguel.

Having done all that walking we rewarded ourselves with *churros* and *taza de chocolate* (donut sticks and a cup of thick hot chocolate) at Chocolatería 1902, and *bocadillos de morcilla* and *de calamares* (blood sausage and squid sandwiches) at Casa Rúa by Plaza Mayor, delicious! Be aware that Madrid gets cold in winter, the odd snowy day isn't unusual from December to February.

Stop #167: Montserrat

Car Park of the Santa Maria de Montserrat Abbey ● GPS: N41.59665, E1.83860 ● Price Guide: £ ● No Services ● Sloping Site ● **Alternative:** Aire in Monistrol de Montserrat, GPS: N41.612573, E1.843524, Price Guide: Free, All Services Except Electricity, Ignore SatNav Instructions to Drive Through the Town (Roads Too Tight)

Having a motorhome allows you to sleep in some bonkers places! While it might not sound salubrius, the car park for the Montserrat Abbey was an unforgettable place for us to spend a couple of nights.

The parking area is carved into the side of a cliff face, below the highest 1,200m peak of the Montserrat mountain range. It's well paved and walled, so you won't roll off down the cliff below, but it slopes and only a handful of places are remotely flat. Bring your ramps. Overnight parking is officially allowed, and if you're unable to get anywhere approaching level, the staff are said to allow use of the flat coach area at the top when the busses have all left for the evening, on the agreement you'll move by 8am.

The Benedictine Abbey with its Virgin of Montserrat statue, is just around the corner. The Abbey was violently surpressed in the Spanish Civil War, with 22 of the monks murdered, but today is again a peaceful and popular spot, clustered along a cliff-face with wonderful views of the Catalan countryside and the Pyrenees to the north. The historic boy's choir (the Escolanía) is popular, singing every day in the Abbey at 1pm (*www.escolania.cat*).

Montserrat is a natural park, with signs marking hiking routes which can be joined together to make an eight mile loop, nothing too technical but a few steps and hills on the way up to the viewpoint on Sant Jeroni, the highest peak in the range. A group of *cabra montés* (mountain goats) added excitement on the way down.

Stop #168: Nerja

Aula de Naturaleza, Cortijo San Miguel Campsite (*www.campingcortijosanmiguel.com*) ● GPS: N36.746946, W3.898696 ● Price Guide: £££, ££ for Month+ Stays ● All Services ●
Alternative: Camper Area MiluCar (*milucar.es*), GPS: N36.732596, W3.942953, Price Guide: ££, All Services, Located In Torrox-Costa 6km from Nerja

Nerja lies to the far eastern end of the Costa del Sol, and retains a relatively low key, low rise ambience. The town's set on small cliffs with a series of sandy bays facing the Mediterranean.

The first time we visited Nerja we arrived outside the gates of the town's only campsite around 1km from the centre, decided it looked too scruffy and carried on driving. The second time we got past the gates, finding it to be an oasis of calm, a family-run site with pitches set beneath avocado, fig, banana and cherimoya (custard apple) trees. The site's mainly used by overwintering 'snowbirds', northern Europeans drawn by the favourable climate with average highs of around 16°C in January.

After touring Europe on and off for several years Nerja was the first place we opted to stay for a full month, almost halving the daily rate on the campsite and getting to know the area well.

In addition to the restuarants, shops and walks in Nerja, regular buses run to the photogenic white town of Frigiliana, just to the north, alongside the Sierras de Tejeda, Almijara y Alhama natural park. The mountains of the park are accessible via trails, with the 1,508m peak of El Cielo providing stupendous views of the eastern Axarquía area. The hike up the Chillar River is a big draw too, but expect very wet feet as the river is often the path!

Nerja's also famous across Spain for the monumental caves in Maro, just to the east of the town (*www.cuevadenerja.es*).

Stop #169: Port Lligat

Restaurant Parking ● GPS: N42.295193, E3.287024 ● Price Guide: £ ● No Services ● 300m from Salvador Dalí House Museum ● **Alternative**: Camping Rodas (*www.campingrodas.com*), GPS: N42.268882, E3.152534, Price Guide: ££ with CampingCard ACSI, All Services, Located In Roses 20km from Port Lligat

After being thrown out of his family home in Cadaqués, the famous surrealist artist Salvador Dalí and his girlfriend (later his wife) Gala bought a fisherman's cabin at the nearby village of Port Lligat, drawn to the location by the landscape, the light and the isolation of the place.

Over the years they bought surrounding properties, expanding the cabin into a seaside villa. Dalí lived there until 1982, when he moved to Púbol Castle, 60km to the south, after his wife's death. Today the villa has been preserved as an intimate museum. The guided tour takes you through the rooms in the house, giving a wonderful impression of the artist and his wife's living and working space, a real privilege for Dalí fans.

Dalí's works aren't on display in his old home, they're spread around the world, but if you're in the area the Dalí Theatre-Museum in Figueres is well worth a visit to see some of them.

We arrived at Port Lligat, which retains its isolated fishing village ambience, after tackling the endlessly twisting road from Empuriabrava, a surreal place in itself, a huge villa-marina complex on the Bay of Roses. The flat parking area in the village is set back from the sea along a short dirt road by the Xiringuito Can Juli, but the restaurant was closed when we visited in December so we were lucky to get a free, quiet night.

Stop #170: Santiago de Compostela

Campsite "As Cancelas" (*www.campingascancelas.com*) ● GPS: N42.889337, W8.524404 ● Price Guide: £££ ● All Services ● **Alternative**: Official Aire "Aparcadoiro de Salgueiriños" (*www.tussa.org*), GPS: N42.894391, W8.531896, Price Guide: ££, All Services Except Electricity

According to legend, Santiago de Compostela in Galicia, north-west Spain, is the burial place of the apostle Saint James. In the 9th Century, 800 years after the saint's death, he is said to have miraculously appeared on a white horse in the midst of a battle helping a Christian army kill over 5,000 of their Islamic foe, leading to the title 'The Moor Slayer'.

While there's no proof the battle even took place, or that James's remains ever came to Spain, the legend was powerful enough for Santiago to become a major pilgrim destination, with walkers taking 'The Way' or 'The Camino', one of dozens of long-distance routes leading to city.

The longest of the six main routes, Camino del Norte, is 514 miles and takes around a month to finish. We travelled to Galicia in a less energetic fashion, driving our motorhome near to one of the main routes across the north of Spain, marked out with the symbol of a scallop shell.

We arrived in December, in awe of the walkers arriving outside the cathedral at the end of their camino. Some were in tears in front of the elaborate Pórtico de la Gloria, hugging one another as the wind howled and rain splattered the ground. A host of carved figures peer out from the façade. Four trumpet-blowing angels symbolise the four corners of the world, from which pilgrims continue to arrive.

On the day of our visit the interior was quiet, the confessionals empty and the famous *Botafumeiro* (the 80kg chain-swinging incense burner) hung smokeless, but the cathedral still exuded history and power, it was quite an experience.

Stop #171: Seville

Official Aire at Port of Gelves (*www.puertogelves.es*) ● GPS: N37.338816, W6.024340 ● Price Guide: ££ ● All Services ● 25-Min Bus to City, or 10-Min via Uber Taxi ● **Alternative:** Official Aire "Parking Caravane" (*parkingcaravane.com*), GPS: N37.410678, W5.940791, Price Guide: ££, All Services, 20-Min Bus Ride to City, 24 Hour Security

Seville is marked out in our memories for its magnificent architecture and lively nightlife! We opted to stay at the marina alongside the Guadalquivir River to the south to avoid driving into the city centre, for a relatively quiet night's sleep and for the 24 hour security. If you'd prefer a campsite, Camping Villsom is the only option relatively close to the city, located at Dos Hermanas, a 40-min bus ride away (GPS: N37.277479, W5.936387).

Seville's the capital of Andalusia, the largest city in the community and the 4th largest in Spain (hence our desire to avoid driving anywhere near the centre). Like much of southern Spain, it can get uncomfortably hot here in summer, regularly topping 35°C in July and August. The aires we've mentioned above have no shade, so we'd recommend visiting outside the summer months, especially if you've children or pets on board.

There's a ton to see in Seville, with the Royal Alcázar, Plaza de España and Catedral de Sevilla, magnificent demonstrations of architecture in their own styles. If Flamenco's your thing, you're spoiled for choice, from intimate and authentic shows to those with a more theatrical, tourist-oriented take on the genre, enjoyed over dinner.

We opted to visit a few bars with friends, enjoying the lively atmosphere and the fact our bill was written on the bar in chalk!

215

Stop #172: València

Camping Coll Vert (*www.collvertcamping.com*) ● GPS: N39.396491, W0.332388 ● Price Guide: ££ With CampingCard ACSI ● All Services ● **Alternative**: Official Aire "Nomadic València" (*nomadicvalenciacampingcar.com*), GPS: N39.548623, W0.344420, Price Guide: ££, All Services, 500m Walk to Metro then 30-Min Into City Centre

València has a great range of secure aires and campsites, all within around 10km from the centre of the city. We opted for the Coll Vert campsite, set back from the beach to the south of the city, low cost with the CampingCard ACSI. From there cycle paths took us all the way to the *Ciudad de las Artes y las Ciencias*, the City of Arts and Sciences, València's iconic sweeping modern white buildings. We visited L'Oceanogràfic, a magnificent ocenarium with over 45,000 marine animals in a series of huge tanks. We spent over six hours in there, absolutely fascinated by the creatures on display.

Along with the other City buildings, L'Oceanogràfic is sited on the bed of the Turia River, dry since it was diverted after a devastating flood in 1957. Continuing along a bike lane towards the centre of València, the Turia Riverbed Park is an oasis of green and calm, filled with gardens, fountains, cafes and games areas. Locals walk, stretch and jog along the paths, their kids (and us) playing on a giant Gulliver.

We enjoyed walking the city boulevards, lined with ornate façades. For lunch we sat outside the town's Mercado Central, munching on a couple of €1 savoury pastries, having eyeballed an array of cured hams, cheeses, dried fruits, a couple of pig's heads, fresh vegetables and other inscrutable packets. The cathedral and Llotja de la Seda (the silk exchange) both attact large numbers of visitors for their architecture and history.

SWEDEN

QUICK FACTS ● **EU**: Yes ● **Schengen**: Yes ● **Language**: Swedish ● **Currency**: Swedish Krona (SEK, £1=SEK 11) ● **Speed Limits ≤3.5t**: Urban/Single/Expressway/Motorway: 50, 70, 110, 110kph ● **Speed Limits >3.5t**: Urban/Single/Expressway/Motorway: 50, 70, 90, 90kph ● **Tolls**: Yes, on Motala, Öresund, Sundsvall and Svinesund Bridges, Pay With Cash or Card (*transportstyrelsen.se*). Charged Access to Stockholm and Gothenburg (Number Plate Read and Invoice Posted) ● **LEZs**: Yes, In Several Cities ● **IDP**: Not Needed ● **Docs**: Driving Licence, Insurance, Passport, V5C ● **Kit**: GB Sticker, Headlamp Deflectors, Warning Triangle ● **LPG**: Reasonable Availability, Dish Adapter, Locally Named Motorgas ● **Time**: UK+1 Hour ● **Daytime Dipped Headlights**: Yes ● **Overnighting**: Campsites, Aires, Free Camping Legal under Everyman's Right (*Allemansrätten*) With Restrictions

We crossed into Sweden overland from Norway, east of Oslo. Coming from Denmark, you can either drive under/over the incredible Öresund tunnel/bridge or take a ferry. There are also popular ferry routes from Germany and Finland.

Swedish food and drink prices are high compared with the UK but are offset by low overnighting costs. Sweden has over 600 campsites, but also has an aire network, and formally allows free camping. Pulling up *park4night.com* or *www.husbil.se*, the country is peppered with places to stay at lakes, towns and cities, marinas, the Göta Canal and in the huge swathes of forest which cover over half the country. Some national parks also allow an overnight stay in their entrance car parks (*www.nationalparksofsweden.se*). There are also free-standing service points so you can empty your tanks and take on fresh water in-transit. Rest areas on the road network also often have 'latrine emptying' points (*www.trafikverket.se*), as do some petrol stations.

If you plan to visit in winter, perhaps to see the Northern Lights you'll need a winterised vehicle, to fit M+S or Alpine-marked winter tyres, practice fitting your snow chains and be prepared to only see a few hours of sunlight per day in the far north.

In summer bring a mosquito net and eye masks, especially if you head to the Arctic where the sun stays above the horizon all night. Sweden's famous Ice Hotel can be visited all year round (*www.icehotel.com*).

217

Stop #173: Älmhult

IKEA Museum Car Park (*ikeamuseum.com*) ● GPS: N56.552499, E14.133515 ● Price Guide: Free (Paid Entrance to Museum) ● No Services ● **Alternative**: Sjöstugans Camping (*sjostugan.com*), GPS: N56.568573, E14.131880, Price Guide: £££, All Services,

When we got wind of the fact the world's first purpose-built IKEA store was close to our route, we couldn't resist. The shop's been a museum since 2016, dedicated to the history of the company. We stayed the night in the car park outside after visiting the museum and checking with the staff that we could sleep there.

Inside the museum we learned about the history of Sweden in the late 19th and early 20th Centuries. Times were hard for the Swedes and one in three emigrated, 1.5 million of them to America. Those who stayed learned to make do and mend, and it is into this background that Ingvar Kamprad was born and built up his business. Even as a billionaire, he wore second-hand clothes and got his hair cut when abroad in developing countries.

The name Ikea is made up of Ingvar's initials, the first initial of the farm he grew up on and the first initial of the parish it was in: Ingvar Kamprad Elmtaryd Agunnaryd. We learned about the struggles faced when other Swedish furniture manufactures forced their suppliers to boycott IKEA and not sell them any stock and prevented him from booking places at trade fairs. Unable to sell just using catalogues and adverts in the paper, they set up a showroom on the first floor of an old wooden building. Expecting around 100 people, Ingvar and his co-workers had to pray the floor wouldn't collapse when over 1,000 people turned up.

The museum was fun too, including a staged area where you can pose for a mocked-up IKEA magazine cover, and a restaurant where you can, of course, eat your fill of meatballs!

218

Stop #174: Karlskoga

Official Aire • GPS: N59.321350, E14.536034 • Price Guide: ££ • All Services • **Alternative**: Garphyttan National Park (*www.nationalparksofsweden.se*), GPS: N59.278691, E14.882939, Price Guide: Free, No Services, One Night Stay Allowed, Start Point of Short Forest Hikes

At the time of our visit, the lakeside aire (*ställplats*) at Karlskoga was free to use, including electricity. After arriving from Norway we were in need of some downtime, and enjoyed staying here for the full 72 hours we were allowed to. We were flanked by Swedish motorhomes, some of whom entertained us by walking their cats on leads each evening, and why not? These days there's a charge to stay, but it's still a great value overnight location.

The town of Karlskoga developed around the Bofors company, originally an iron works and later an arms manufacturer. The company's most famous owner was Alfred Nobel, who was instrumental in changing the company focus and spent his summers in Karlskoga at the company-owned Björkborns Herrgård, now a museum to the creator of the Nobel Prize.

The prize is actually five prizes, created according to Nobel's will after his death using 94% of his wealth and awarded "to those who, during the preceding year, have conferred the greatest benefit to humankind".

It came as a shock to us to discover that Nobel was heavily involved in the arms industry, was the inventor of dynamite, and was accused of treason in France for selling explosives to Italy. One French newspaper referred to him as "the merchant of death", presumably in reference to the 90 armaments factories he created. We'd often find this as we travelled: that we really didn't know a great deal about our native continent!

After almost three months in Norway, where we avoided eating out most of the time to keep our costs down, we enjoyed a meal at a restaurant in Karlskoga (probably the only time eating out will feel cheap in Sweden!).

Stop #175: Stockholm

Camping Klubbensborg (*www.klubbensborg.se*) ● GPS: N59.307714, E17.960344 ● Price Guide: £££ ● All Services ● Open May to Sep ● **Alternative**: Mixed Parking "Långholmen Parkering", GPS: N59.320235, E18.030688, Price Guide: £, No Services, 3.5km Walk to City Centre, Next Door to Official Aire (*www.husbilstockholm.se*), Inside the LEZ

We were lucky on our visit to Stockholm, although it didn't feel that way at first. We'd a tip off that we could sleep on the Isle of Skeppsholmen, which lies right in the centre of the city and seemed an unlikely place we'd be allowed to stay.

The stress of city driving caused us to drive across a 'width trap' designed to only allow larger vehicles to cross. Our van is big, but not big enough and one set of wheels fell off the rails and into the 'trap' beneath. Somehow we got away with zero damage and when we got to the beautifully calm parking area, facing live-aboard boats moored on the calm sea, we couldn't believe our luck.

Sadly that area is off-limits now and if we return to Stockholm during the summer, we'll use a campsite as the mixed parking and official aire on Långholmen are both inside the city's low emission zone (site details above).

We really enjoyed Stockholm, a series of sea islands linked by bridges, it had a relaxed, nautical, easy going and safe feel to it. During the two days we were there we visited the Vasa Museum, ambled around Gamla Stan (Stockholm's old town), watched the changing of the guard at the Royal Palace, ate herring from the famous stand near the Slussen T-Bana station and wandered the Livrustkammaren (the Royal Armoury). We didn't make it to the Abba Museum (*abbathemuseum.com*), but friends who did loved it there.

SWITZERLAND

QUICK FACTS ● **EU**: No ● **Schengen**: Yes ● **Languages**: German, French, Italian, Romansh ● **Currency**: Swiss Franc (CHF, £1=CHF 1.2) ● **Speed Limits ≤3.5t**: Urban/Single/Expressway/Motorway: 50, 80, 100, 120kph ● **Speed Limits >3.5t**: Urban/Single/Expressway/Motorway: 50, 80, 80, 80kph ● **Tolls**: Yes on Motorways, ≤3.5t Windscreen Sticker, >3.5t 'PSVA' Payment via Smartphone App (*www.ezv.admin.ch*). Great St. Bernard and Munt la Schera Tunnels Both Toll ● **LEZs**: Stick'AIR Scheme in Geneva ● **IDP**: Not Needed ● **Docs**: Driving Licence, Insurance, Passport, V5C ● **Kit**: GB Sticker, Headlamp Deflectors, Warning Triangle, Spare Glasses/Contact Lenses, Snow Chains in Winter ● **LPG**: Good Availability, ACME and Dish Adapters ● **Time**: UK+1 Hour ● **Daytime Dipped Headlights**: Yes ● **Overnighting**: Campsites, Aires, Free Camping Legal under Everyman's Right With Restrictions (Rights Vary by Canton According to The Swiss Civil Code)

Switzerland is a first-class motorhome destination. The country is clean and safe, with a very good public transport network, some of which is spectacular! There's a widespread network of campsites, although you may want to come out of season and armed with a CampingCard ACSI, choosing sites in the scheme to keep costs down.

There are also plenty of stellplatz/aires which are cheaper than campsites and often in fantastic locations. Some are attached to businesses, giving the opportunity to get a little closer to the locals (*swissterroir.ch*). One tip: you can only use special pre-taxed rubbish bags in Switzerland. These are quite expensive, and available from grocery stores and campsites.

Finally, free camping is possible in the mountains and in more remote parking areas, offering some unique overnighting opportunities. During summer heatwaves in the valleys below, high altitude locations bring much cooler air too.

If you plan to use your motorhome for winter skiing in Switzerland, bear in mind mountain roads can be snowbound over winter and spring (*www.alpen-paesse.ch*). You may also want to book into campsites ahead of your visit, as some close over the winter and not all resorts allow overnight parking at lifts.

Switzerland has stupendous scenic railways, funiculars and cable cars, but you may need to save up a little before you come. None are cheap, but in our opinion they're all worth the money (*www.myswitzerland.com*).

Stop #176: Bern

TCS Camping Bern (*www.tcs.ch*) ● GPS: N46.963745, E7.384183 ● Price Guide: £££ ● All Services ● **Alternative**: Camping Platz Eichholz (*www.campingeichholz.ch*), GPS: N46.932912, E7.455686, Price Guide: £££, All Services, 3km Walk to City Centre

Switzlerland is split into 26 regions called *cantons*, run under a federal system with Bern as the de facto capital. With four languages, multiple religions and a wide range of landscapes, the federation approach has proved itself well suited to Swiss democracy. Decisions over national defence, foreign police and so on are taken in Bern, while each canton decides the level of income tax its citizens pay, education and health policy, anything which isn't set at federal level.

Off-site parking is, we were told, actively policed in Bern and the city has no aires so the two city campsites were the only choices available. We opted for TCS Camping Bern, 7km east of the centre, up against the Aare River and 20 minutes on the bus to the city. It was very easy to drive to, just a short distance off the A1 motorway with no city driving needed.

Bern's a clean and easy-going river-side city with gardens, a cathedral (with great views from one of the towers), museums, art galleries (including one dedicated to Paul Klee), and a very attractive old town.

We were drawn there by a round of the Formula E Championship which was taking place (*www.fiaformulae.com*), an electric car racing series held on temporary street circuits. We headed into the city on two consecutive days, to see the practice session first and then the excitement of the race the following day.

The city itself is, like all of Switzerland, immaculate, and with the added adreneline and pazzazz of the racing was an unforgettable experience for us.

Stop #177: Chur

Stellplatz Attached to Camp Au Chur (*www.campingtrin.ch*) ● GPS: N46.862124, E9.507369 ● Price Guide: ££ ● All Services ● **Alternative**: Camping Trin (*bad-blumenstein.ch*), GPS: N46.827867, E9.347431, Price Guide: £££, All Services, 17km West of Chur

Chur's one of the oldest settlements in Switzerland, having been inhabited since around 3,500BC. We arrived here one October afternoon to find the town's only campsite Camp Au Chur was full, but they did have space in an attached stellplatz outside, a basic parking area with a lower overnight price.

We were happy with that as we were a tad tired after a day's exploring. We had woken in the morning at a lovely little mountain campsite by the River Inn called Camping Chapella, just outside Cinuos-Chel (GPS: N46.632510, E10.014339, *www.campingchapella.ch*). It was -4°C and our waste water tank slung under the van was frozen, so we decided to head to a lower altitude and warm up.

A good quality road carried us quickly to St Moritz, snow-free at this time of year where we were attracted by the echoes of glamour attached to the name. The first car park we came to had a big No Motorhomes sign, so we carried on to Sankt Moritz Bad, where we discovered we could park for free at the cable car lift as the machine was broken (GPS: N46.483171, E9.831359)! The town's glitzy shops were all closed, so we peered through the windows at all the designer gear before heading to the start of the Cresta Run, a bonkers ice racing track rebuilt each winter which riders fly down head first at up to 80mph.

Leaving St Moritz, the Julier Pass carried us up into the snow where we stopped at the top to mess about in it and grab some photos with Charlie, our snow-loving pooch, before heading down to Chur.

223

Stop #178: Furkapass

Mixed Parking at 2,429m, Top of Furka Pass ● GPS: N46.572326, E8.415006 ● Price Guide: Free ● No Services ● **Alternative**: Mixed Parking at Hotel Alpenrösli at Top of Grimselpass (*www.grimselpass.com*), GPS: N46.562092, E8.338024, Price Guide: £, No Services

Motorhomes can often stay in the mixed parking areas provided at the top of Switzerland's serpentine mountain passes. Sometimes a restaurant might collect a fee, but other times they're free to use, although none have services and they can be very windy so high up.

At the eastern end of the Rhône Valley you'll find two great examples, at the top of the Furka and Grimsel Passes, both above 2,000m and set in spectacular scenery. We drove up the Grimsel Pass having first experienced the bonkers 106% steep Gelmerbahn, a cable railway built to help create the Gelmersee reservoir and hydro-electric power plant (*www.grimselwelt.ch*). In July the Grimsel Pass parking, and the entrance to the *Panoramastrasse Oberaar*, were very busy (and we'd already stayed there on another occasion), so we opted to carry on. After descending to the valley we climbed back to the top of the Furka Pass which was free to stay and much quieter. Even in midsummer there were walls of snow and ice 2 to 3m high alongside the road. Beneath the Grand Tour sign pictured above (placed by the tourist board, *www.myswitzerland.com*) we spotted a hidden gun emplacement, a reminder that Switzerland's stayed neutral in 19th Century wartime partly by being very well defended (the country still has mandatory military service).

The following day we got up early and drove a short distance down to the Hotel Belvédère, which provides access to the Rhône Glacier, the source of the famous river, for an entrance fee. An ice tunnel lets you walk inside the glacier, touching the pale blue walls formed by compressed snow, quite an experience.

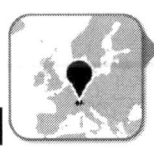

Stop #179: Gurnigel Pass

Mixed Parking (*gantrischparking.ch*) ● GPS: N46.722284, E7.445951 ● Price Guide: £ ● Composting Toilet, No Other Services ● **Alternative**: Campingplatz Blumenstein (*bad-blumenstein.ch*), GPS: N46.744922, E7.520027, Price Guide: £££, All Services

Sitting on a rock in mid-June, staring out over the wide expanse of the Gantrisch Nature Park, we couldn't have felt more content (*www.gantrisch.ch*). We do our best to capture these kind of views with our camera, but it never quite works. The only way to fully take in the beauty in the world is to see it with our own eyes.

Our motorhome was standing a couple of miles away, in the parking area at the top of the Gurnigel Pass, with broad Alpine meadow views from the windscreen. The parking area is only an hour south of Bern and was packed with cars at the weekend, but almost empty come Monday morning. The roar of motorbikes and sports cars was replaced with the bong-bong of cowbells and the ting-ting ringing from smaller bells carried by herds of goats.

The parking area is the start of a network of hiking trails in superb countryside. It's unsurprisingly hilly around here, and a 6 mile hike took us five hours, albeit with a good amount of resting to absorb the views and a bit of goat stroking. It's about 1,600m above sea level here, and in the summer heat we needed factor 50 sunscreen and hats to avoid being sunburned. If you've the skills and nerve, there's a *via ferrata* to try, a climbing route rendered safer by metal fixed to the rock which you harness yourself to.

We stayed here for three nights, flanked by local motorhomes, one of which interestingly deployed the array of poles and cables of a huge radio antenna alongside their rig. Other locals entertained us by flying model aircraft above us, swooping and gliding in the clean air.

Stop #180: Lauterbrunnen

Camping Breithorn (*campingbreithorn.ch*) ● GPS: N46.568123, E7.909601 ● Price Guide: ££ With CampingCard ACSI ● All Services ● **Alternative**: Campsite Rütti (*www.campingruetti.ch*), GPS: N46.546314, E7.902175, Price Guide: ££ With CampingCard ACSI, All Services

The village of Lauterbrunnen lies in one of the most impressive valleys in the Alps, with giant cliffs slicing upwards towards the base of the towering Jungfrau, Mönch and Eiger mountains (the Virgin, Monk and the Ogre).

The main north-south valley, and the side valley leading to Grindelwald, have a good network of campsites, all of which get good reviews. The Breithorn and Rütti sites are the only ones to currently offer the CampingCard ACSI discount, which makes them great value for money as Swiss campsites tend to be expensive.

We arrived in the valley in October, getting settled into the campsite and entertained by head-butting goats in the meadow next door. The following morning we woke to find the whole valley filled with mist, through which bright coloured parachutes emerged from time to time, landing from their take-off point on the cliffs above. Checking the webcams at Mürren above us we could see the weather was glorious up there. A short ride on the gondola from Gimmelwald and we were up in the sunshine. As we admired the magnificent mountains on the opposite side of the valley a helicopter dramatically landed alongside us. Expecting some kind of medical emergency, we were surprised to see it was being used to lift materials onto a nearby building site, a sight we later saw several times in Switzerland.

If time and funds allow, the famous Jungfraujoch railway and Schilthorn cableway are both in this area. There's plenty of hiking to be had too (most routes require a reasonable level of fitness).

Stop #181: Sion

Official Aire ● GPS: N46.256962, E7.344131 ● Price Guide: Free ● Fresh Water and Black Water Disposal ● **Alternative**: Official Aire in Saint-Léonard, GPS: N46.255597, E7.426023, Price Guide: £, All Services Except Electricity, Service Point Closed in Winter

Sometimes digging around in the comments on apps like *park4night* reveals something really interesting. Looking for somewhere to stay along the Rhône Valley this aire popped up, free to use and with lots of good reviews, always a good sign. Some mentioned the great views, looking south across to the 4,358m high Dent Blanche, and one said they'd enjoyed walking the nearby Bisse du Torrent Neuf.

Firing up Google we discovered the aire is in the car park at the start of a famous three-hour out-and-back walk (*www.torrent-neuf.ch*). The accompanying photos showed cliff-side paths linked with a series of suspension bridges, all set high on the side of a valley.

The path follows a 600-year-old channel built to carry water for irrigation high on the valley sides. It's called the *Torrent Neuf* (the new torrent), as it was built in place of even older waterways.

The channel ran in wooden aquaducts anchored into sheer cliff faces, some of which have been reconstructed, through tunnels carved in the stone and along ledges on the steep slopes. All along the route signs tell you to look out for goats on the cliffs above you, as their movement can lead to rocks being dislodged and sent down in your direction. Small stone fragments were falling off all the time, but our caps were enough to protect us from them. There's a small café at the start of the route with a box for donations towards its upkeep.

We enjoyed the walk so much that when we returned to Switzerland the following year we repeated it and can highly recommend it.

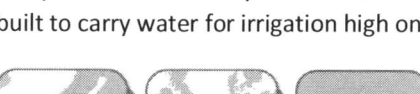

227

Stop #182: Steingletscher

Mountain Parking "Parkplatz Umpol" ● GPS: N46.713384, E8.415560 ● Price Guide: £ ● No Services ● **Alternative**: Parking at Top of Sustenpass, GPS: N46.729798, E8.446404, Price Guide: Free, No Services, 2,224m Above Sea Level, Open Roughly June to October

A Swiss couple tipped us off about this parking area below the Stone Glacier, accessed via a 3km toll road, which starts a few curves below the top of the Susten Pass. The scenery on the drive and at the parking area is nothing less than spectacular. The parking area is the start of serious hikes up to the glacier and the Tierberglihütte mountain hut, whose tiny lit windows gave away its position in the heights at night. There are less serious walks too, with incredible views of the Susten Pass as it zig zags back and forth, clawing its way up the epic landscape.

On our first trip a few years ago we came in October and the signs at the bottom of the pass had shown a snowflake symbol, gulp! We were there alone and nervous we'd wake to find the road snowbound and us stuck, but thankfully no snow fell that night.

The second time we stayed in June during a heatwave, with maybe 50 motorhomes and campervans spread along the toll road, every one of them with a stunning view. Climbers were out in force, and a couple of intrepid Czech skiiers carried their equipment on foot, using skins (material which slides in one direction but grips in the other) to climb up the snowy slopes as there are no lifts. Local kids were using the snow to slide into semi-frozen mountain lakes, a tough lot these Swiss!

There are no services or toilets up here in the wilds so its important to only come if you're carrying your own facilities and can leave no trace of your stay. For low-cost services, the riverside "Stellplatz an der Reuss" is around 25km east and gets great reviews (GPS: N46.730603, E8.625471).

Stop #183: Täsch

Camping Alphubel (*www.campingtaesch.ch*) ● GPS: N46.065809, E7.775033 ● Price Guide: £££ ● All Services ● **Alternative**: Parking Attached to Matterhorn Golf Hotel in Randa (*www.matterhornparking.ch*), GPS: N46.093010, E7.780012, Price Guide: £, No Services

The village of Täsch is as far south as you can drive along the Zermatt Valley, towards the border with Italy, high in the Alps. To reach the famous mountaineering and ski resort of Zermatt, you'll need to either hike the remaining 6km, or take one of the frequent trains from Täsch, the final section of the Glacier Express.

If you're making the trip to Zermatt, we highly recommend taking the 33-minute train from there to Gornergrat at 3,135m. Tickets don't come cheap, but we've managed to take the train several times for free, although not without effort as the tickets were included in the Gornegrat Zermatt Marathon entry fee. One summer option to keep the cost down is to take the train up and hike back down to Zermatt, although obviously you'll need to be in good physical shape to do this.

From alongside the Gornergrat observatory you've an incredible viewing area, with the 'Toblerone' Matterhorn and 19 other peaks over 4,000m, plus the sweeping Gorner Glacier.

The Alphubel campsite at Täsch is fairly expensive and doesn't have marked-out pitches, but is very convenient for the train station next door and for a hike to the longest suspension bridge in the world.

We've also stayed at Camping Attermenzen a little further north towards Randa and a couple of kilometres walk or cycle to the nearest train stations (GPS: N46.085542, E7.780985). We've not yet used the relatively low-cost parking at the Matterhorn Golf Hotel (details above) but it looked like a good budget option when we've walked past.

TUNISIA

QUICK FACTS ● **EU**: No ● **Schengen**: No ● **Languages**: Arabic, Berber, French ● **Currency**: Tunisian Dinar (£1=TND 3.6) ● **Speed Limits**: Urban/Single/Expressway/Motorway: 50, 70, 90, 110kph ● **Tolls**: Yes on Motorway, Pay with Cash ● **LEZs**: None ● **IDP**: 1968 ● **Docs**: Driving Licence, Insurance, Passport, V5C ● **Kit**: GB Sticker, Headlamp Deflectors ● **LPG**: Available from Some Agil and Total Stations ● **Time**: UK+1 Hour ● **Daytime Dipped Headlights**: No ● **Overnighting**: Campsites, Business Parking, Marinas, Youth Hostels, Wild Camping

Unlike Morocco, which attracts thousands of motorhome travellers, Tunisia is a relatively unvisited North African motorhome destination. We spent six weeks touring the country in 2013, visiting Julie's grandfather's WW2 grave as part of our trip, and at the time it felt like we had the place to ourselves.

Tunisia underwent a revolution as part of the Arab Spring movement in 2011. It was still in a state of emergency two years later and tourism had collapsed as a result. In 2015 terrorist attacks on the Bardo museum in Tunis and at hotels in Sousse received international attention and damaged the industry again, although visitor numbers had recovered well by the time the COVID-19 pandemic hit in 2020.

For us Tunisia was a 'stretch' destination, about as far out of our comfort zone as we wanted to go. We found the people to be friendly and helpful, the landscapes jaw-dropping, and the heritage fascinating. Having arrived on a ferry from Sicily poorly prepared, we quickly pulled together a network of places we could stay across the country.

We completed a circular route, from the north Atlantic down across the mountains and plains to the dry salt lakes in the south (*chotts*), then further to desert oasis towns. Not wanting to cross into Libya we turned north first to the isle of Djerba, then to the cities, medinas, Roman ruins and holy sites of the east and all the way back to the capital at Tunis and our ferry back to Palermo.

Tunisia's closer to being an 'overlander' destination to us, the next stage in adventure from the easier, more relaxing motorhome touring countries in Europe, but it gave us experience after experience, none of which we'll ever forget.

Stop #184: Aghir

Centre des Stages et Vacances on Isle of Djerba ● GPS: N33.757712, E11.014324 ● Price Guide: £ ● All Services ● 22km South-East of Houmt Souk

In converting the Arabic language, places tend to acquire more than one similar-sounding spelling when written in Latin. The isle of Djerba is also written as Jerba or Jarbah as a result, and you'll see similar 'transliteration' spelling differences everywhere across the Arabic world.

We drove onto the island across the road bridge to the south, later leaving via a short ferry on the west coast. Our research revealed a holiday centre among the tourist resorts on the east coast which had an area for motorhomes to park facing the beach and the calm blue Mediterranean Sea. It was a perfect spot which we had all to ourselves, the closest we got to other motorhomers was chatting with some German tourists who'd flown to their hotel, who had a *wohnmobil* at home and were interested what it was like to tour Tunisia by motorhome.

We used the holiday centre as a base for a few days, exploring the small island on day trips out. Having spotted flamingos and duckbills from afar, we took off down dirt roads to get a better look. We headed up to Houmt Souk, the largest town on the island (حومة السوق in Arabic). After a wander through the souk and the fish auction house we nipped to the Tower of Skulls, an obelisk memorial to an Ottoman-empire victory over a Spanish fleet. A macabre tower of skulls fashioned from the vanquished dead was torn down in 1848 under French pressure.

On another foray we took in Jerba Explore, a large complex with a museum and heritage centre but the main attraction was the area holding 400 crocodiles of all ages (*www.djerbaexplore.com*). Feeding time was quite a sight.

Stop #185: Bulla Regia

Guarded Parking Besides the Bulla Regia Archaeological Museum • GPS: N36.556676, E8.754872 • Price Guide: £ • Black Waste Disposal and Fresh Water

Tunisia was historically a major trading and military centre, based around Carthage near present day Tunis. This came to an end when the Romans finally destroyed Carthage in 146BC and took control of the country for the next 800 years. The archaeological site of Bulla Regia in north-west Tunisia preserves a city occupied by the Carthaganians and Romans, before eventually being destroyed by an earthquake. The site was protected by drifting sand until being rediscovered and excavated in the 20th Century.

In most Roman ruins we find ourselves walking among low walls, trying to imagine what the full rooms might have looked. In Bulla Regia many villas were built underground though, around a courtyard opening to the sky above. This was to protect the inhabitants from fierce summer heat above. A number of these houses have been excavated, allowing you to walk down into them and walk besides the masterpiece in-situ mosaics inside a full room, like the original inhabitants.

When we visited some of the signs at the site were so worn nothing could be read, so paying for a guide or doing your research before you arrive will enrich the experience. Above ground you'll find the baths, Byzantine churches, the forum with its Temple of Apollo, the market, a theatre and other smaller temples.

We asked at the ticket office whether we could stay for the night and they arranged for us to stay in the compound after it was locked, even calling in a security guard who stayed on site all night.

Stop #186: Douz

Camping Club Desert Douz ● GPS: N33.453041, E9.025500 ● Price Guide: £ ● All Services ● Located Just Inside the Oasis, Under Palms on Packed Sand, Best Site We Visited in Tunisia

In times past Douz was an important resting place for trans-Saharan caravans, and is still known as the *Gateway to the Sahara*. The town's campsite is a short walk away, set just inside a huge palmerie made up of 500,000 trees producing *deglet nour* (finger of light) dates. We shared the site with just a couple of other motorhomes, two 4x4s returning from a two week stint in the desert and an American English teacher staying in a tent, between jobs.

We stayed here a few days while we waited for the town's weekly *souk* (market). The oasis made for fascinating walks, spotting people adjusting flows of water or tending to the crops grown beneath the towering trees. Each winter the International Festival of the Sahara is held to the south of the palms, marked out with a grandstand. A little further south we found an *erg*, an area of sand dunes.

We enjoyed the downtime in Douz, haggling over scarves, buying camel meat, battling with Arabic keyboards in the Internet café (there was no mobile data signal down here on the edge of the desert), and enjoying the local *brick à l'oeuf* and *brochettes*.

Come market day one of our fellow motorhomers from the Netherlands ran his own stall in the souk. He attracted a huge crowd to buy the bits and bobs he'd brought from home, old electrical equipment mainly, an entertaining business for everyone. The wider souk was well worth the wait, a frenetic affair with huge piles of vegetables, lace-less unmatched shoes, murky olive oil, blankets and goats, sheep and even a few camels being traded.

233

Stop #187: El Jem

Municipal Car Park at El Jem ● GPS: N35.297544, E10.705123 ● Price Guide: £ ● No Services
● Short Walk to Roman Amphitheatre

The Roman amphitheatre at El Jem is among the largest in the world, added to the UNESCO World Heritage list in 1979, one year before the Rome Colosseum. The Colosseum is by far the larger of the two though, holding 50,000 spectators while El Jem would have held maybe 30,000 to 35,000 but it's still mangnificent, the largest Roman monument in Africa.

After managing to get lost on the way to the town, being directed down dirt roads by locals, we were relieved to see the amphitheatre standing tall above the sea of olive trees covering the plain around us. Coming to a rest in the town's municipal car park, a guardian arrived and requested 2 TND, less than €1 for the night, leaving plenty of funds to purchase pizzas from a nearby restaurant for that evening's meal.

El Jem's well preserved, other than damage caused by being shelled in the 17th Century when it was being used as a citadel. Unlike the Colosseum, which was built in a mixture of brick (inside) and stone (outside), El Jem was built entirely from cut stone. It was a real pleasure to explore, just us and a handful of other tourists.

Our entrance tickets included a nearby museum, whose walls and floors are covered in huge, detailed Roman mosaics, some patterned, others depicting mythological scenes or animal fights inspired by what took place on the floor of the adjacent amphitheatre. Signs informed us that workmen who laid the original mosaics would have been paid two chickens per day, while the artists who drew the designs earned four chickens each day. Next door to the museum stands a reconstructed Roman African villa.

Stop #188: Ksar Ghilane

Campement le Paradis ● GPS: N32.986907, E9.638046 ● Price Guide: £ ● All Services ● Access via Unsealed Road, May Be Inaccessible Due to Sand, Check First ● Short Walk to Swimming In Oasis Source and Sand Dunes, Approx 3km Walk to Ruins of Roman Fort

The oasis at Ksar Ghilane lies on the edge of the Grand Erg Oriental, an enormous sea of sand dunes making up part of the Sahara Desert. Heading from Douz towards Matmata, we knew we had to turn south onto the 'pipeline road', the C211, when we reached a small café, the only building for miles in the stony, barren desert. The pipe must be buried, as all we saw for the next 70km was road, stones and dust. The road rolled up and down with the land, and we found ourselves zoning out until a small patch of orange started to grow in the distance, the sand dunes of the erg.

Before we could park and relax we'd a few more small challenges to overcome, the first being young soldiers manning a roadblock with machine guns strapped across their backs. A quick passport inspection saw us waved on our way to the next problem, the fact the sealed road ended at Ksar Ghilane and all the campsites were accessed via a sandy dirt road. Our two wheel drive motorhome got through the sand, leaving us just a quick negotiation over prices once we were in the oasis so we could decide which site to stay in. Finally we were parked in an oasis on the edge of the desert in the south of Tunisia, phew.

Ksar Ghilane was once the southern edge of the Roman Empire, and the stone remains of a fort are within walking distance of the oasis. We made do with fooling around in the dunes, our dog Charlie getting a full workout attempting to run up their fast-collapsing sides. The oasis also has a pool you can swim in, and we cooled Charlie off with a dunk in an irrigation channel, later regretting it when he dried off by rolling in the sand and filling the inside of our van with it!

235

Stop #189: Matmata

Parking at Chez Abdul Restaurant ● GPS: N33.544874, E9.966981 ● Price Guide: Negotiated, Free When Buying Meals ● Fresh Water ● Facing onto Area of Pit Dwellings

The road into Matmata offered spectaular desert views, the hills around us having eroded into layers, giving the appearance of being 'combed' like the Anti-Atlas Mountains in Morocco. In places we could see a series of walls built between the hillsides. These *jessour* structures help capture rainwater in the *wadis*, ravines which only run with water during floods. Other than a sparse few palm dates, nothing grew in the *jessours*, a lot of building and mainteance work for seemingly little reward.

At Matmata we were enthusiastically waved into the parking area besides Chez Abdul, by Abdul's friend Mohammed. Another motorhomer who'd passed this way a few days earlier told about a deal struck he'd struck to buy a meal and get a free night's stay as a result. We agreed the same deal before settling in.

Despite being obviously full of cold, Mohammed was still working as a guide and later took us over to the town's famous Hotel Sidi Idriss, the underground pit home used as part of Luke Skywalker's home in Star Wars.

Next we were shown around another pit dwelling by the lady who lived there. She proudly showed us her bedroom (with en-suite shower!), living room and kitchen. Mohammed explained how they built the homes in the soft sandstone, and in the 1950s everyone still lived in a pit dwelling. In 1959 the government started to build a new town 15 kilometres up the road to house the growing population. At the time we visited in 2013 only 25 families still lived in pit dwellings in Matmata.

Stop #190: Metameur

Parking at Hotel Les Gorfas ● GPS: N33.369089, E10.437328 ● Price Guide: £ ● Electricity, Black Water Disposal and Fresh Water ● Located in Courtyard of Fortified Grain Store

Two words we learned in southern Tunisia: *ghorfa* and *ksar*. The former is a fortified grain store used by the native Berbers to keep valuable food secure from thieves and the latter is a collection of these ghorfas, arranged into a kind of fort around a central courtyard. Preserved ksars in Tunisia were used in Star Wars as slave quarters, so they were easily recognisable.

Our first ksar was at Metameur, at the Hotel Les Gorfas, where we were able to park and sleep inside the courtyard. Unsure whether the hotel was open we moved a barrier to get in, the owner arriving the following day laughing and hugging us when we explained we'd just winged it. She made us mint tea, and on a second visit cooked a delicious couscous *tagine* which we ate in the van.

As well as being an extra-ordinary place to spend the night, the hotel was a safe haven after pushing our comfort zones touring the less-visited, stony hills and deserts in Tunisia's south, not far from a turbulent Lybia. Our Lonely Planet, written during more stable times, suggested the Maztouria Loop south of Tataouine was worth a visit and we opted to give it a go.

Our first stop was the abandoned Beni Barka hilltop town, where workmen showed us around and we peered out from the walls at the magnificent views of the surrounding desert. From there the thin strip of tarmac headed down to Ksar Ouled Soltane, before looping back north through simply incredible landscapes, like being in a Hollywood film.

237

Stop #191: Sidi Bou Said

Parking at Sidi Bou Said Marina ● GPS: N36.868243, E10.351703 ● Price Guide: £ ● Electricity and Fresh Water ● Negotiated Overnight Fee with Guards ● Convenient for Train to Carthage and Tunis, and La Goulette Ferry Port

The pleasure port of Sidi Bou Said is a safe and quiet place to spend a couple of nights, convenient for the blue-and-white town on the cliffs above above. The La Goulette ferry terminal is within easy reach, as are trains into Tunis, the capital of Tunisia and the Carthage archeological area. We arrived with another motorhome, an imposing green rugged 4x4 which looked like it could drive straight up a mountain, and the guards at the marina negotiated a price for us both to stay, hooking us up to the electrical points for the yachts.

We took the train and tram into Tunis, taken aback by youths hanging onto them from the outside as they sped between stations. Our visit was two years after the country's dictator Zine El Abidine Ben Ali was overthrown, and a state of emergency persisted. An armoured car sat outside the Bardo National Museum, a bored-looking soldier inside (*www.bardomuseum.tn*). In 2015, two years after our visit, terrorists killed 21 people at the museum, an act mourned as a national disaster.

The Bardo, pictured above, is a beautiful building in itself, partly a 15th Century palace. The floors and walls were covered in huge, spectacular Roman mosaics. The ceilings were decorated with Islamic art, pattened, painted or gilded.

Outside the rain poured into the city medina. We refuelled with chicken and chips in bread rolls, eyeballed some of the stalls and headed for home.

Stop #192: Tozeur

Camping Les Beaux Rêves (*beauxreves.koi29.com*) ● GPS: N32.927332, E10.446817 ● Price Guide: £ ● All Services ● Small Aire-Like Parking Area on Packed Sand by Reception, Main Campsite Not Accessible to Motorhomes

On the way south to Tozeur we stopped at Metaloui to ride the Lézard Rouge train. Made in France and once owned by the Tunisian monarch, the train now carries tourists through desert scenery. It wasn't running the day we arrived, but we had fun entertaining the locals with our dog's tricks, as not many Tunisian's have pets, and a couple of guides offered to show us around the carriages for free.

At Tozeur we rolled into the campsite and got ourselves hooked up to the electricity and the WiFi. The owner arranged for a friend with a 4x4 to take us to the scenery in the desert used as the spaceport Mos Espa in Star Wars (GPS: N33.994251, E7.842689), a bizarre but memorable excursion which also took us past Camel Head Rock, also featured in the film. Our guide, who claimed to have three houses and two wifes, 'forgot' to take us out towards the Algerian border to see the small white building used as Luke Skywalker's homestead, so we drove out in the van and peered at it from the road (GPS: N33.842787, E7.779150). The underground part of the house, shown adjacent to it in the film, is actually 250km east at Matmata.

A couple of British round-the-world bikers rode into the campsite one day, on their way south through Africa. We enjoyed sharing a drink and a meal with these fun, fascinating and inspiring people before they headed east into Libya.

After leaving Tozeur we crossed the dry Chott el Djerid salt lake via a causeway on our way to to Douz, stopping for photos on this unforgettable stretch of road.

239

UNITED KINGDOM

QUICK FACTS ● **EU**: No ● **Schengen**: No ● **Languages**: English ● **Currency**: Pound Sterling (£) ● **Speed Limits Unladed Weight ≤3.05t**: Urban/Single/Expressway/Motorway: 30, 60, 70, 70mph ● **Speed Limits Unladen Weight >3.05t**: Urban/Single/Expressway/Motorway: 30, 50, 60, 70mph ● **Tolls**: Yes on M6 Toll Motorway, Some Bridges and Tunnels (Some Paid Online) ● **LEZs**: Central London ● **IDP**: Not Needed ● **Docs**: Driving Licence, Insurance, V5C ● **Kit**: None ● **LPG**: Widely Available, Bayonet Adapter ● **Time**: UK Time ● **Daytime Dipped Headlights**: No ● **Overnighting**: Campsites, Business Parking (Pubs in Particular), Small Number of Aires, Wild Camping Not Legal But Discrete Off-Site Parking Tolerated in Places (Especially Scotland)

According to *statista.com*, almost 20 million nights were spent on UK campsites in campervans, motorhomes and touring caravans in 2019. Another 12 million nights were spent under canvas. It's fair to say we love our camping in the UK and we've around 4,000 sites to choose from. The UK's two main camping clubs, the Camping and Caravanning Club and Caravan and Motorhome Club, offer both large, well-equipped sites, and smaller, basic, lower cost locations called Certified Sites (CSs) and Certified Locations (CLs).

Many sites operate independently of these clubs but are easy to track down with websites and apps like *search4sites.co.uk*, *pitchup.com* and *ukcampsite.co.uk*. These each have different features but allow you to look for sites which accept dogs, are adult-only, by the sea or within walking distance of a pub, for example.

One type of overnight location the UK isn't known for is aires. This system of official overnight, no-frills parking places provided across many Western European countries doesn't extend to the UK, although there is the odd one like the Canterbury Park 'n' Ride aire, and a few more are starting to be built to meet demand. Also, the Britstops scheme sees businesses with parking areas offer them for overnight motorhome stays (*www.britstops.com*).

Unofficial off-site parking tends to be frowned upon in the UK, although it's more widely tolerated in more remote parts, especially for a single night away from people's homes and other campervans and motorhomes. We live in the UK but due to the ease of finding low cost overnight places, we tend to spend most of our time abroad.

Stop #193: Canterbury

Official Aire at New Dover Road City Park 'n' Ride (*www.canterbury.gov.uk*) • GPS: N51.261338, E1.100110 • Price Guide: £ • All Services Except Electricity • **Alternative**: Canterbury Camping & Caravanning Club Campsite (*www.campingandcaravanningclub.co.uk*), GPS: N51.276722, E1.112340, Price Guide: £££, All Services, 40-Minute Walk or 6-Minute Bus to Canterbury

Canterbury City Council is one of the few authorities in England to have created an official aire, and the city attracts a good number of motorhome tourists as a result.

The aire is located at the New Dover Road Park 'n' Ride facility, either a two mile walk into the city or you can take the shuttle bus which runs every few minutes and is included in the parking fee. The aire has a grey and black water drain and provides fresh water. It's also convenient for the ferry and Eurotunnel routes to and from France, just a 30-minute drive away.

Canterbury's a major tourist destination, one of the most-visited cities in the UK, and a UNESCO World Heritage site. The city's been the seat of the spiritual head of the Church of England for nearly five centuries. Its cathedral, one of the oldest Christian buildings in England, was founded in 597, rebuilt in 1077 and again in 1174 following a fire. It became a major destination for pilgrims who came to see a shrine to Archbishop Thomas Becket, murdered in the cathedral by followers of a contentiously-crowned English King. The shrine and the archbishop's bones were later destroyed by King Henry VIII.

The city has a good range of pubs and shops and is a great place to stock up before a long trip outside the UK, especially on any English-language books, magazines and maps you want to take with you.

Stop #194: Edale

Newfold Farm Campsite (*www.newfoldfarmedale.com*) ● GPS: N53.370347, W1.816834 ● Price Guide: ££ ● All Services ● **Alternative**: Waterside Farm Camping, GPS: N53.361070, W1.824796, Price Guide: ££, All Services, 15-Minute Walk to Edale

The village of Edale lies in the Peak District (*www.peakdistrict.gov.uk*), the first of 15 UK National Parks. As most land in the UK is privately owned, the public had little access to the countryside before the parks were created. It took decades of lobbying and a mass trespass across the hills close to Edale in 1932 before the park was finally established in 1951.

The result of our forebears efforts is a hiker's paradise. Trails lead out from the village, immediately into sweeping hills, babbling brooks, and up to rocky outcrops with wonderful views across the valley. Serious hikers have the Pennine Way National Trail to tackle, 431km from Edale all the way up to and over the Scottish border.

We stayed at Newfold Farm Campsite, previously Cooper's Farm, a well-known site located in the centre of the village with its own café and close to the The Old Nags Head, a 1577 stone-built traditional country inn which serves delicious food and drinks (*www.the-old-nags-head.co.uk*). One tip: stick to the main A roads where you can and try to arrive and leave at quieter times, as the final stretch of road to the campsite is narrow and often lined with parked cars. We got stuck three times on our last weekend visit, having to reverse and squeeze past cars and tractors.

To the south of the village you'll find the Mam Tor hill, the Blue John Cavern and the towns of Castleton and Hope. To the east lies the Ladybower Reservoir, whose dam was used for practice by 'the dambusters' Lancaster bombers, another bucolic walking and cycling destination.

Stop #195: Edinburgh

Mortonhall Caravan and Camping Park (*www.meadowhead.co.uk/parks/mortonhall*) ● GPS: N55.903622, W3.179673 ● Price Guide: ££ ● All Services ● **Alternative**: Drummohr Holiday Park (*www.drummohr.org*), GPS: N55.949660, W3.007035, Price Guide: ££, All Services, 10-Minute Walk to Bus Stop Then 1 Hour to Edinburgh

Edinburgh, the capital of Scotland, is easy to visit in a motorhome. We opted to use the Mortonhall Campsite four miles to the south, as always looking for security around a big city. If you don't want to camp, the Newcriaghall Park 'n' Ride site to the east gets good reviews as a budget option (GPS: N55.933779, W3.093481).

Fairly frequent buses ran from the road outside our campsite into the city, taking payment on-board with the correct change or a contactless card. As soon as we'd arrived and were settled in we took a bus into the city to see it at night, wandering up the Royal Mile to the castle before heading down into the streets below to join the weekend revellers.

The following day the November skies were heavy so we wrapped up warm before taking the bus again. This time we walked up Arthur's Seat, an ancient 251m volcano above the city which, when it's not covered in cloud, offers fantastic views of the city and the sea to the north.

Back down the hill we passed the Scottish Parliament building and headed for the National Museum of Scotland, which works on a donation-entry system. The exhibits inside were fascinating, showcasing not just natural wonders and Scottish achievements and heritage, but has exhibits from across the World.

We rounded off the day with a delicious meal in one of Edinburgh's 190-or-so pubs.

243

Stop #196: Fionnphort

Fidden Farm Campsite ● GPS: N56.308598, W6.363622 ● Price Guide: ££ ● All Services Except Electricity ● **Alternative**: Coastal Wild Camp on Mull, GPS: N56.356096, W5.874327, Price Guide: Free, No Services, Tea Room Nearby at Old Post Office

Our first motorhome was an old Talbot Express Autosleeper Harmony, which we used to tour England, Wales and Scotland before venturing over to continental Europe. We unimaginatively called him Harvey the RV, and in the above picture he still has his awning attached. A few nights later we accidentally let the wind rip it off, a lesson learned to always wind it away at night, even if its calm when we go to bed.

We reached the Isle of Mull on a ferry from Oban, docking at Craignure and taking the single-track road across the island, pulling up at passing places (marked with striped poles) to allow the occasional car to pass.

When we arrived at Fidden Farm Campsite we were given a free choice on where to park. There are no marked-out pitches so

we picked a spot overlooking a small sandy cove and the Isle of Iona, the birthplace of Celtic Christianity in Scotland, with the sound of waves gently lapping on the beach below.

With our fridge and gas bottles full, we had everything we needed with us and had a great sensation of being far away from the hectic world we'd left behind. It was a pleasant feeling which we'd later get in places like Icht on the edge of the Sahara in Morocco and on the Mani Penisular in the Peloponnese in Greece.

Mull has a whiskey distillery at Tobermory, the picture-postcard colourful fishing village also known through the children's TV programme *Balamory*. We caught our ferry off Mull from here, disembarking at Kilchoan on our way north towards Skye.

244

Stop #197: Sango Sands

Sango Sands Oasis Campsite (*sangosands.com*) ● GPS: N58.568579, W4.743323 ● Price Guide: ££ ● All Services ● **Alternative**: Kinlochbervie Loch Clash Campervan Stopover (*klbcompany.wordpress.com*), GPS: N58.459711, W5.056868, Price Guide: ££, All Services, Located on Sea-Facing Dock

The North Coast 500 is Scotland's take on America's iconic Route 66. The 516-mile NC500 is a circular route around the scenic coast and highlands north of Inverness, first marketed in 2015 by a Prince Charles-backed tourism initiative. You don't have to drive the full route, of course, and might instead want to use the various NC500 books *or www.northcoast500.com* to research which parts you want to cover.

The Sango Sands campsite at Durness lies directly on the NC500 route, facing a pristine sandy beach and cliffs. It closes its shower block out of season and operates more like an aire, with a very low nightly price including electricity.

From the campsite we took a walk across the tracks and beaches to Faraid Head with views across the Kyle of Durness to Cape Wrath, the most north-westerly point in mainland Britain.

Back towards Durness we came across the old church and graveyard at Balnakeil, resting place of the Gaelic poet Rob Dunn, John Lennon's Aunt Elizabeth Parkes and Donald MacLeod who is said to have murdered 18 people and disposed of their bodies in nearby Smoo Caves.

Further on, we couldn't resist stopping at the Cocoa Mountain chocolatiers (*www.cocoamountain.co.uk*). The thick hot chocolate topped with cream and yet more melted chocolate was unforgettable, the best we've ever tasted!

Stop #198: Whitby

Whitby Holiday Park (*www.whitbypark.co.uk*) ● GPS: N54.485114, W0.590069 ● Price Guide: ££ ● All Services ● **Alternative**: High Straggleton Farm Campsite (*www.highstraggleton.co.uk*), GPS: N54.490899, W0.652189, Price Guide: ££, All Services, 2 Mile Walk to Whitby

Facing out onto the bleak North Sea, Whitby is a much-loved seaside resort in Yorkshire, England. It's served by a number of campsites which accept touring motorhomes and campervans, plus one which 'pops-up' each summer behind the ruined abbey. We opted to stay at Whitby Holiday Park, located on a cliff top a mile or so walk along the Cleveland Way path and down the 199 steps by the abbey to the centre of town. A much shorter path takes families from the park to the sandy beach of Saltwick Bay below, a famous spot for finding Jurassic fossils and jet, a black jemstone made into jewellery and on display in shops in the town.

Besides playing on the beach, there are a whole host of quintessentially English seaside activities to take part in: pleasure boat rides and sea fishing trips, catching crabs from the quayside, playing the slot machines and other arcade games, buying 'rock' (a hard-boiled sugar confectionery) and eating fish and chips from one of the many competing chippies.

You can also visit a museum to Captain James Cook who lived in Whitby. Two of Cook's ships were also built and launched here, Resolution and Endeavour, which took him across the world on his historic voyages of discovery. The town still has a boat builder, and we watched a fishing boat being slowly lowered for the first time into the harbour's still waters.

Six miles scenic hiking south on the Cleveland Way (*www.nationaltrail.co.uk*) brings you to Robin Hood's Bay, where you can refresh yourself at the sea-facing Bay Hotel.

UKRAINE

QUICK FACTS ● **EU**: No ● **Schengen**: No ● **Languages**: Ukrainian ● **Currency**: Ukrainian Hryvnia (£1 =38UAH) ● **Speed Limits**: Urban/Single/Expressway/Motorway: 50, 90, 110, 130kph ● **Tolls**: None ● **LEZs**: None ● **IDP**: 1968 ● **Docs**: Driving Licence, Insurance, V5C ● **Kit**: GB Sticker, Headlamp Deflectors, First Aid Kit, Fire Extinguisher ● **LPG**: Widely Available, Dish Adapter ● **Time**: UK Time+2 Hours ● **Daytime Dipped Headlights**: Yes Between 1 October and 1 May ● **Overnighting**: Limited Number of Campsites, Parking Attached to Some Businesses, Wild Camping Allowed But Avoid Nature Reserves and Border Crossing Areas

Crossing the border from Romania to Ukraine felt like stepping back in time, into a cold war film, as stern-faced border guards in military-like uniforms rifled through the reams of paperwork carried by lorry drivers, ink stamping them again and again. Our motorhome insurance didn't cover us in Ukraine, so we went to one of the insurance agent's cabins just inside the border, leaving clutching a sheet of paper in Cyrillic, having only the slightest idea what we'd bought.

We'd done far too little research beforehand, having to buy a map at the first petrol station we came to and assuming we'd be able to simply drive across a corner of the country to Poland, stopping in car parks or perhaps the occasional campsite overnight.

We soon learned the roads in Ukraine are rough! Very rough in places, almost unpassable without risking serious suspension damage. There are few campsites too, and we ended up sleeping on the drive of a guest house, in the car park of a hotel and in the grounds of a horse racecourse.

Ukraine's population have had an incredibly difficult history, including enduring the *Holodomor*, the deliberate starvation of millions of people by the Soviets in the 1930s and the Chernobyl nuclear disaster in 1986. More recently in 2014 Russia annexed Crimea using 'masked troops' whose uniforms carried no identifying insignia.

We were shocked at how poor Ukraine's infrastructure, towns and inhabitants were, its living standard clearly below those of the surrounding ex-Soviet countries, reputed to be caused by endemic corruption. The people we met though went above and beyond to make us feel welcome, something we often find in economically poor countries.

Stop #199: Kolomyia

Driveway to On the Corner Guesthouse ● GPS: N48.522937, E25.029449 ● Price Guide: £ ●
Black Waste and Fresh Water ● May No Longer Be Available

Our guidebook told us that Kolomyia in Western Ukraine was one of the more tourist-oriented towns on our route, and we found a guesthouse online with glowing reviews. We emailed the owner the night before, asking whether we could park on their driveway, waking up to a very welcoming email the following morning. The drive to Kolomyia was testing as the road surface would quickly shift from fairly smooth to almost unpassable, potholed for a mile or two in places with old cars, buses and trucks weaving all across the road and onto the pavements to try and find a safe way through. We crawled along in first gear being overtaken by Ladas, wincing at each bang and shudder as our aging motorhome was punished by hole after hole in the ground.

You can imagine our relief when we arrived at the guesthouse and the owner Vitaly greeted us with smiles and handshakes, helping us reverse onto the driveway, showing us where we could empty our loo, and inviting us to eat home-cooked dinner later that evening.

Later he walked with us to the town, past the eye-catching 14m high egg-shaped Pysanka Museum to the Hutsul Museum. Here he explained the ethnographic exhibits, including a belt with bells which he told us hunters' wives would wear to walk behind them, so they'd know if a bear had attacked them. We weren't sure if he was joking! It was great to be able to ask Vitaly all our questions about life in Ukraine. At dinner that evening we got to meet some US Peace Corps volunteers from Crimea taking a weekend break, a fascinating group of young selfless people.

Stop #200: Lviv

Hotel Jockey Parking at Race Course ● GPS: N49.840961, E24.039621 ● Price Guide: ££ ● Showers and Toilets in Hotel Available ● Bus or Uber 10km Into the City ● **Alternative**: 24 Hr Guarded Parking in Central Lviv, GPS: N49.840961, E24.039621, Price Guide: £, No Services

Lviv is one of Ukraine's easiest cities to access from the EU, just 70km of relatively good quality road from the border with Poland. Compared with the towns we'd passed through to get there, the city felt far more affluent, clean and architecturally impressive. Lonely Planet describes the city as "the country's least Soviet" saying it "exudes the same authentic Central European charm as pretourism Prague or Kraków once did" (*www.lonelyplanet.com*).

We stayed at the horse racing circuit and took the bus into the city. As the bus filled up, passengers behind us passed their money forwards to the driver from person to person. The change and ticket came back the same way.

Lviv has had a turbulent past, being faught over time and again through the centuries. Being part of Poland for hundreds of years, before WW2 two-thirds of the inhabitants were Poles. In 1939 the city was occupied by the Soviets, taken by the Nazis in 1941 and re-occupied by the Red Army in 1944, being incorporated into the Soviet Union. Forcible exile of the city's Poles and the holocaust reduced the Lviv population by 80 to 90%.

We only had a few hours in the city, so opted to walk the old town, admiring the architecture such as the National Opera (pictured above). Many choose to visit the Lychakiv Cemetery or visit Rynok Square, climbing the steps to the city hall observation deck for panoramic views from above.

Destination Maps

Maps below show the locations of all 200 stops. Page 14 has an overview map.

Maps A, C: Norway

Stop	Location	Page	Stop	Location	Page
120	Aurlandsfjorden	157	126	Oldedalen	163
121	Bergen	158	127	Oslo	164
122	Dalsnibba Plateau	159	128	Saltstraumen	165
123	Eggum	160	129	Sand	166
124	Holmvassdammen	161	130	Steinsvik	167
125	Nordkapp	162	131	Trollstigen	168

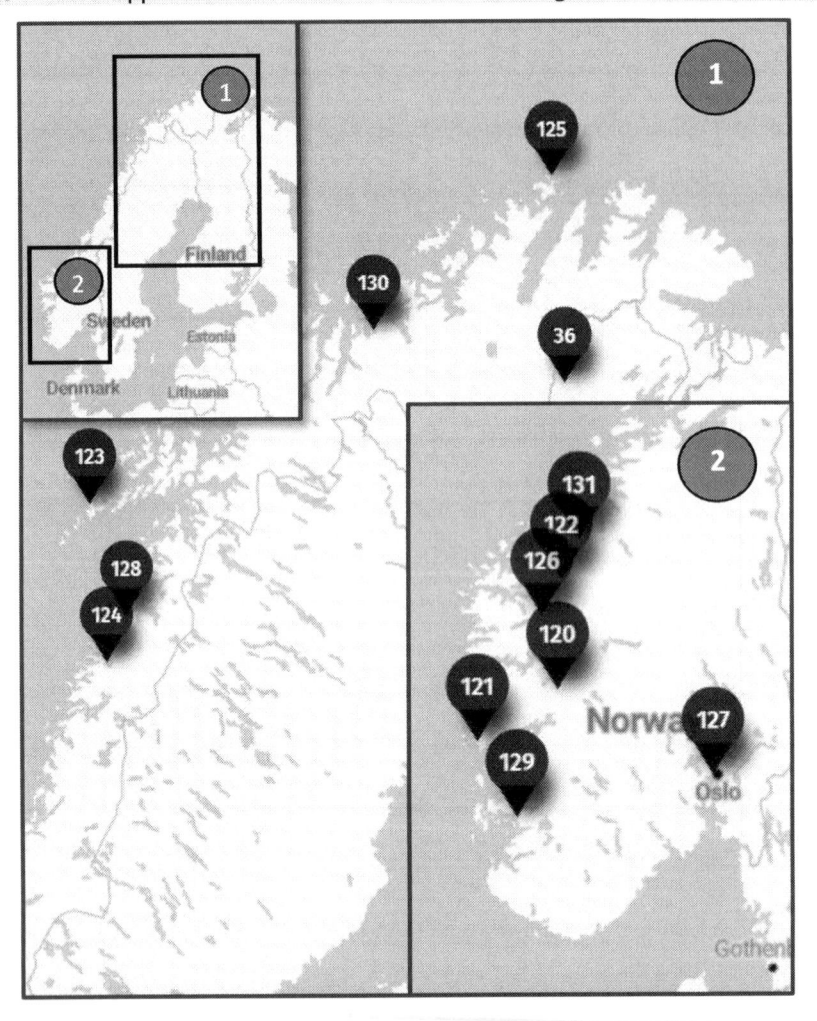

Maps B, D: Finland, Sweden

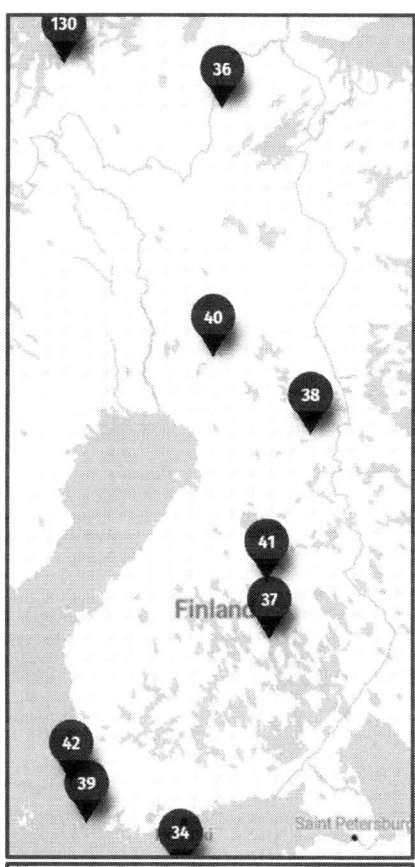

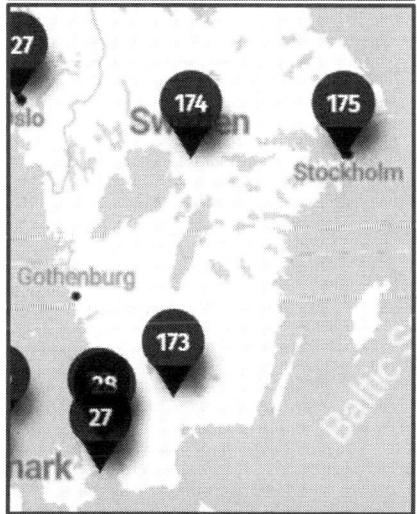

Map B: Finland

Stop	Location	Page
36	Kevo Nature Reserve	60
37	Kuopio	61
38	Kylmäluoma	62
39	Nagu/Nauvo	63
40	Rovaniemi	64
41	Sonkajärvi	65
42	Uusikaupunki	66

Map D: Sweden

Stop	Location	Page
173	Älmhult	218
174	Karlskoga	219
175	Stockholm	220

Map E: Estonia, Latvia, Lithuania

Stop	Location	Page	Stop	Location	Page
32	Rõngu	55	101	Raiskums	132
33	Soomaa National Park	56	102	Rīga	133
34	Tallinn	57	104	Druskininkai	137
35	Viljandi	58	105	Jurgaičiai	138
99	Jūrmala	130	106	Vilnius	139
100	Klapkalnciems	131			

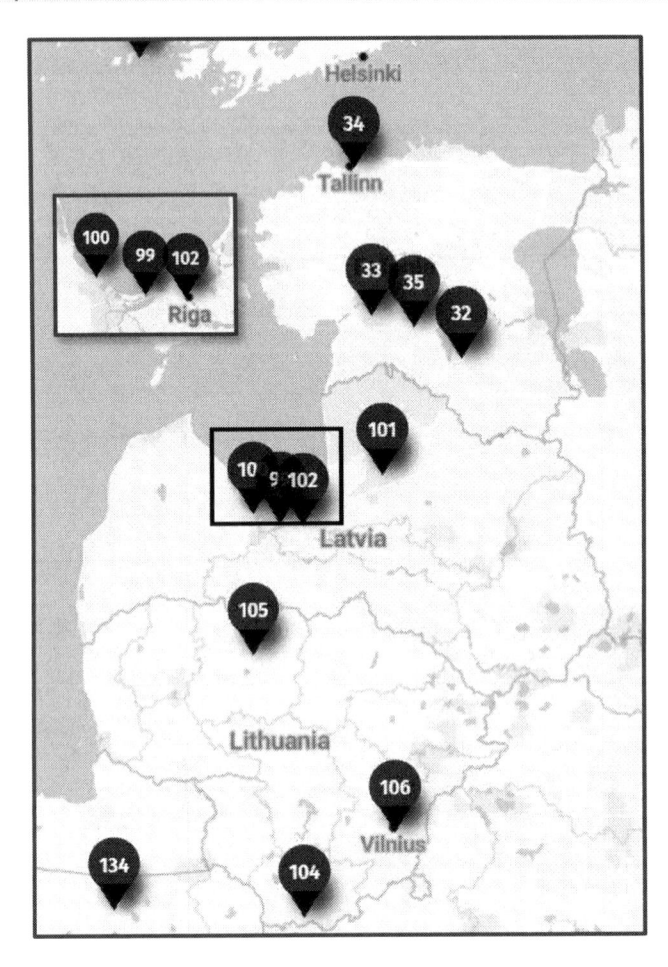

Maps F, J: UK, Netherlands, Belgium

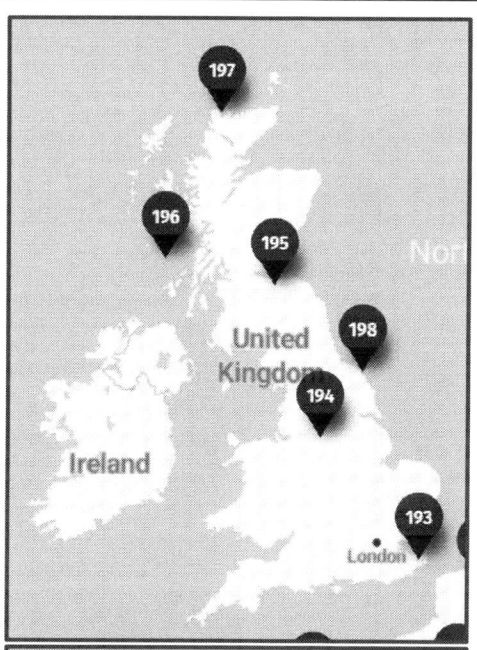

Map F: United Kingdom

Stop	Location	Page
193	Canterbury	241
194	Edale	242
195	Edinburgh	243
196	Fionnphort	244
197	Sango Sands	245
198	Whitby	246

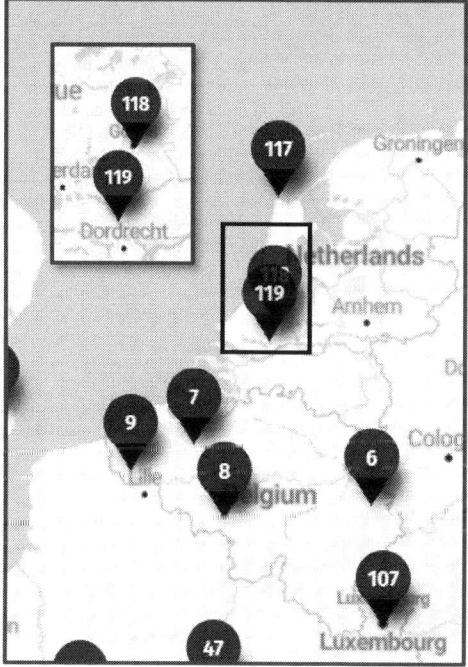

Map J: Netherlands

Stop	Location	Page
117	Den Helder	153
118	Gouda	154
119	Kinderdijk	155

Map J: Belgium

Stop	Location	Page
6	Barrage de la Gileppe	23
7	Ghent	24
8	Thieu	25
9	Ypres	26

Map G: Denmark

Stop	Location	Page	Stop	Location	Page
26	Aarhus	48	29	Hornbæk	51
27	Copenhagen	49	30	Jelling	52
28	Helsingør	50	31	Vandel	52

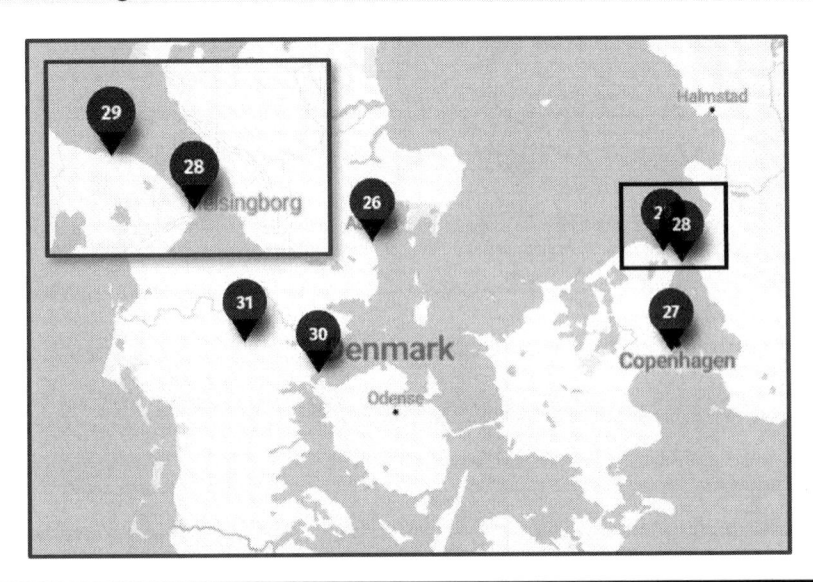

Map N: Hungary

Stop	Location	Page
80	Balatonberény	109
81	Budapest	110

Map H: Germany, Luxembourg, Czechia

Stop	Location	Page	Stop	Location	Page
23	Český Krumlov	44	62	Hamburg	88
24	Mariánské Lázně	45	63	Munich	89
25	Prague	46	64	Nuremberg	90
58	Bastei	84	65	Oberwesel	91
59	Berchtesgaden	85	66	Würzburg	92
60	Berlin	86	107	Luxembourg City	141
61	Dresden	87			

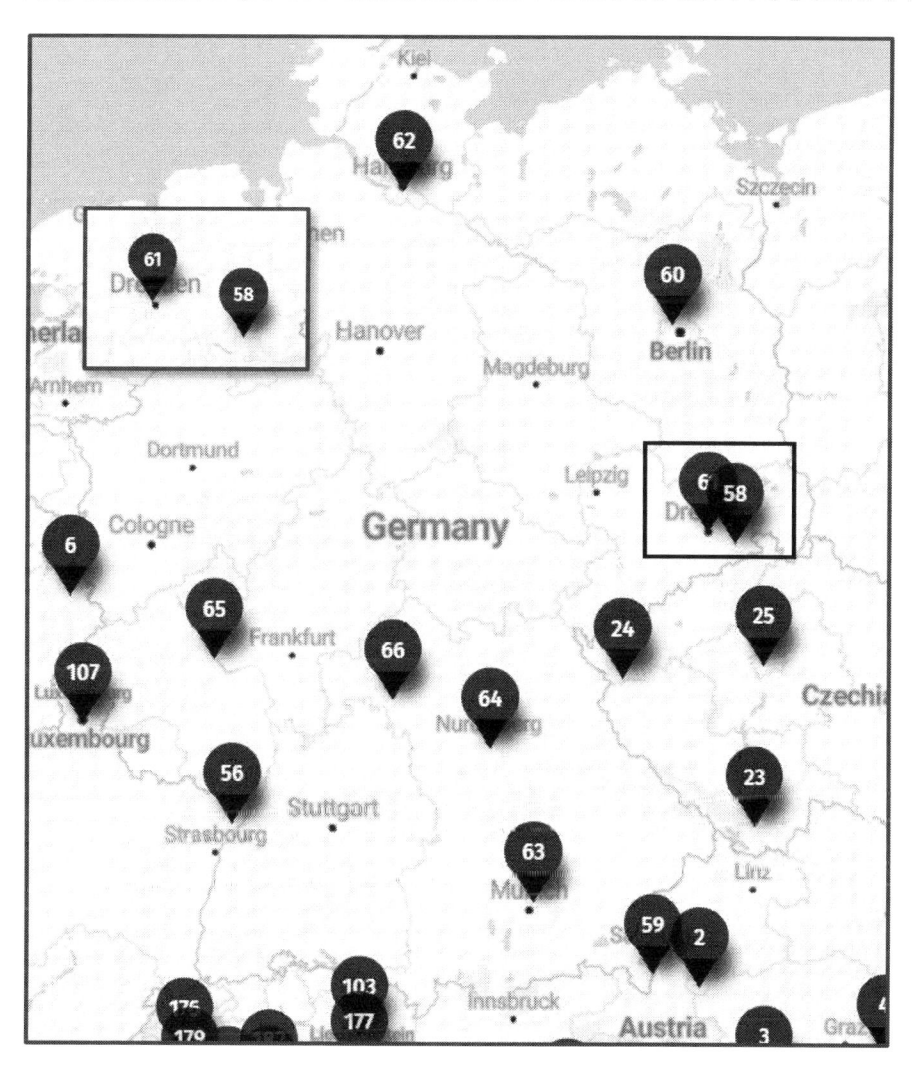

255

Map I: Poland, Ukraine, Slovakia

Stop	Location	Page	Stop	Location	Page
132	Kazimierz Dolny	170	136	Wieliczka	174
133	Oświęcim	171	152	Tatranská Lomnica	194
134	The Wolf's Lair	172	199	Kolomyia	248
135	Warsaw	173	200	Lviv	249

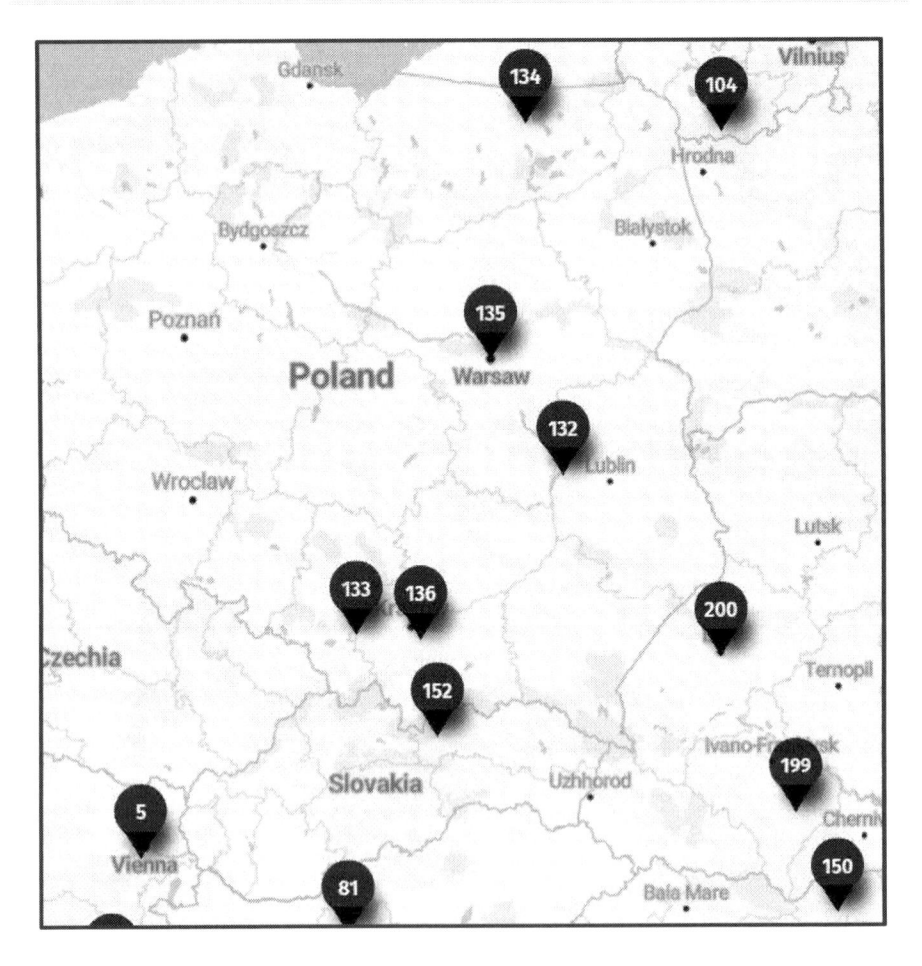

Map K: France

Stop	Location	Page	Stop	Location	Page
43	Beynac-et-Cazenac	68	51	Port Grimaud	76
44	Capbreton	69	52	Rothéneuf	77
45	Col du Lautaret	70	53	Saint-André-de-Rosans	78
46	Comps-Sur-Artuby	71	54	Saintes-Maries-De-La-Mer	79
47	Épernay	72	55	Saint-Jean-en-Royans	80
48	Le Reposoir	73	56	Soufflenheim	81
49	Monbazzilac	74	57	Taninges, Le Praz de Lys	82
50	Paris	75			

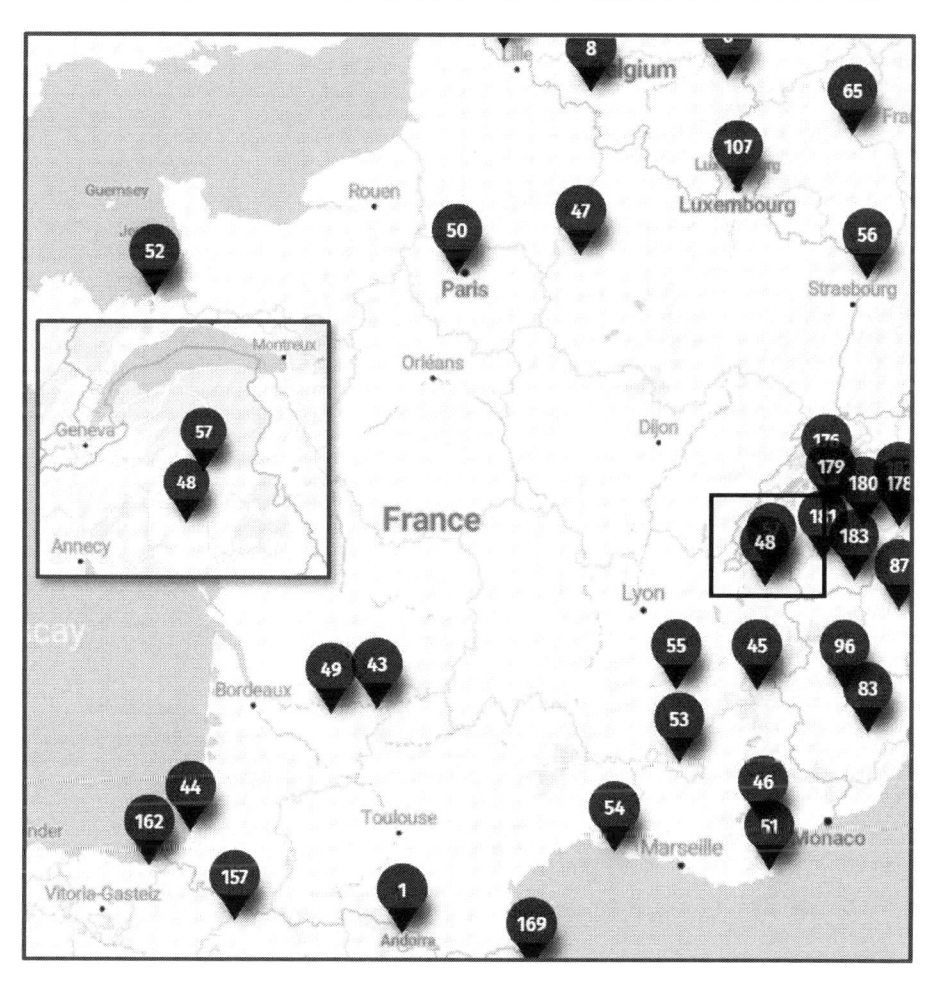

257

Map L: Switzerland, Lichtenstein

Stop	Location	Page	Stop	Location	Page
103	Vaduz	135	180	Lauterbrunnen	226
176	Bern	222	181	Sion	227
177	Chur	223	182	Steingletscher	228
178	Furkapass	224	183	Täsch	229
179	Gurnigel Pass	225			

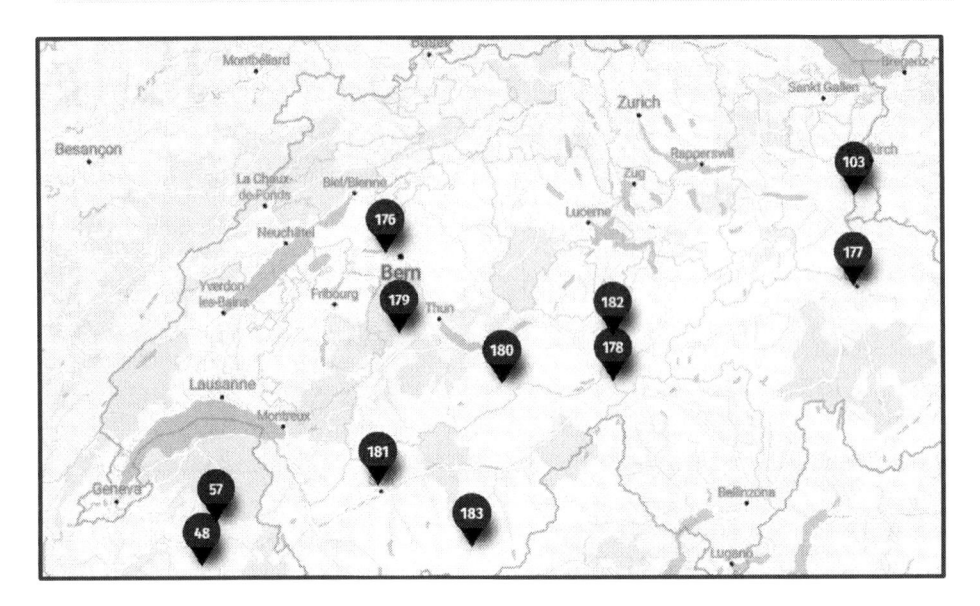

Map M: Austria & Slovenia

Stop	Location	Page	Stop	Location	Page
2	Hallstatt	18	153	Bled & Vintgar Gorge	196
3	Hochosterwizt Castle	19	154	Izola	197
4	Riegersberg Castle	20	155	Kočevski Rog	198
5	Vienna	21	156	Ljubljana	199

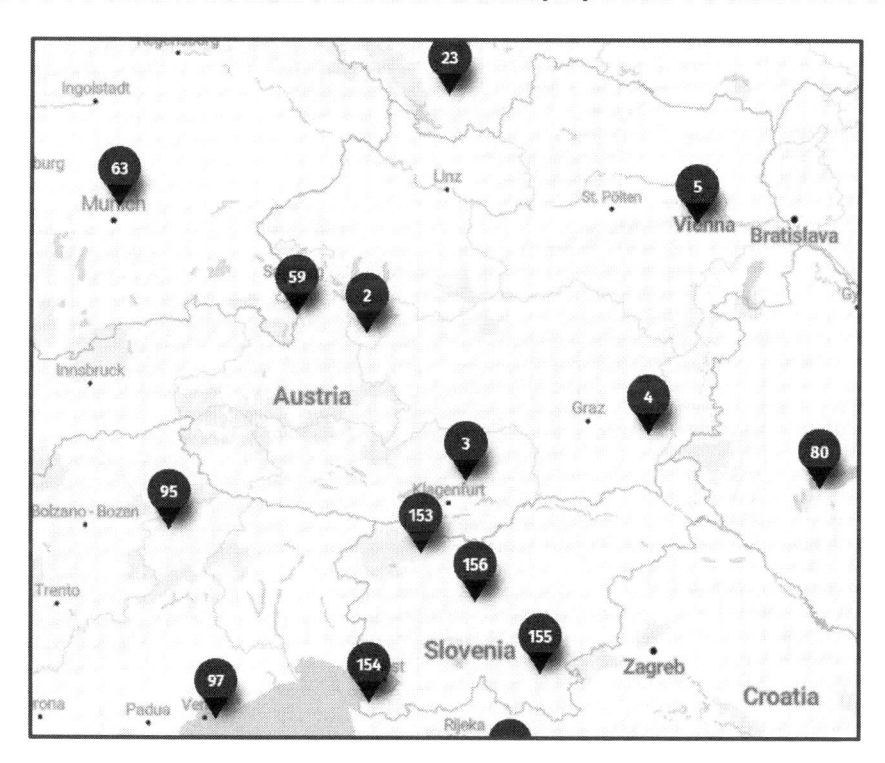

Map O: Romania

Stop	Location	Page	Stop	Location	Page
146	Bucharest	186	149	Transfăgărășan Pass	189
147	Sibiu	187	150	Vatra Moldoviței	190
148	Sighișoara	188			

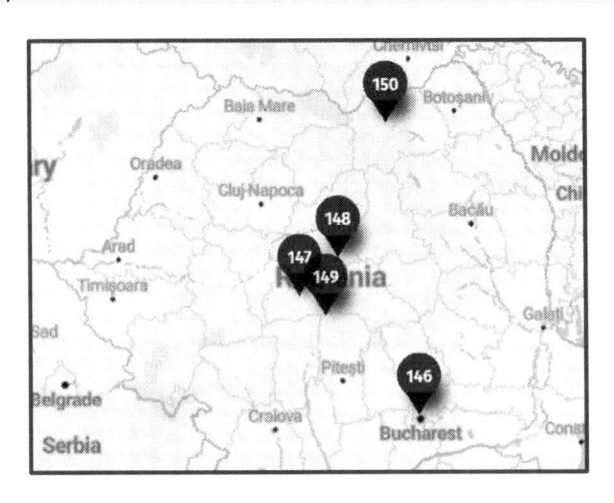

Map S: Bulgaria

Stop	Location	Page	Stop	Location	Page
13	The Rila Monastery	32	15	Veliko Tarnovo	34
14	The Seven Rila Lakes	33			

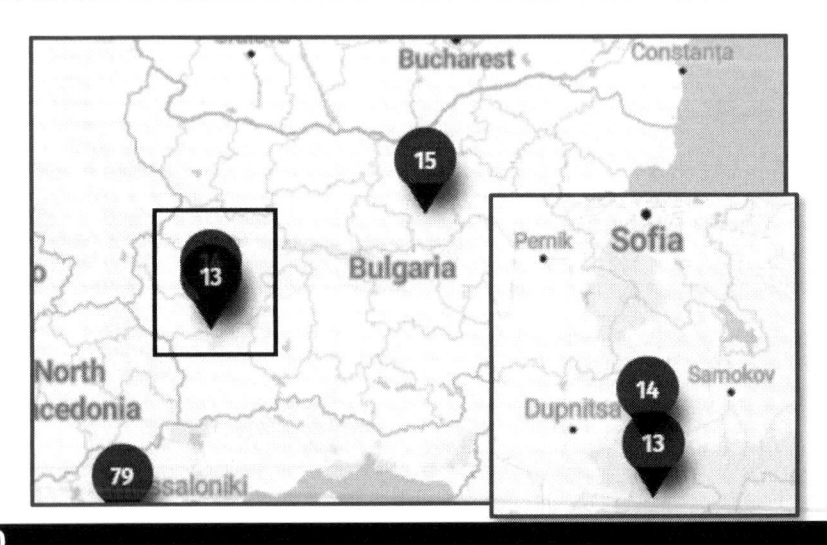

Maps P, T: Italy, San Marino

Stop	Location	Page	Stop	Location	Page
82	Alberobello	112	92	Pisa	122
83	Castiglione Falletto	113	93	Rome	123
84	Florence	114	95	Syracuse	125
86	La Spezia	116	96	The Giau Pass	126
87	Lake Orta	117	97	Venice	127
89	Montepulciano	119	151	City of San Marino	192
91	Palermo	121			

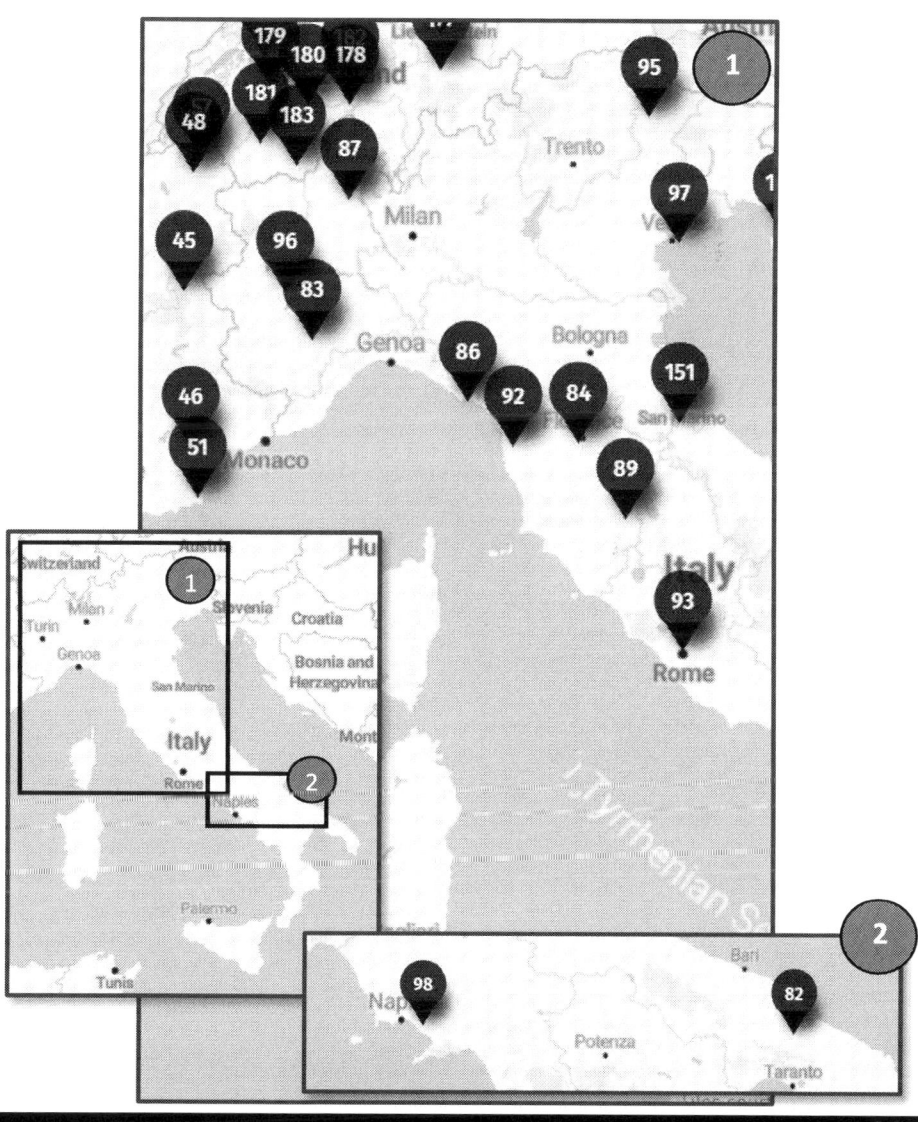

Map Q: Croatia, Bosnia & Herzegovina

Stop	Location	Page	Stop	Location	Page
10	Kravica	28	18	Pag Island	38
11	Mostar	29	19	Plitvice Lakes	39
12	Sarajevo	30	20	Povile	40
16	Hvar Island	36	21	Split	41
17	Krka	37	22	Trogir (Okrug Gornji)	42

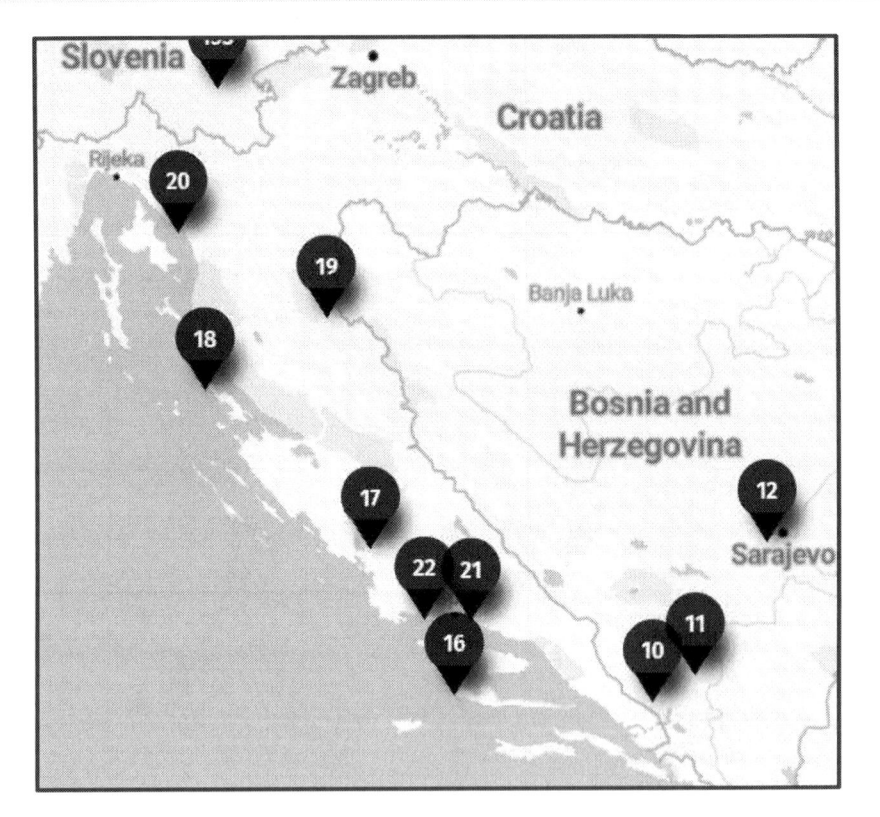

262

Map R: Andorra, Gibraltar, Portugal, Spain

Stop	Location	Page	Stop	Location	Page
1	Ordino Arcalis	16	160	Cangas de Onís	204
67	Gibraltar	94	161	Córdoba	205
137	Alvor	176	162	Donostia-San Sebastián	206
138	Braga	177	163	Granada	207
139	Cascais	178	164	Guadix	208
140	Coimbra	179	165	La Jarosa Reservoir	209
141	Évora	180	166	Madrid	210
142	Faro	181	167	Montserrat	210
143	Porto	182	168	Nerja	212
144	Silves	183	169	Port Lligat	213
145	Tomar	184	170	Santiago de Compostela	214
157	Ansó	201	171	Seville	215
158	Barcelona	202	172	València	216
159	Benarrabá	203			

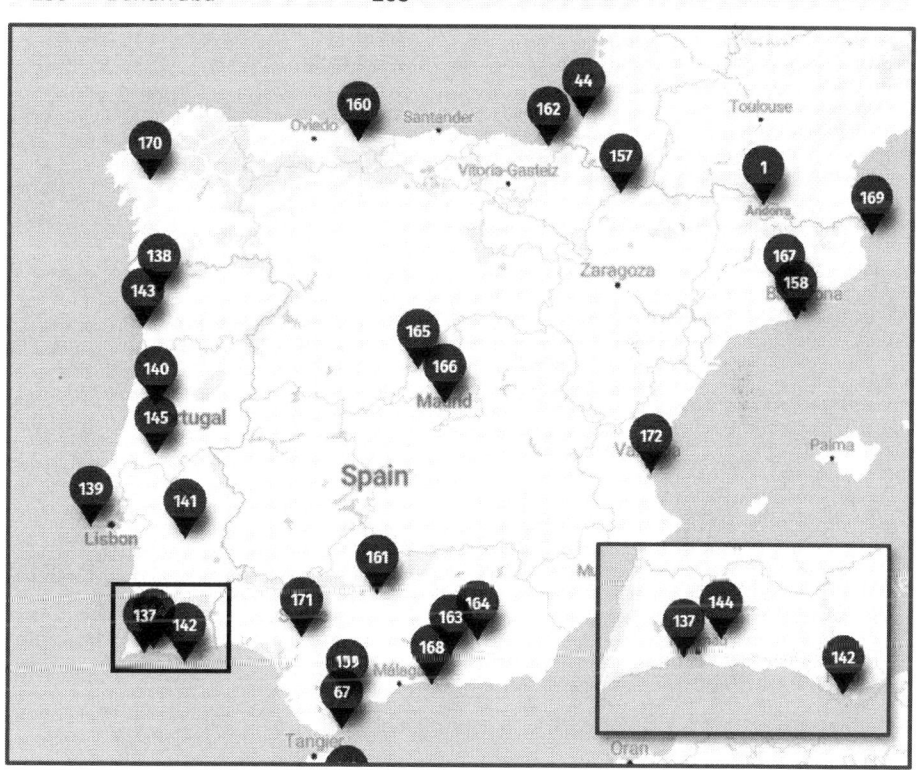

263

Map U: Greece

Stop	Location	Page	Stop	Location	Page
68	Acrocorinth	96	74	Meteora	102
69	Athens	97	75	Methoni	103
70	Diakofto	98	76	Mezapos	104
71	Diros	99	77	Monemvasia	105
72	Galaxidi	100	78	Porto Káyio	106
73	Katakolo	101	79	Vergina	107

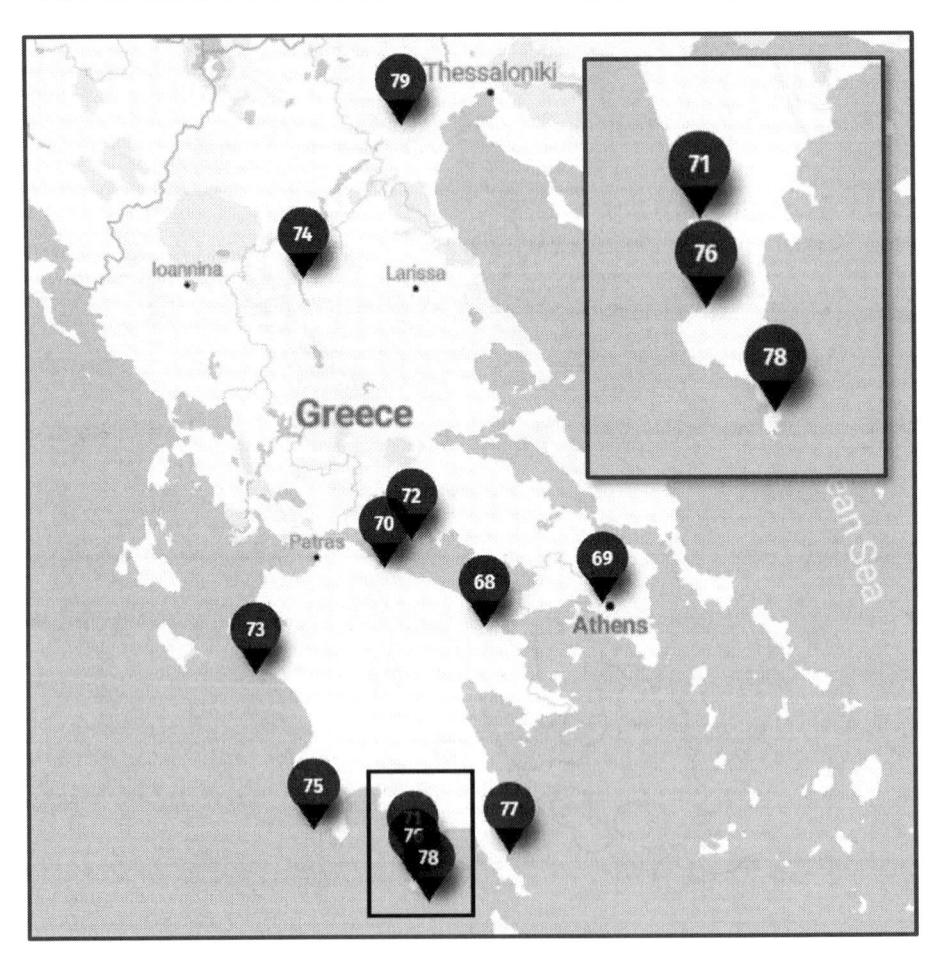

Map V: Sicily

Stop	Location	Page	Stop	Location	Page
85	Giardini-Naxos	115	91	Palermo	121
88	Marina di Ragusa	118	94	Syracuse	124
90	Mount Etna	120			

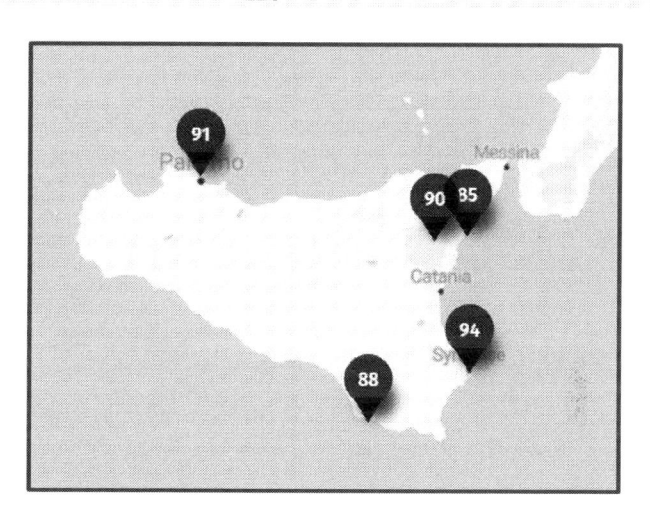

Map: W Tunisia

Stop	Location	Page	Stop	Location	Page
184	Aghir	231	189	Matmata	236
185	Bulla Regia	232	190	Metameur	237
186	Douz	233	191	Sidi Bou Said	238
187	El Jem	234	192	Tozeur	239
188	Ksar Ghilane	235			

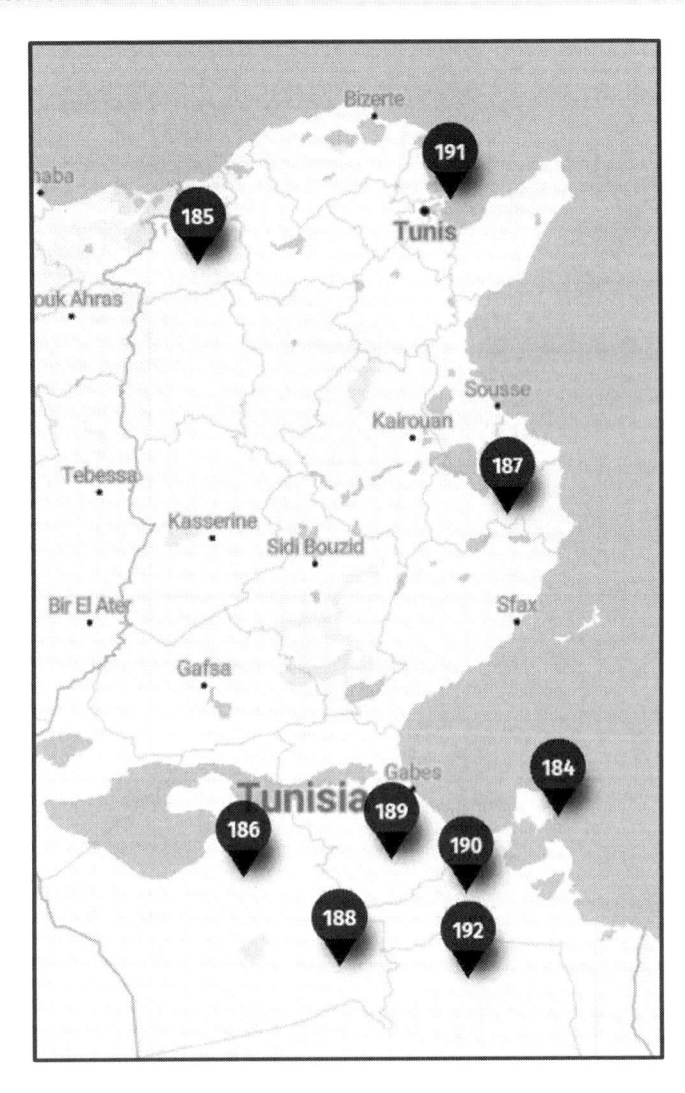

Map X: Morocco

Stop	Location	Page	Stop	Location	Page
108	Aït Mansour	143	113	Marrakech	148
109	Azrou	144	114	Meski	149
110	Chefchaouen	145	115	Tafraoute	150
111	Erg Chebbi	146	116	Tata	151
112	Fez	147			

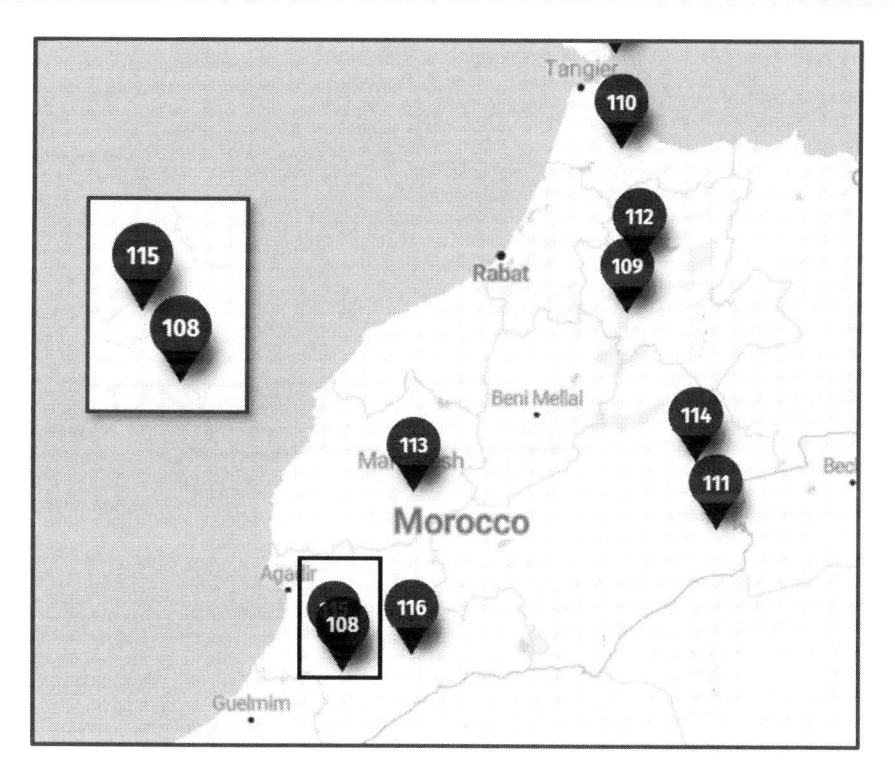

And For More Inspiration...

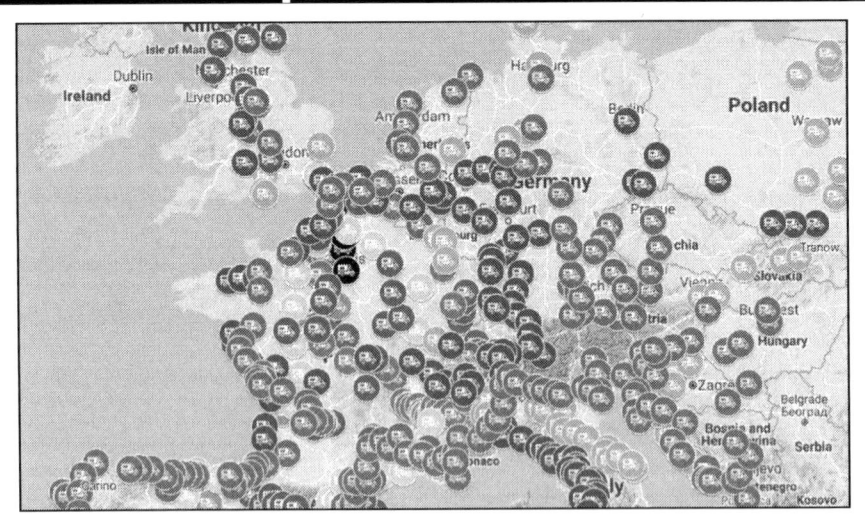

That's just 200 of the thousands of amazing places you can stay in your motorhome or campervan across Europe and North Africa. We hope you're now feeling inspired to plan your own motorhome adventure.

We really struggled to narrow this list down to 200, from the 1,000+ places we've stayed in our motorhome. If you're hungry for more, you can check out our blog where we have a map showing all of the places we have stayed: *ourtour.co.uk/home/all-tours*.

There's a marker for each place and if you click on it, you'll see a link to the blog post we wrote while we were there, including GPS co-ordinates, photos and videos.

We aren't the only ones out there exploring Europe by motorhome, and lots of people choose to blog or vlog about their journeys too.

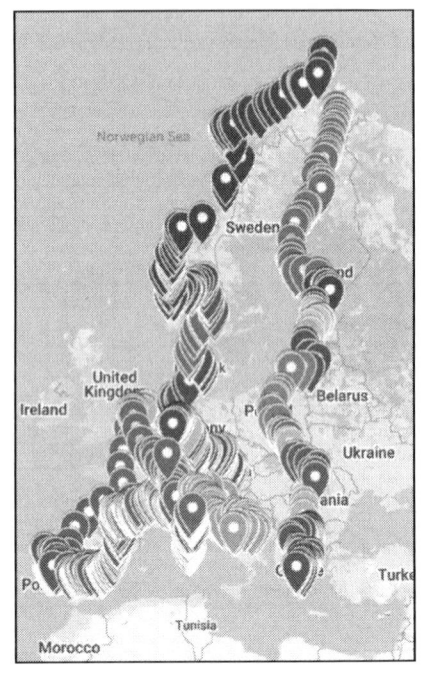

For further inspiration we've pulled together a collection of their tour maps here: *ourtour.co.uk/home/google-tour-maps-from-motorhome-bloggers*.

About the Authors

Julie and Jason Buckley quit work just before they turned 40 to take a once in a lifetime, one-year tour of Europe in their motorhome, starting the *ourtour.co.uk* blog in 2011. Two years later they finally returned home and set a goal to change their lives and become financially free, enabling them to travel whenever they wanted to. Aged 43, they 'retired' and took to the road once more to explore from the North Cape in Norway to the Sahara Desert. They now mix up their time between motorhome life and their base in Nottinghamshire, England. Julie and Jason have written several books to help and inspire others to follow their own motorhome dreams or to start the journey to financial freedom.

The Motorhome Touring Handbook 
Packed full of practical advice from choosing a motorhome and touring the UK to travelling abroad or planning for and enjoying a year-long tour.

The Non-Trepreneurs 
A practical guide explaining how we think about and manage our personal finances to enable us to retire aged 43, and travel whenever we want to.

Motorhome France 
A helping hand for anyone wanting to take their motorhome across the channel for the first time to explore this motorhome friendly country.

Motorhome Morocco 
The book we wanted to buy when going to Morocco for the first time! It guides you through the process of planning and enjoying a tour of this incredible North African country.

A Monkey Ate My Breakfast 
A travelogue of our first motorhome tour of Morocco in 2011, an eye-opening adventure onto a new continent, and into a new and exotic culture.

OurTour Downloaded 
All the blog posts from our first year of full time motorhome touring, handily gathered into one book.

If you have enjoyed this book, please pop a review on Amazon. Your feedback will be much appreciated by us and very useful for other readers.

Printed in Poland
by Amazon Fulfillment
Poland Sp. z o.o., Wrocław
19 July 2023

0eeb3818-8d1a-4377-b548-9d31115e8706R01